Insights into Professional Development in Language Teaching

A language teacher's work is never really done. From entering a teacher education program for initial qualifications onwards, language teachers must always be on the lookout for new approaches, methods, and insights into their teaching and development. This need for ongoing professional development is not a reflection of any inadequate initial teacher education or training deficits, but rather a reflection that the knowledge base of language teaching is constantly expanding, and the world changing (e.g., we are in the midst of the COVID-19 pandemic that has pushed us all to quickly pivot to online platforms for teaching and development), and we must try to keep up with our own development. Insights into Professional Development in Language Teaching is about how we can continue with our professional development as language teachers and examines a variety of approaches (individual and collaborative) to professional development for language teachers. The book is intended as a practical introduction for language teachers, and a guide for administrators and other stakeholders, who wish to implement a coherent and strategic approach to language teacher development.

Thomas S.C. Farrell is Professor of Applied Linguistics at Brock University, Canada. Professor Farrell's professional interests include Reflective Practice and Language Teacher Education and Development. Professor Farrell has published widely in academic journals and has presented at major conferences worldwide on these topics. A selection of his work can be found on his webpage: www.reflectiveinquiry.ca.

Language Teaching Insights Series
Series Editors: David Nunan & Glenn Stockwell

Burston & Arispe: *Mobile-Assisted Language Learning and Advanced-level Second Language Acquisition*

Eginli: *Insights into Emotional Well-Being of Language Teachers*

Farrell: *Insights into Professional Development in Language Teaching*

Horwitz: *Becoming a Language Teacher (2nd ed.)*

Khezrlou: *Insights into Task-Based Language Teaching*

Lai: *Insights into Technology and Autonomy in Language Teaching*

Leis: *Insights into Flipped Classrooms*

Mohebbi (Ed.): *Insights into Teaching and Learning Writing*

Tanaka-Ellis: *Insights into Teaching and Learning with Technology*

More information about titles in this series can be found at
https://www.castledown.com/academic-books/book-series/language-teaching-insights/

Insights into Professional Development in Language Teaching

Thomas S.C. Farrell
Brock University

Melbourne – London – Tokyo – New York

www.castledown.com

4th Floor, Silverstream House, 45 Fitzroy Street Fitzrovia, London W1T 6EB United Kingdom

Level 9, 440 Collins Street, Melbourne, Victoria 3000, Australia

2nd Floor Daiya Building, 2-2-15 Hamamatsu-cho, Minato-ku, Tokyo 105-0013, Japan

447 Broadway, 2nd Floor #393, New York NY, 10013 United States

First published 2022 by Castledown Publishers, London

Information on this title: www.castledown.com/academic-books/view-title/?reference=9780xxxx
DOI: 10.29140/9781914291036

Insights into Professional Development in Language Teaching

© Thomas S.C. Farrell, 2022

All rights reserved. This publication is copyright. Subject to statutory exception and to the provisions of relevant collective licencing agreements, no reproduction, transmission, or storage of any part of this publication by any means, electronic, mechanical, photocopying, recording or otherwise may take place without prior written permission from the author.

Typeset by Castledown Design, Melbourne

ISBN: 978-1-914291-03-6 (Paperback)
ISBN: 978-1-914291-05-0 (Digital)

Castledown Publishers takes no responsibility for the accuracy of URLs for external or third-party internet websites referred to in this publication. No responsibility is taken for the accuracy or appropriateness of information found in any of these websites.

Contents

Preface	*ix*
1 Language Teaching Professional Development	**1**
Teaching: Job or Profession?	3
Effective Language Teaching	5
Professional Development	8
Career Cycles	10
Goals	14
Reflective Practice	16
"Doing" Professional Development	19
Writing	19
Dialogue	21
2 Approaches to Language Teacher Professional Development: Individual	**24**
Self-Monitoring	26
Critical Incidents	33
Case Study	40
Teaching Portfolios	44
Action Research	48
Language Awareness	50
3 Approaches to Language Teacher Professional Development: Collaborative	**53**
Critical Friends	55
Team Teaching	58
Peer Coaching	63
Peer Observations	68
Teacher Development Groups	76
4 Teacher Development Needs	**82**
Novice Teacher Needs	82
Experienced Teacher Needs	88

5 Implementing and Sustaining Professional Development — 95

Implementing Professional Development:
   Institutional Perspective — 95
Implementing Professional Development:
   Individual Teacher's Perspective — 99
Sustaining Professional Development through
   Practitioner Research — 102
Sustaining Teaching and Development in an Online World — 106

6 Ten Professional Development Scenarios For Reflection — 110

Scenario 1 — 110
Scenario 2 — 111
Scenario 3 — 112
Scenario 4 — 113
Scenario 5 — 114
Scenario 6 — 115
Scenario 7 — 116
Scenario 8 — 118
Scenario 9 — 119
Scenario 10 — 120

References — *123*

Index — *132*

Preface

A language teacher's work is never really done. From entering a teacher education program to study for initial qualifications onwards to mid and end of career, a teacher must always be on the lookout professionally for new ideas, approaches and methods, and insights into his or her profession. This need for ongoing professional development is not the result of any inadequate initial teacher education or any training deficits, but rather a reflection that the knowledge base of language teaching is constantly expanding, and the world always changing (e.g., we are in the middle of the COVID-19 pandemic as I write this book, that has forced all language teachers to quickly pivot to teaching on online platforms and also to seek development opportunities online as well), and we must try to keep up with all these changes throughout our teaching careers. This book, *Insights into Professional Development in Language Teaching*, will assist language teachers of all experiences to keep up with an ever-changing professional world as it outlines and discusses a variety of approaches (individual and collaborative) to professional development. The book is intended as a practical introduction for language teachers of all levels of experience, and also a guide for administrators and other stakeholders, who wish to implement a coherent and strategic approach to language teacher development within their own institutions.

A key element of this book is that any approach to teacher professional development should involve a reflective approach where practitioners reflect critically on their own practices both inside and outside the classroom. Such a reflective approach will ensure that language teachers will always strive to be the best they can be, and that they will thrive throughout their teaching careers. The contents of this book include such a reflective approach to teacher professional development through the use of Time Outs (that include practicing teachers' own examples with professional development) after each section within each chapter, as well as a chapter dedicated to ten different development scenarios (Chapter 6) where readers can reflect on the contents based on their own personal experiences within their particular contexts. Such reflections can be carried out through the mediational reflective tools of dialogue with the self and other teachers as well as through writing for their own reflections and perhaps sharing these with other teachers.

Insights into Professional Development in Language Teaching offers language teachers eleven different procedures they can use individually (e.g., self-monitoring, analysis of critical incidents and case studies, reflection with teaching portfolios, and through action research, and development of individual teacher's language awareness), and/or collaboratively (development through critical friends, team teaching, peer coaching, peer observations, and teacher development groups).

The opening chapter of the book presents an overview of professional development and discusses conceptions of effective language teaching, teacher professional career life cycles and development goals, as well as why, and how, language teachers can implement reflection as part of their professional development. Chapters 2 and 3 offer different procedures for professional development that teachers can use individually (Chapter 2) and/or collaboratively (Chapter 3). Chapter 4 outlines and discusses both novice and experienced language teacher professional development needs, as well as how they can determine their own needs throughout their careers. Chapter 5 outlines and discusses implementing and sustaining professional development from both an institution and individual teacher's perspectives and includes how language teachers can sustain their teaching and professional development in an online world. Chapter 6, the final chapter in the book, offers ten different scenarios for language teachers to reflect; all are based on real examples I accumulated while working with language teachers worldwide during my 40+ years as a language teacher educator. Each chapter is written in a clear, non-technical and accessible style and assumes little previous background knowledge about professional development.

As mentioned above, you are all busy teachers thus, a main objective of Insights into Professional Development in Language Teaching is to provide you with instantly workable procedures and activities most relevant to your personal teacher professional development needs depending on where you are along your teacher career cycle (see Chapter 1 for more). I hope this book can provide some insights into YOUR professional development as you continue to thrive as a teacher throughout your career.

Thomas S.C. Farrell

1
Language Teacher Professional Development

Introduction

When language teachers hear the term "professional development," some may roll their eyes with dismay because of possible negative past experiences with mandated professional development days (or the dreaded school PD Day!). One reason for this feeling of apprehension may be because attendance is compulsory, and/or where an outside (so-called) expert comes in to tell the teachers what they have been doing incorrectly and then proceed to show them how it should be done. Such an approach to professional development is top-down because it is executed on teachers taking a deficit approach to what teachers are currently doing. Thus, we should not wonder why many teachers really do not look forward to these mandated PD days. However, as the contents of this book will show you, there are alternative approaches to professional development that can be more beneficial for language teacher professional growth if they are carried out *with* and *for* teachers. This more bottom-up approach includes the teacher in the decision process of what he or she considers important for him or her to develop rather than any external institutional agenda. Such an approach to teacher development includes each teacher's "personal and moral dimensions" (Mann, 2005, p. 104), where each teacher systematically examines who they are, what they do, how and why they do it, what the outcomes are (especially in terms of student learning), and what professional development actions they will take as a result of knowing all of this information. This chapter introduces teachers to the concept of professional development as it outlines and discusses various aspects of language teaching, conceptions of effective language teaching, professional development, teacher career cycles and teacher plateauing, professional development goals, reflective practice and "doing" professional development.

Time Out

- Do you think language teaching is a job or a profession? What is the difference between the two?
- Read the following real experiences of a language teacher's first steps into professional development and compare this with your own first steps as written in the teacher's own words.
  - Like many teachers, I recall my first lesson with horror. Having only taken a one-week training course as preparation and forced to follow an audiolingual coursebook, I followed the teacher's book religiously and the lesson was an embarrassing flop. The next few months were spent frantically trying to build a repertoire of activities by picking my colleagues' brains. Within a week, I learnt that you could use pair work (and I still remember what a massive revelation this was), and I slowly got to the point where I could deliver a varied and enjoyable (if rather purposeless) lesson. For the next few years of teaching, there were two main inputs to my development. Firstly, colleagues were still vitally important. In addition to picking their brains, I've also found it useful to see how colleagues work, and to try out those things that colleagues do that seem applicable to me. For example, one colleague would spend every free moment at work preparing supplementary activities, and they ended up with a large file of useful materials. Although I lacked the dedication to design so much material, I did start developing a few (I have to admit rather poor quality) supplementary materials, and consequently I became interested in how learners reacted to them. Since passing the stage where I was mainly concerned with classroom survival, I became interested in the learners and looked for feedback on my teaching. Much of the time, this was gathered informally through chatting to learners at break times – it's only in the last few years that I have learnt more formal methods for evaluating my own teaching. From my experience, two key issues in dealing with feedback are firstly, that it's important to pay attention to positive feedback as well as to criticisms, and secondly, that some qualitative comments can have an influence far beyond their face value (reminiscent of critical incidents theory). More recently, after taking a master's degree, I

became interested in reading about teaching. Although I rarely read an ELT book from cover to cover, skimming tens of books and journals each year (to add to my database which gives me a purpose in reading) means a continual flow of input raising awareness, stimulating ideas, and encouraging me to think about my teaching. I am now in the fortunate position where, to some extent, I can choose what work to do. As a general rule, I choose those things which I believe I will learn from (as opposed to quick money-earners). I am therefore constantly facing new challenges, and if I continue working in this way, I believe that I will have a wealth of opportunity for further development.

Teaching: Job or Profession?

Is teaching a job or a profession? Why ask such a question to begin a book on language teacher development you may correctly wonder? One answer may be that if you believe that teaching is just another job, then you do what is required to get by day by day and pick up your paycheck as a result without much reflection. The general requirements of the "job" may be outlined on a document you are given the first day and/or someone (a mentor) may take you through your first day (or more) to show you what to do. After a short time of such "learning" you are then on your own to do the job each day of your shift. The job rarely changes each day as routine kicks in and you "get through it" without much reflection.

However, if you consider teaching a profession, then you may expect to have some status attached to it, specialized training involved from "approved" schools/institutions where you probably obtain a certificate and/or degree, and resultant standards to follow when you are finally qualified. This is the common notion when teaching is considered a profession where "qualified" teachers are recruited because they possess and can implement a specialized type of knowledge related to the subject they are teaching. Thus, if we assume teaching is a profession, then central to this premise is that a particular and legitimate body of knowledge exists that sets it apart from other professions, and that possession of this knowledge base is what grounds the practice of teachers. In order to become a "professional" teacher it is assumed that you have gained this knowledge through education and training that has been provided by some professional body that speaks for the profession of teachers.

Leung (2009, p. 49) distinguishes between the terms "professional" and "professionalism" and points out that a "professional" is a "trained and qualified specialist who displays a high standard of competent conduct in their practice", whereas "professionalism" refers to a practitioner's [i.e., a "professional"] knowledge, skills, and conduct. So, for teaching to be considered as a profession, where professionals exhibit professionalism, something must be known (a knowledge base) and such knowledge should ground practice. As Leung (2009, p. 49) puts it, issues related to professionalism in teacher education involve questions such as "what should teachers know?" and "how should teachers go about their business?" Thus, it can be considered that professional language teachers have been trained and educated in some recognized language teacher education institution.

Freeman (2016, p. 9) has maintained that the function of language teacher education should be to act as "a bridge that serves to link what is known in the field with what is done in the classroom, and it does so through the individuals whom we educate as teachers." However, over the years there has not been much agreement or uniformity as to "what they need to know" (disciplinary knowledge) and "how they should go about their teaching" (pedagogical content knowledge). As Richards (2014, p. 23) has noted, "the central issue of what constitutes appropriate disciplinary knowledge and pedagogical content knowledge remains an unresolved issue." Indeed, some programs (especially the shorter ones) still focus on providing teaching methods (e.g., Communicative Language Teaching (CLT) still among the most popular), while other programs (the longer ones) are more academically focused (e.g., Education foundational courses and/or linguistic oriented courses depending on which faculty they are housed). That said, it is beyond the scope of this book to discuss what and how language teachers should be trained and educated to become professionals. In fact, my main point in considering if teaching is a job or a profession, is that I wanted to point out that as a professional you will have received a particular body of knowledge from your teacher education program that you can and should examine (i.e., what disciplinary knowledge and pedagogical content knowledge did you obtain?) so that you are aware of what currently grounds your teaching and the time out below will help you reflect on this.

Time Out

- What kind of language teacher education program did you take? Was it a BA, MA and/or certificate?
- What courses were you asked to take in these courses (list them all)?
- Which ones would you consider to be disciplinary knowledge (e.g., second language acquisition, methods, sociolinguistics, phonology, etc.)?
- Which ones would you consider to be pedagogical content knowledge focused (e.g., curriculum planning, assessment, teaching young learners, etc.)?
- What are the uses of each of the above courses in terms of your teaching?
- Are there any courses you wish you could have taken but were not provided?
- Do you think you received a balance between theory and practice in the language teacher education program you took? Why or why not?
- Do you feel you were prepared adequately for a career as a language teacher? Why or why not?
- What are the most important things a teacher needs to know to be able to teach a second or foreign language (in general or a specific one)?
- Where can they get information about these things?
- Do you think you know everything you need to know about language teaching now that you have been teaching for some time?

Effective Language Teaching

The previous section sought to seek your reflections on the type and content of your initial language teacher education experiences so that you can be aware of the disciplinary knowledge and the pedagogical content knowledge that backs up your current practice. This section examines different conceptions of effective language teaching that you can explore related to your previously acquired disciplinary and pedagogical content knowledge. The reason for this exploration is because different conceptions of language teaching can lead to different views of what the essential skills of teaching are. However, it should be recognized that it is difficult to define exactly what "effective" language teaching is. As Richards (2010: 102) has noted, "the nature of what we mean by effectiveness in teaching is not always easy to define because conceptions of good teaching differ from culture to culture." Thus, the way each individual teacher teaches will be a representation of that person's personal history: his or her cultural background, and prior experiences as well as the context he or she is teaching in that includes students, colleagues, administrators, parents and others. Freeman and Richards (1993) adapted Zahorik's (1986) three major conceptions of teaching to the language teacher profession that demonstrate different conceptions of effective language teaching that are useful for our reflections. These are Science/Research; Theory/Values; Art/Craft.

Science/Research

As the name suggests, the science/research conception is derived from research and supported and "tested" by some kind of experimentation. For this dimension, a "tested" model of learning informs "effective" teaching, and to succeed, teachers must learn specific acts of teaching (such as "effective" questioning). "Effective" teachers (defined as those whose students get high scores on tests) are observed, and their actions documented so that others can do what they do. Within language teaching, early Audiolingualism, and a currently popular approach, Task-Based Language Teaching (TBLT), are such examples of the application of research to language teaching. The popular TBLT approach is derived from second language acquisition (SLA) research and maintains that "successful" language learning happens when learners are engaged in negotiation of meaning, and where different tasks practice language forms and communication skills. Thus, for the science/research conception, effective language teachers understand the learning principles, develop tasks based on these learning principles and then monitor to see that the desired performance is being achieved.

Theory/Values

The theory/values conception bases teaching on what ought to work or "what is morally right to do" (Zahorik, 1986, p. 22). There is no real empirical research information backing up any of these conceptions of effective teaching, so the "theory" behind the method is obtained through reason or rational thought. CLT, for example, is derived from the idea of operationalizing communicative competence and was a direct reaction to grammar-based approaches (e.g., grammar/translation method). This is called a "principled approach" because it does not produce evidence of its effectiveness as the theory itself is only used to justify the approach.

A value-based approach views certain methods as politically justifiable and therefore good, while other methods judged not justifiable based on incorrect morals, and therefore bad. Teaching through action research is a value-based approach as it is justified on a social values system. Following a learner-centered approach to teaching is another value-based approach because teachers value the idea that learners should be self-directed and responsible for their own learning. Teachers using this approach supply learners with learning strategies and get them to develop their own ways of learning and evaluation. Although all of these are very popular with language teachers, again, no empirical research information exists to back up any of the conceptions in a values-based approach. Thus, for the theory/values conception, effective language teachers understand the theory, principles and values, select syllabi, material, and tasks based on the theory or value, and monitor to see that it conforms to the theory or value.

Art/Craft

The Art/Craft conception of effective teaching suggests that a teacher's individual skill and personality influences his or her instructional approach. Each teaching situation is viewed as being different and unique and thus each language teacher will decide what to do based on his or her teaching skills and personality. Such a teacher does not follow any one method and chooses from a range of options to teach. As Zahorik (1986, p. 22) notes: "A good teacher is a person who assesses the needs and possibilities of a situation and creates and uses practices that have promise for that situation." Thus, the art/craft conception suggests that each teacher will define what is best for his or her particular context and not what research/science results, or theory/values suggests they do. Consequently, for the art/craft conception, effective language teachers view each situation as unique, try different teaching strategies for each and then monitor each for effectiveness as each teacher develops his or her own approach to as a language teacher.

Time Out

- Do you follow a science/research conception of language teaching? Why or why not?
- Do you follow a theory/values conception of teaching? Why or why not?

- Do you subscribe to CLT within a theory conception? Why or why not?
- Do you subscribe to a learner-centered approach within a values-based conception? Why or why not?
- Do you follow an art/craft conception of teaching? Why or why not?
- How do you know what is best for your context and your students?
- I would strongly suggest that you now read Freeman and Richards' (1993) article for more details on these very interesting and relevant conceptions of teaching for language teachers.

Professional Development

So far I have pointed out that language teachers who consider themselves "professionals" will want to engage in some kind of professional development opportunities throughout their careers. This is not a reflection that they have been inadequately prepared, but a response to the fact that not everything a language teacher needs to know can be provided during their initial teacher education programs (Richards & Farrell, 2005). In addition, and as Tsui (2003, p. 80) points out, after several years of teaching, teachers can begin to experience some self-doubt caused perhaps by such factors as the "monotony of classroom teaching, and unpleasant working conditions." Thus, in this book professional development can be seen as a continuous process where teachers as Guskey (2000, p. 16) notes, enhance their "professional knowledge, skills, and attitude so that they might, in turn, improve the learning of students." Thus, teacher development can be considered as a process that never really ends for teachers who want to become the best that they can be (Underhill, 1999). The form of professional development that a teacher takes will vary for each teacher, and as Senior (2006, p. 67) has noted, the exact pattern will be unique, and the rate of development will vary with each teacher in that "some teachers develop quickly, others more slowly."

So, what should language teachers develop? The answer to this question will vary with each teacher and will depend on each teacher's prior knowledge, interests and previous experiences throughout their teaching careers. Richards and Farrell (2005) provide a useful overall summary of what language teachers may be interested in exploring as part of their own development:
- *Subject-matter knowledge*: knowledge related to the disciplinary basis of language teaching such as English grammar, discourse analysis,

phonology, testing, second language acquisition research, methodology, curriculum development and the other areas which define the professional knowledge base of language teaching.
- *Pedagogical expertise*: mastery of new areas of teaching; adding to one's repertoire of teaching specializations; improving one's ability to teach different skill areas to learners of different ages and backgrounds.
- *Self-awareness*: knowledge of oneself as a teacher, of one's principles and values, of one's areas of strength and weakness.
- *Understanding of learners*: deeper understanding of learners, learning styles, learners' problems and difficulties, ways of making content more accessible to learners.
- *Understanding of curriculum and materials*: deeper understanding of curriculum and curriculum alternatives, use and development of instructional materials.
- *Career advancement*: acquisition of the knowledge and expertise necessary for personal advancement and promotion, including supervisory and mentoring skills.

Time Out

- Have you ever engaged in professional development before? If yes, explain how you did this. If no, why not?
- Where do you get ideas about teaching methods/techniques?
    - Talks/demonstrations by other teachers (brown bag lunches).
    - Talks by invited speakers.
    - Workshops.
    - Short courses.
    - In-service courses at your institution.
    - ESL/EFL textbooks teachers' manuals.
    - Conferences.
    - Teacher resource books on teaching theory.
    - Academic journals.
    - ESL/EFL magazines.
    - Other?
- What have you done in the past year to develop yourself as a language teacher? [Mark all that apply]
    - ☐ Attended workshops.

- ☐ Attended talks/demonstrations by other teachers (e.g. brown bag lunches).
- ☐ Attended talks by invited speakers.
- ☐ Attended short courses.
- ☐ Attended in-service courses at your institution.
- ☐ Attended conferences.
- ☐ Worked with a colleague.
- ☐ Observed other teachers.
- ☐ Read language textbook teachers' manuals.
- ☐ Read teacher resource books on teaching theory.
- ☐ Read academic journals.
- ☐ Read language teaching magazines.
- ☐ Other?

- What aspects of your professional life are you interested in exploring and why?

Career Cycles

As already mentioned, each language teacher's professional development requirements will be different and may depend on what stage or phase of their career cycle they are located. One influential approach to teacher career life cycles is that of Huberman's (1989, 1993) where he suggested that teachers do not pass-through career phases in a linear manner; rather he noted they pass in and out of phases in response to both personal, institutional and social requirements. Huberman (1989) suggests that teachers pass through the following phases: from novice (early, mid, late novice) to mid-career (stabilization, experimentation, taking stock) to late-career (serenity, disengagement). Figure 1 below gives a visual outline of Huberman's (1989) phases that teachers pass through during their careers.

According to schematics of Huberman's (1989) model outlined in Figure 1, there is a single arrow flow at the point a teacher starts his or her career (career entry) moving to the stabilization phase. Then, there are multiple routes or streams throughout the career cycle that ultimately converge again onto a single flow/path at the end, which may either signify teacher serenity or bitterness depending on the previous career trajectory. The "flow" of the career cycle is represented by a single arrow stream at the point a teacher starts his or her career (career entry) moving to the stabilization phase. Then, there are multiple routes or streams throughout the career cycle that ultimately converge again onto a single flow/path at the end, which may either signify teacher serenity or bitterness, depending on the previous career trajectory. The different trajectories are represented on the left and the right sides of the model with the most harmonious sequence running along the left side of the model: Experimentation/diversification → serenity → (serene) disengagement; and the most problematic sequence running along the right side of the model: Reassessment/self-doubt → conservatism → (bitter) disengagement.

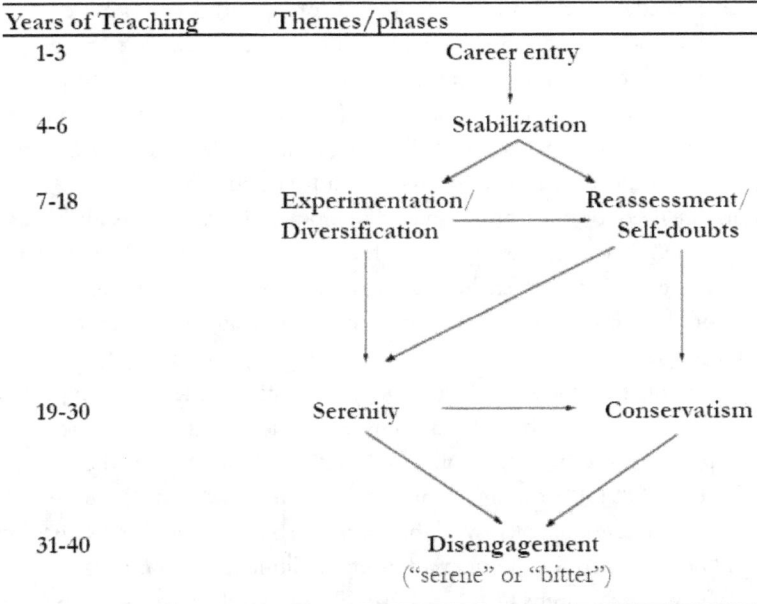

Figure 1.1 *The Professional Life Cycle of Teachers (adapted from Huberman, 1989)*

For example, he has suggested that years one to three, called the novice years, are characterized by the novice teacher's primary concern of surviving in a new environment. This is then followed by a period of discovery of the act of teaching and its impact on student learning. The mid-career years follow and are characterized by some years of stabilization where teachers have committed to the profession and begin to experience "greater instructional master and comfort" (Huberman, 1989, p. 34). Teachers are now more experienced and feel more confident about their teaching skills and follow a more settled pattern inside and outside the classroom. Some teachers may even begin to experiment with new approaches and activities in order to make their teaching more interesting or exciting. In mid-career Huberman (1989) suggests that some teachers may also begin to take stock of their careers and reflect on their past and future as teachers. Beyond these years, teachers can find job satisfaction or not. For those who do find satisfaction, they become content and eventually retire feeling fulfilled. For those who do not find job satisfaction, they become disengaged and retire feeling bitter.

Knowledge of this cycle is important for educators because it explains that a teacher's progression through his or her career cycle is filled with "plateaus, discontinuities, regressions, spurts, and dead ends" (Huberman, 1995, p. 196). Indeed, Huberman (1989) suggests that mid-career (somewhere between the 10-to-15-year mark in their careers) is where teachers can be most vulnerable to plateauing and thus burnout and so may be in dire need for some professional development initiatives. As Huberman (1989, p. 34) notes, "having been a few times around the block, teachers may be ready for new challenges, new stimulation." Thus, teachers are susceptible to growing stale, a problem more associated with teachers in the latter stages of their careers. So, at this stage Huberman (1989, p. 43) suggests some teachers can begin to notice a shift in their thinking where they "feel the stale breath of routine." Teachers then become more susceptible to the phenomenon of plateauing at this stage of their careers (Milstein, 1989). Plateauing, according to Milstein (1989, p. 3), can occur if teachers perceive that their work has become so routine and repetitive that they "become skeptical about ever finding fulfillment in our careers."

Meister and Ahrens (2011, p. 770) suggest that the term "plateauing" is used "to describe the frustration and disillusionment some teachers may experience over the course of their tenure in the classroom" and that it usually happens to teachers in their mid-career years. Milstein (1989) has pointed out that teachers can be considered to reach a level of either "high-plateauers" or "low-plateauers." "High-plateauers" tend to have negative feelings, and are more skeptical about their work as teachers, while "low-plateauers" tend to have more positive feelings and are less skeptical about their work as teachers. Milstein (1989) has pointed to several factors that can lead to a teacher experiencing both types of plateauing such as the nature of teaching where teachers work in low-growth organizations with little career advancement (they must leave the classroom and go into administration to advance), age (those over the age of forty can experience job stagnation); as well as job longevity (the longer one is in the same job, the more likely he or she will experience some form of plateauing). Thus, it is in these mid-career years that language teachers especially may feel the need to take stock and engage in some form of teacher development (Garton & Richards, 2008). So, an important question is how teachers can become aware of the real possibility of the phenomenon of plateauing so that their enthusiasm for teaching can be sustained throughout their careers. Meister and Ahrens (2011) maintain that one way of making teachers aware of such issues in mid-career is by encouraging them to reflect on their practice.

Time Out

- Huberman identified several stages in the career cycle of Swiss secondary school teachers, which are summarized below with associated approximate years. What phase of your teaching career are you at?
    - *1–3 years*: Career entry—painful or easy beginnings; survival, discovery, reality shock.
    - *4–6 years*: Stabilization—taking on adult responsibilities; making a commitment to a defined professional goal; giving up other options.
    - *7–18 years*: Experimentation/Activism—experimenting with different materials, student groupings, sequencing; attempts to make institutional changes.
    - *7–18 years*: Reassessment/Self-doubts—growing sense of monotony (between the 12th and 20th year of teaching); thoughts of leaving teaching; realizing that other careers will have to be ruled out if they do not move quickly.
    - *19–30 years*: Serenity/Relational Distance—more mechanical, relaxed, self-accepting.
    - *19–30 years*: Conservatism—resistance to innovation, nostalgia for the past; concern with holding on to what one has rather than with getting what one wants.
    - *31–40 years*: Disengagement—disengaging from investment in work; serene or bitter.
- Do you agree with Huberman's descriptions above and are they relevant to your career stage?

- Do you think any particular phase of a teacher's career is more important than another? Why or why not?
- Kelchtermans (1993) did not present a sequence of phases in a cycle by years of experience, but he identified some common trends and recurring themes among Flemish primary school teachers that he interviewed, including the following:
  o Teachers reported a shift in emphasis in their work over time.
  o Certain events or persons functioned as "turning points" (critical incidents or critical persons) in the teachers' lives.
  o Teachers had a primary concern with stability in the job situation.
  o Teachers perceived themselves as vulnerable to the outside world.

  What is your understanding of this themes approach above and is it relevant to your career stage now?
- Have you ever thought deeply about your teaching at any particular phase of your career than others? Why or why not?
- Do you think all teachers plateau at some stage of their careers?
- If you experienced plateauing, were you a "high" or a "low" plateauer?

Goals

Within the scope of teacher professional development, two broad kinds of goals can be distinguished, training or development (Richards & Farrell, 2005). Training is normally thought of as the starting phase in a teacher's professional development. When the goal of professional development is training, the main emphasis on development is concerned with transmitting the required, "correct" knowledge and skills to the teacher to be able to copy in practice. As Freeman (1982, p. 21) has observed, in such a training approach "the teacher learns to teach the same way as I learn to ride a bicycle." Wallace (1991) has called the training approach the "craft model" of teaching in which the master teacher tells the apprentices what to do, and shows them how to do it, with the apprentices imitating it exactly. The content of training is usually determined by experts and is often available in standard training formats (e.g., in the form of methods) or through prescriptions in methodology books.

However, such a training view of teaching leaves language education at the level of knowledge and skill and where teachers are trained in prescribed ways of teaching; knowledge in the form of what is being taught, to whom and where; skill, the basic component, in what to do in the classroom (e.g., give instructions, present materials). The training model is also limited by the fact that we still do not know exactly what the cause and effect of teaching to learning outcomes is because not enough is known about how teaching behaviors result in student learning (Richards & Farrell, 2005). In addition, teachers cannot really reflect on their beliefs and their consequences on their practices and vice versa nor how they provide or block opportunities for their students to learn.

Another goal within the scope of teacher professional development is development. Within the language teacher education and development literature in the 1990s, there was a move away from a training approach to a development approach. Although we can talk about the "craft" of teaching (see above), such as checking attendance, we cannot really say exactly what the "art" of teaching entails. However, a "developmental" view of teaching recognizes this "art" aspect of teaching as well as the "craft" of teaching, recognizing professional development as a continual intellectual, experiential, and attitudinal growth of teachers. As Green (2002, p. 7) maintains, "development, with its focus on growth, relates to the knowledge, skills, and attitude people need to do their next job or a different form of their current job, usually with greater responsibility."

A development approach serves a longer-term goal of professional development and seeks to facilitate growth of a language teacher's ability to make their own informed decisions about teaching and a general understanding of himself or herself as a teacher. Such a view of professional development sees a changing role of teacher educators, supervisors, and workshop leaders from a prescriptive mode (training) to that of providing opportunities for teachers to participate in a variety of activities (Farrell, 2013). As Head and Taylor (1997, p. 1) point out, the main goal of a development approach is "personal awareness of the possibilities for change and of what influences the change process."

Most educational institutions will have both training and development goals and provide opportunities for teachers to develop using both approaches. However, many schools and institutions tend to focus on supporting their teachers on building specific skills that they think their teachers need for the good of the school or institution. However, as Richards and Farrell (2005) point out, any school or institutional comprehensive plan for professional development should not just focus on training, but also focus on the individual teacher's long-term growth that will also benefit the school or institution. Please note much of what is presented in this book takes the development goal of professional development for language teachers through a self-reflective process of "questioning old habits" so that "alternative ways of being and doing are able to emerge" (Head & Taylor, 1997, p. 1).

Time Out

- What is your understanding of a training goal related to professional development?
- Which of the following examples of goals from a training perspective would you like to learn (from Richards & Farrell, 2005)?
  - using peer feedback in writing classes
  - using an interview for oral language assessment
  - using a video to teaching listening comprehension
  - using cooperative-learning techniques in an ESL class
  - developing strategies to use with disruptive students
  - using a course book with large classes
  - using computers in the classroom
  - giving error feedback in a speaking class
  - Others?
- What is your understanding of a development goal to professional development?
- Which goal interests you the most and why?
- Which of the following examples of goals from a development perspective would you like to learn (from Richards & Farrell, 2005)?
  - understanding how teachers' roles change according to the kind of learners he or she is teaching
  - understanding the kinds of decision-making that occurs during lessons
  - reviewing one's own theories and principles of language teaching
  - developing an understanding of different styles of teaching
  - determining learners' perceptions of classroom activities
  - Others?

Reflective Practice

Professional development that takes an applied science model (or what Schön, 1983, called "technical rationality") has prevailed for a long time and is still enacted in many professional development programs today because it gives stability with discipline specific standards, and systemized knowledge that can provide general solutions to problems through training and applications of research. Professional development from such a perspective is the learning of such scientific knowledge and skills as applied to teaching in a "one-size-fits-all" approach. Such "transmission-oriented" models for teacher development suggest that teachers isolate, practice, and eventually master discrete teaching behaviors such as teacher talk, wait time, and use of questioning techniques.

However, over recent years scholars have noted that such generalizations of professional development practice are not appropriate for more complex problems of practice that are unique to teachers in specific contexts that call for more specific and unique solutions. Such a reflective view of professional development is based on the assumption that language teachers can learn from experience through systematic reflection on the nature and meaning of their teaching experiences (Schön, 1983; Farrell, 2015, 2018, 2019a, 2019b, 2021). Indeed, within many professions today (e.g., science, law, medicine, nursing and education), engaging in reflective practice is recognized as a mark of professional competence. Within the field of Education, reflective practice offers teachers a way to articulate what they know, and what they do as they (re)consider what they learn in and through their teaching. As Zwozdiak-Myers (2012, p. 3) put it, reflective practice is central to a teacher's development because it helps teachers "to analyze and evaluate what is happening" in their classes so that they can not only improve the quality of their teaching, but also provide better opportunities for their students to learn. I agree with Lange (1990, pp. 249–250), who sees an intimate relationship between teacher reflection and teacher development:

> The reflective process allows developing teachers latitude to experiment within a framework of growing knowledge and experience. It gives them the opportunity to examine their relations with students, their values, their abilities, and their successes and failures in a realistic context. It begins the developing teacher's path toward becoming an "expert teacher."

Wajnryb (1992, p. 9) has also linked reflective practice to language teacher professional development, and she considers reflective language teachers as those who are "discovering more about their own teaching by seeking to understand the processes of teaching and learning in their own and others' classrooms." Kumaravadivelu (2003, p. 17), too, has suggested that language teachers should enter into "a continual process of self-reflection and self-renewal" so that they can "construct their own personal theory of teaching." Its inclusion in language teacher development programs, according to Freeman (2016, p. 221), is based on two premises: (1) "Improvement in teaching comes when teachers can turn actions that are automatic and routine into ones that are considered. (2) This shift from automatic to considered actions supports a more professionalized view of teaching." More recently Chung (2021) has pointed out that traditional means of providing professional development for teachers such as through courses, seminars, and workshops, have been shown to be inadequate to fulfil the needs of practicing teachers. In other words, Chung (2021, p. 2) suggests that professional development is not just the acquisition of new content knowledge but that the inclusion of reflection "is positively related to teachers' professional development."

Teachers who engage in reflective practice can develop a deeper understanding of their teaching, assess their professional growth, develop informed decision-making skills, and become proactive and confident in their teaching (Farrell, 2019). Professional development through reflective practice can be seen as an opportunity for teachers to enter a process of "mental growth spurred from within" (Feiman-Namser & Floden, 1986, p. 523), a process in which teachers can expand their knowledge of their practice and thus be in charge of their own growth. Thus, teachers actively construct their own knowledge through self-awareness, they can begin to question their knowledge and develop more ideas as they evolve as teachers.

Time Out

- What does "reflective practice" mean to you?
- How can you engage in your professional development through reflective practice?
- Freeman (2016) noted above that reflective practice can help improve teaching especially when teachers consider their actions. How can you improve your teaching skills?
    - Observing yourself and/or other teachers?
    - Being observed by other teachers?
    - Writing about teaching?
    - Talking about teaching?
    - Taping (video and/or audio) your classes?
    - Getting student feedback?
    - Attending seminars/workshops/conferences?
    - Other?

"Doing" Professional Development

When language teachers take part in, or "do" professional development, they have various reflection tools available to help with the two most common being writing and discussion. Both of these can be used individually or with another teacher (pair) or with a group of teachers. For example, the Time Outs that appear in this chapter and other chapters can be responded to in written form or discussed with a colleague or a group of colleagues. In fact, the activities in the remaining chapters of this book can also be carried out individually or collectively with a colleague or a group and can be in written form or through discussions.

Writing

One of the most popular methods of "doing" professional development using a specific tool is by writing about your experiences and reflections. Teachers already do a lot of writing within their workday, be it on lesson planning, reports on students' progress, writing to parents or any other means of communicating to others about their work. However, teachers seldom write for or about themselves as teachers reflecting on their practices. Writing as a tool for professional development has its own built-in reflective mechanism because you must stop, however briefly, to consider what you are thinking about, and this helps organize all the passing thoughts that flow at high speeds. Then after writing (with a pen or computer processor), you can actually "see" your thoughts and this gives us another chance to consider if they remain relevant for the issue you are reflecting on. This is called reflective writing (Farrell, 2012). Such reflective writing can include written accounts of thoughts, observations, beliefs, attitudes, and experiences about practice both inside and outside the classroom. Teachers can include records of critical incidents, problems, and insights that occurred during lessons in order to gain new understandings of their own learning and practices. Thus, when teachers take the time to write about their practice they can express their opinions, hypothesize about their practice and of course reflect later on what actually happened during their practice and compare results.

Teachers can consider different reflective levels of writing they can engage in. Hatton and Smith (1995, p. 85) identified four levels of writing.

- Descriptive writing (not reflective) reports events that occurred or is a report of something you have read in the literature. There is no attempt to provide reasons or justifications for the events. Its main purpose is to provide a support or a starting point for the framework.
- Descriptive reflection attempts to provide reasons and justifications for events or actions but in a descriptive way. Although there is some recognition of alternative viewpoints, it is mainly based upon personal judgment.
- Dialogic reflection demonstrates a "stepping back" from the events/actions leading to a different level of mulling about discourse with oneself through the exploration of possible reasons.
- Critical reflection demonstrates a level of awareness that actions and events in the classroom (and beyond) are explained by multiple perspectives. It involves giving reasons for decisions or events, which takes into account the broader historical, social, and/or political contexts.

Teachers can choose to structure their writing in a kind of developmental sequence from the non-reflective, descriptive writing to descriptive reflection, becoming more able to give a range of reasons for acting as they do. Then they can take a more exploratory examination of why things occur the way they do and engage in dialogic reflection. Or, as Hatton and Smith (1995) note, teachers can take a more critical perspective depending on where they are reflectively. Language teachers can write about countless different topics related to their practice such as group work in class, giving of instructions, the use of teacher questions, giving feedback/correction of errors, to more macro concerns such as: lesson planning, textbook selection, curriculum development, administration influences. After writing for some time on whatever topic that interests you most, you can then look for patterns that emerge and when you have noticed a pattern, you can investigate it in more detail by engaging in an action research project (see Chapter 2 for more on action research) that critically explores whatever theme or pattern that has emerged.

Although I said that writing is an individual reflection tool, it can also be shared with others with or without a request for feedback. When you write for yourself, you can include more personal/private thoughts and feelings as well as facts about your practice that you may not want others to see. You can read these for later reflection with the idea that you look for patterns in these writings over time for more ideas on your professional development. You can also share these with other teachers and ask them to write their own comments on your reflections.

There are also different modes of writing that can include teacher journals and online writing in blogs, chats, and forums. Teaching journals provide language teachers with a written record of various aspects of their practice and thus enables them to later review, interpret, and reflect on them so that they can gain a deeper understanding of their work. Another more modern mode of writing is technology based and makes use of the internet and online formats for writing. Such online formats are easy to use (does not require understanding of HTML or web scripting), interactive and can be continuously updated. Indeed, a language educator made use of his laptop to keep an "electronic journal-cum-diary" to record his own reactions and observations of his students' learning during a course and found this form of reflective journal writing very successful (Towndrow, 2004, p. 175). Other online formats such as blogs are a way for language teachers to express and share their thoughts, emotions, opinions, and reflections online with other professionals. Twitter is also fast becoming very popular as a form of communication (bites of information that appear usually in one or two sentences with a maximum of 140 characters in a tweet) and interaction for language teachers in many different contexts. Teachers use twitter to seek advice about a particular way to teach one of the skills or to undertake research or to find out if others had similar experiences with a particular method of teaching. Indeed, some language teachers report that online writing formats are better than engaging in dialogue (see below) because teachers can challenge peers online easier than when discussing issues face-to-face. Actually, online blogging can provide an emotional outlet for teachers interested in writing as a mode of professional development and can lead to dialogic blogs between teachers and teacher groups wishing to develop together (see below for more on dialogue).

Dialogue

Dialogue can be a very important mode of professional development for many language teachers because each individual teacher brings a different perspective to the discussion. As Mann and Walsh (2017, p. 8) point out, dialogue "is a crucial part of the reflection-action-further-action cycle, since it allows for clarification, questioning and ultimately enhanced understanding." Thus, discussions with other teachers can result in a teacher gaining new knowledge, new perspectives, and new understandings that may have been difficult to achieve by reflecting alone. Certainly, such gatherings can generate more connections between teachers—which is important for such an isolated profession where individual teachers spend most of their day in one room (door usually closed) with different groups of students. However, when they gather in pairs or groups to discuss their practice, this isolation is reduced as teachers share their knowledge, with the result that they can all provide better learning opportunities for their students.

When language teachers come together either in pairs or in groups, there is no set format in terms of process or content discussed. However, Mann and Walsh (2017) maintain that discussions with other teachers can be enhanced if artifacts are included such as video analysis and other such recordings of teaching to promote more systematic dialogue (see Chapter 2 for more on this). In addition, trust is an important aspect of dialogic reflections because these discussions (and for writing above) involve a certain amount of risk-taking as you share your ideas with others, and others may challenge you through dialogue (and/or writing) that may be outside our comfort zone. The main point in this section is that you decide which tool, or combination of tools, will best assist your professional development.

Time Out

- Do you like to write about your teaching? If yes, why? If no, why not?
- Do you like to share your writing with other teachers?
- Richards and Farrell (2005) report that teachers should set a time frame for the writing activity as there is a danger it may fizzle out without such allocated time. How and when will you allocate time for you to write regularly about your work?
- Do you like to talk to other teachers about your teaching? If yes, why? If no, why not?
- Which do you prefer, talking with one other teacher (pair) or with a group of teachers?
- What topics are important for you to talk to other teachers about and why?
- Which areas would you like to develop in your teaching?
    - Obtaining new ideas for classroom activities?
    - Getting more experience teaching different courses?

- Developing your communication skills?
- Improving your English language abilities?
- Improving your teaching methods?
- Becoming more aware of what is happening in your classroom?
- Learning more about the theory behind language teaching and learning?
- Other?

Conclusion

Most, if not all, language teachers are doing great work every day, and most are probably very comfortable with their current practices that they have most likely developed on their own over the years. However, as time goes by we sometimes follow routines that can obscure these tried and trusted practices to the point where we may feel somewhat uneasy if we are asked to explain what we do and why we do it. Indeed, I have felt this many times during my career when someone asks me what I am doing and why because I may have been following my own routines without much reflection. If we do follow our routines without much reflection or development, we may become more susceptible to some kind of plateauing during our teaching careers. Thus, engaging in professional development throughout our careers can help us avoid plateauing and maintain interest, enthusiasm, creativity and curiosity so that we can become the best teacher we can be. In the remaining contents of this book, I offer a professional development plan that includes a wide variety of methods and procedures for all levels of experience. As noted above in this chapter, these activities can be carried out at the individual level and or with a colleague or a group of colleagues. I hope you have a pleasant professional development journey with the contents of this book.

2
Approaches to Language Teacher Professional Development: *Individual*

Introduction

As mentioned in the previous chapter, teachers have a wide variety of approaches, methods, and procedures at their disposal for teacher development, which can be explored individually and/or collaboratively. This chapter explores approaches to professional development activities that can be carried out individually, while the chapter that follows (see Chapter 3) focuses on approaches that can be carried out collaboratively. The focus of this chapter includes development through *self-monitoring*, *critical incident* and *case study* analysis, reflection with *teaching portfolios*, and through *action research* projects, as well as development of a teacher's *language awareness*.

Time Out

- What activities have you used in the past for your individual professional development?
- Read the following example of the professional development experiences of a non-native English-speaking teacher (NNEST) in Thailand as written in the teacher's own words and comment on her experiences:
  - *What did I do for my professional development?*
    There are many methods that I have used to improve myself as a language teacher. Getting involved is the key method of my professional development. When I first started the career, I didn't know much about teaching at all. So, I started off with a lot of teaching hours. Later on, more complex jobs started coming my way, such as writing materials, presenting papers, giving talks, setting

up self-access centers, co-advising theses, conducting research, and so on. I rarely declined any jobs assigned. In doing these assignments there was always somebody, normally experts in the field, to lead the group. Working with high caliber people has allowed me to observe and learn a lot, more than any courses that any universities could have provided. I always find time to attend workshops and seminars of my interests. And the other way round I've forced myself to present papers at conferences or to give a talk when invited at least twice a year. Doing presentations has allowed me to sit down and study something seriously, synthesize the knowledge gained and explain it to other people. I started my career by teaching Foundation English to non-English major students, and then I moved further to teach English major students. Now I'm in teacher training. I feel grateful to the experience I have had from my earlier years of teaching undergraduate students. Even though I have a lot of experience in teaching, running self-access centers, developing curriculum, writing classroom materials, self-access materials and web-based materials, I still lack a theory to back up when I teach my MA students. One of the ways I did to bridge the gap is to ask my colleagues if I could possibly sit in their MA classes. I've learned both the theory and the training methodology. This has proved very useful to me. I've realized that teaching methodology is not enough for me to be a good teacher, and I also need to be proficient in English as well. I take all opportunities available to use the language so that I can be fluent when communicating with my students. One example is to at least find some time during the day to talk, discuss, and share ideas with my colleagues who are native speakers of English.

- *What did I find helpful?*
  I find that all of the methods I have used are very helpful for my professional development.
- *What do I still need to do?*
  I haven't got time to read seriously. Reading more research papers, or textbooks can help me to grasp the theory to balance it off with my experience for my teacher training career. Being a teacher trainer, I need to strike a balance between theory and experience. So, at the moment I need more theory to support.

Self-Monitoring

In the previous chapter the concept of reflective teaching applied to teacher professional development was introduced, and it was noted that an individual teacher's professional development can be enhanced greatly by engaging in self-monitoring. In this chapter, self-monitoring involves more than just thinking about our teaching after class because we can have a selective memory about what we think occurred in our lessons. Self-monitoring means that we must collect as much information (called data) as we can about our actual practices and then consider our findings in light of our teaching beliefs and theory of practice. In such a manner we can make more informed decisions about our practice that are based on the data rather than our feelings about what we think occurred. As Richards and Farrell (2005) maintain, language teachers can engage in more objective self-monitoring by documenting what actually occurs in lessons, rather than what we think occurs without gathering any data. More objective methods of engaging in self-monitoring include the use of lesson reports, questionnaires and checklists, as well as collecting samples of teaching through audio-recording and video-recording our lessons.

Lesson Report

One simple way language teachers can engage in self-monitoring and obtaining information about their teaching is to write a report on their lesson after the event. A lesson report is basically as detailed as possible written description of what happened during the lesson. Thus, it is important to complete such a report soon after the lesson, because our memory can become selective as time passes after any event. In fact, I have often taken my own notes while I was teaching so I would not forget these at the end, and when I was writing my own lesson reports, I found these notes very helpful. Richards and Lockhart (1995) suggest the following procedures (modified for individual use here) for preparing self-report forms:

- First, identify in as much detail as possible the philosophy underlying the course and the different kinds of teaching activities, procedures, and resources that you expect to use in the course.
- Next, prepare a lesson report form.

- Use the lesson report form on a regular basis to record the activities, procedures, and resources used throughout the course.
- Monitor your own teaching using self-report forms, thus gathering important information that will be useful the next time you teach the same course.

When individual language teachers write such reports, they obviously focus on lesson events that were meaningful for them, such as how the materials and activities were received by the students, and/or any difficulties they may have had with them during the lesson, or things that did not go according to what you had planned as you compare your report with your previously prepared lesson plan. In this manner, you can reflect and evaluate why any unanticipated events occurred so that you can learn more about your lessons. You can also use the results of your lesson report to reteach any lesson you consider did not go according to your plan, and/or you can consider how you would teach it differently if you had such an opportunity in the future. Thus, a lesson report can be a short note you write after class, or a more detailed written account of everything that happened in the lesson, but the main idea is the same: individual language teachers can use this data as a source to self-monitor for their future learning, development, and teaching.

Time Out

- What kind of information would you like to include in your lesson report and why?
- Richards and Lockhart (1995) suggest language teachers write answers to the following questions after class as a basic approach to reporting on their lesson; try to answer these questions after teaching a lesson:
    - What were the main goals of the lesson?
    - What did the learners actually learn in the lesson?
    - What teaching procedures did I use?
    - What problems did I encounter and how did I deal with them?
    - What were the most effective parts of the lesson?
    - What were the least effective parts?
    - Would I do anything differently if I taught the lesson again?

Checklists, Surveys, Questionnaires

Language teachers can also include checklists, surveys, and questionnaires to help self-monitor what happened during their lessons. They can develop their own checklists or use predetermined lesson observation checklists, many of which are published on the internet for free but should be adapted to suit your own needs. Many such checklists cover main points in a lesson such as the lesson opening, the main activities used, the level of interaction among all the participants including teacher talking time, the lesson closing and whatever else a teacher is interested in monitoring during the lesson. As with lesson reports, these should be filled out as soon as possible after each lesson for a more accurate recollection.

Language teachers can also survey or administer a questionnaire to their students for their self-monitoring as well as to obtain even more information about what their students experienced during their lessons. Of course, there are endless topics that language teachers can survey their students about, however one popular topic is how their students' view working with their peers in a group in a language lesson. The questionnaire or survey can be designed to ask students about their attitudes towards the use of group work and if they find it useful and enjoyable regarding their learning of the target language (see also Time Out below). One point to remember when administering questionnaires or surveys to students, however, is the issue of confidentiality, and so the degree of confidentiality about learners' responses should be considered each time they are used. One way of assuring anonymity is not to require the students to put their names on these instruments.

Time Out

- What are some aspects of teaching or learning that you are interested in investigating using checklists, surveys and questionnaires?
- How can you design a checklist, survey or questionnaire to suit your need for obtaining information about your teaching?
- One example (from Farrell, 2019a) is a questionnaire designed by a language teacher who wanted to include her students' voices about their language learning experiences, and especially their attitudes towards her use of group work. She was particularly interested in knowing more about how her learners feel about homogeneous grouping (being grouped with classmates of similar levels) compared to heterogeneous

Individual Approaches to Teacher Professional Development

grouping (being grouped with classmates of different levels). In addition, she wondered about how these different groupings affect the degree of student participation. So, this language teacher set about developing a questionnaire with a mixture of closed (Likert-scale) and open-ended questions to garner feedback on group dynamics and student participation at the end of her lesson as outlined below:

- 1) Think about how you worked in your group today. Please rank your feelings about each aspect of today's group.

1. Strongly disagree; 2. Disagree; 3. Neither agree nor disagree; 4. Agree; 5. Strongly agree

I felt comfortable working with the members of today's group.	1 2 3 4 5
I am happy with my participation in today's group.	1 2 3 4 5
I found it easy to work in today's group.	1 2 3 4 5
Communication in today's group was good.	1 2 3 4 5
Working in today's group helped my learning.	1 2 3 4 5
I felt adequately challenged working in today's group.	1 2 3 4 5
I was comfortable with the pace that my group worked at.	1 2 3 4 5
My group members respected my opinion.	1 2 3 4 5
I was able to share my ideas with the group.	1 2 3 4 5

2) Did you enjoy working in today's group? Why/why not?

3) Did you have any problems working in today's group? If so, explain.

- Try to administer the questionnaire about group work above (or adjust it in any way you like to suit your needs) with your students and see what the result is.
- How could the information from your checklists, surveys and questionnaires be used?

- Who should have access to this information?
- Should you, and how can you, account for anonymity for your students' responses?
- Read and comment on the following account of one ESL teacher's development and use of observation checklists as part of his teacher development as written in his own words.
  - Once after being observed for the purpose of evaluation, the observer pointed out a few problems with my teaching methodology and said I was doing too much grammar-translation and no communicative teaching. I had to remind the observer that the institution demanded grammar-translation methods even though I was well aware of all the communicative learner-based methodologies. Since then, I always ask the observers beforehand what they know about teaching practices the school requires, and I also give my own personal opinions about methodologies and the school policies. So, over the years I have developed many classroom observation checklists because one thing that I have realized is that an observation checklist should be very teacher friendly and must not contain too many items, this is a lesson I learnt from my above experiences. I think that rather than put too many items on a checklist to check off and make the checklist concise and stick to the most important points you are interested in checking.

Audio & Video-Recording Lessons

Another method language teachers can use to self-monitor is to audio and/or video record lessons. One advantage of recording your lessons is that these are retrievable at any time (and can be used to show teacher growth over time) so that you can continuously check (replay) different lesson events that you are interested in self-monitoring. In addition, both types of recording are more objective in nature than the previously outlined self-reflection techniques above that depend on an individual's recollections. With recordings, however, you can get a detailed and real account of the actual lesson as long as you record in ways that can capture the voices of the participants you are interested in.

Video recordings add the visual and nonverbal talk to the audio and thus can provide even more details of what occurred in the lesson. Placement of any video recorder will of course determine the amount of detail and number of participants you want to capture. I have used both audio and video recordings over the years with my own classes. For audio recording, I have found that placing a recording device in the middle of the room can capture only those voices who are in close proximity unless the device is so powerful as to capture the entire room. Thus, I have used audio differently than video in that I prefer to use it to capture the teacher's voice by placing a mic on the teacher's lapel during the lesson. This way the teacher can capture all of his or her talk during the lesson. In the same vein I have placed video cameras either directly focusing on the teacher throughout the lesson, or at the front of the room directly focusing on the students' interactions (with their permission of course). Over the years, as technology has progressed audio and video have developed in terms of digitalization, storage, edition, and annotation with much more sophisticated software available for teachers to manipulate.

Once you decide if you want to record all or part of your lesson (Walsh (2013) argues that short "snapshot" recordings may have more value in heightening awareness of lessons rather than more longer recordings) you are interested in monitoring, you will then need to review the recordings. When reviewing both audio and video recordings of your lesson, you can simply listen and watch both audio and video as well as transcribe all or parts of the lesson for a more detailed analysis. You can take notes while listening to the tape and viewing the video, make short or long transcripts, and/or tally specific behaviors you are interested in monitoring. Since you are engaged in self-monitoring, the amount of detail of what you transcribe will be your decision, but if you want to use this transcription with other teachers later (see Chapter 3), then the written transcription will need to be more detailed and formal. Given that professional development is an opportunity for you to become more aware of your teaching, engaging in self-monitoring with the use of audio and video recordings can help you identify hidden aspects of your teaching that may be difficult for you to "see" while you teach, and as a result once identified, can be improved. As one ESL teacher in South Korea noted:

> Videos have made me aware of some bad habits that developed and helped me watch my own treatments. As an example, I found that I had developed a "restless pacing" pattern. I concluded this was from my own desire to stay away from a "lecture from the podium" format, but that it was surely disconcerting to the learners.

Self-monitoring using lesson recordings that can generate samples of your teaching style is often a good starting point in planning any individual professional development initiatives, since it can be used to identify particular issues that might be further explored through collaboration with other teachers through for example, critical friends, peer coaching, team teaching, classroom observations, and/or teacher groups (see Chapter 3).

Time Out

- Audio and/or video record a lesson. Replay each (listen to the audio and listen and view the video):
    - What did you learn about you and your teaching style?
    - Did anything surprise you as you listened and viewed?
    - What were the positive aspects of your teaching?
    - What were the negative aspects of your teaching?
    - How was the pace of your lesson?
    - Who is doing most of the talking in the lesson?
    - What kinds of questions did you ask most often? (e.g., Yes-no? Either-or, Wh-? Tag Questions?)
    - How long did you wait after asking a question to get a response?
    - How did you give instructions?
    - Do students know what to do after being given the instructions?
    - How much talking time did you engage in?
    - What did you notice about your students' participation?
    - What did you notice about your students' nonverbal behaviors?
    - Was anyone off task?
    - What type of language was used and was this part of your overall lesson plan?
    - What did your students learn?
    - What helped them learn?
    - What got in the way?
    - What specific evidence can you quote to back up your claims?
    - What did you learn from this analysis?
    - What aspects of the lesson were easy for you to capture with both recordings and what were difficult?

Critical Incidents

The previous section outlined and discussed how individual language teachers can engage in self-monitoring through the use of surveys, checklists and questionnaires, as well as gathering information about their teaching with the use of audio and/or video recordings. Another method of engaging in individual professional development for language teachers is to focus on particular events, actions or episodes that occur in lessons. These "critical incidents" may interrupt or even highlight a teacher's taken-for-granted ways of viewing his or her teaching. Such interruptions and/or highlights can be examined intensely so that the teacher can begin to uncover the values and beliefs that really underpin his or her perceptions about teaching.

Whereas the previous section introduced you to self-monitoring that explores your overall beliefs and practices, this section encourages you to recall and review specific classroom events and experiences that you "vividly" (Brookfield, 1990, p. 84) remember well after the lesson has ended. As Woods (1996, p. 375) has noted, such classroom events are "critical" for the teacher because they are "flash-points that illuminate in an electrifying instant" that the teaching status quo has been interrupted. Tripp (1993, p. 8) suggests that a critical incident is an "interpretation of the significance of an event ... a value judgment we make, and the basis of that judgment is a significance we attach to the meaning of the incident." When a teacher analyzes and reflects on such "critical incidents" or "flash-points" in depth, he or she can begin to question underlying assumptions, habits, and routines about his or her teaching. Analyzing critical incidents in depth allows teachers to not only identify both practical dilemmas, but also to explore opportunities that occur during lessons (Richards & Farrell, 2005).

The following summarize how analyzing critical incidents can help facilitate teacher development (adapted from Richards & Farrell, 2005):

- *Create a greater level of self-awareness*. By writing and talking about and reading critical incidents, we can become more aware of our underlying beliefs, values and assumptions about language teaching and learning, gaining greater self-understanding and personal growth. The following example explains how a teacher gained awareness about differences in culture by reflecting on a critical incident that happened in his class (adapted from Richards & Farrell, 2005): One day a student raised her hand and asked if she was allowed to use Korean during the class. I realized that when the student sought permission to speak her native language in class, it raised a conflict with my belief system about what education should be about. My different cultural background led me to assume that all students could lead autonomous lives within the school in that they are responsible for their own actions. I said that it was up to her if she wanted to clarify something with a friend during the class.

- *Prompt an evaluation of established routines and procedures.* Analysis of critical incidents raises important issues about how our students respond (or do not respond) to our teaching techniques and activities. Thus, we can become more aware of how we teach, the impact of our teaching on our students' learning and how our students learn so that we can fine-tune our teaching. The following is an example of such awareness (adapted from Richards & Farrell, 2005): One day when I was teaching, I realized that when I ask questions to EFL students, I am actually asking them to perform a complicated task. It was when I was teaching the class a student misspelled the word, promote, on the board during a dictation exercise. After he corrected it, I asked him if he understood the word, but he couldn't hear it in the sentence that I had just read. This experience showed me again that listening to directions is not an easy task for an EFL student. I now realize that EFL students must first listen and understand the language in order to understand the directions for the activity, and how to do the activity. Finally, the students must choose and organize the appropriate words in the foreign language to express the understanding response.
- *Learn how to pose critical questions about teaching*: By becoming more aware of the complexities of language teaching, we can begin to pose more meaningful questions about the consequences of specific teaching activities and approaches. The following incident is an example of how one teacher posed questions that led him to make specific changes in his teaching: I had this student in an essay writing course. His name was Alfredo. The course involved students in writing 250–500-word essays. Alfredo was a good writer, and his essays were clearly better than the other students in the class. His grasp of sentence structure was excellent, he explained his ideas well through examples and details, and he organized his ideas effectively. I would read his essays and mark them with an "A," happy that there was such a good writer in the classroom.

All this while the other students were struggling with writing their essays, and indeed would often have to rewrite them to get a decent grade. At the end of the semester, Alfredo told me one day, "If you had marked my essays lower, I would have worked harder." I was very surprised to get a remark like that from a student, and also upset to think that he felt he hadn't been pushed enough in my classroom, that he hadn't learned very much. From this, I learned then that I couldn't judge students only by comparing them with the others—that I needed to judge them on their own terms. I needed to grade them in comparison with the work they were doing and were capable of doing. Otherwise, I wouldn't be doing these better students a favor—I wouldn't be helping them grow in their writing. Since then, I make sure that even if I think an essay is good, I give the student plenty of feedback as to what kind of changes or additions can be made to make the essay even better. I work with the students on not concentrating so much on grades and concentrating more on their development as writers. I find that I am more relaxed in the writing classroom now, as the focus is more on the writing process, and not on simply putting marks on the final written product. So, I enjoy teaching writing much more now than before I got this comment from Alfredo.

- *Bring beliefs to the level of awareness.* By writing, reading, analyzing and interpreting critical incidents, we can become more aware of our beliefs and decide if any of them should be changed. Our beliefs are generally fixed and therefore difficult to change and so by analyzing such incidents, our beliefs become clearer. The following (adapted from Tripp, 1993, p. 4) is such an example that involves a novice teacher attempting to control a noisy class. He enters the classroom to start the lesson, but it is very noisy.

Teacher: Rick, is that you making all the noise?
Rick: No, Sir!
Teacher: Well then, who is making all the noise?

The class noise then subsides as students take interest in the conversation between the teacher and Rick. The teacher looks round all areas of the classroom. An analysis of this incident reveals that when the teacher entered the classroom, he immediately singled out an individual in an attempt to manage the situation by showing he was in control.

The interaction between the teacher and a single student becomes the focus for the whole class. The teacher controls the event, and thus controls the whole class revealing his underlying principle of classroom management. Rick realized that he had not given a great deal of thought to this before he read what he had written in his journal.

- *Develop an awareness of teaching/learning complexities.* Analysis of critical incidents raises important issues that occur while teaching, and teachers can come to realize that in some cases there are no easy answers that can solve all these issues because teaching is a complex undertaking. The following is an example of how a teacher realized just how complex teaching can be (adapted from Richards & Farrell, 2005): My students in a lower intermediate listening/speaking class were assigned a pair activity. The first part of the lesson had focused on examples, working through the language needed. I gave them a handout, with clear step-by-step instructions. We had gone over the instructions on the handout, and I asked them if they understood what they were to do. I answered a few questions and the class started to work. I walked around to check that everyone was on track, and to answer any other questions. It looked like the pairs were off to a good start, but as I got to the back of the room, one pair asked, "Sir, what do you want us to do?" This incident not only made me scratch my head at the time, but also it reminded me of how complex teaching is given we have students with different cultural backgrounds, language proficiency abilities and interests. I never take things for granted in my classes again.
- *Realize that there are no simple answers.* We often realize that there are no simple answers to dilemmas in classrooms when we reflect on our (and others) critical incidents. We also realize that we must examine the viability of alternative solutions and the consequences of these solutions. The following example is from an ESL teacher who was teaching in a university language program in the USA and shows how there are no easy answers to solve problems that occur in classes (adapted from Richards & Farrell, 2005): I was teaching intensive writing in an EAP program in the US and my students were mainly from countries that bordered each other in a certain region of the world. I had two younger boys in my ESL class who were from the same country and the rest of the students were from different, but nearby countries as the boys. One day during class there were exchanges between these boys and the other students. One of the other students

suddenly spat at one of the boys and I was shocked and really did not react for a few minutes. They then began shouting at each other in a language, which I couldn't understand. Then I stood in and made them stop before they started fighting. I stopped class then and told the other students to go. I kept the younger boys back and they told me that in their country they would settle the situation with knives but didn't wish to do so there. I was really shaking now but I realized that I had to keep my class and my teaching intact as these were fee-paying students, so I went to my boss for help.
- *Create opportunities for case study analysis and action research projects.* Critical incident analysis can be the starting point for follow up research such as a case study (see below) or action research (see below).

In practical terms of describing critical incidents, I have found the following procedures useful (Farrell, 2007, 2013): when you experience and identify an incident you consider critical to you, write (to keep a record—see journal writing previous chapter) a brief description of it describing who was involved, where it took place, when, and what happened exactly. At this first stage, do not attempt to explain or interpret the incident. After reflecting on the incident, you can then attempt to explain and interpret the meaning and its implications for you as a teacher.

An important consideration for critical incidents for language teachers is the type of incident they choose to examine because many teachers tend to only look for negative (a teaching "low", Theil, 1999) classroom events and ignore more positive incidents (a teaching "high", Theil, 1999). For example, a teaching "high" could be a successful spontaneous intervention or change the teacher made to a lesson plan that had a positive effect on the lesson by increasing student participation. A teaching "low" could be a specific classroom incident that was immediately problematic and perplexing, such as reflecting on one student who suddenly stopped talking in a conversation activity for no apparent reason but is usually the first student to participate normally. In addition, you can use the audio and/or video to recall such particular incidents in the lesson that you consider critical for your professional development. If you are meeting regularly with other teachers, you can share your incidents and interpretations and see if you have the same understanding of them (see Chapter 3 for more on collaborative professional development).

Time Out

- Reflect on an unanticipated, unplanned moment, event, and/or incident that was "critical" for you as a language teacher (remember it can be a positive ("high") or negative ("low") moment). Write up the incident in as much detail as you can recall and use audio and video analysis (if you have them) to help you recall. Now try to answer the following questions about the incident:
  - What happened directly before the event?
  - What happened directly after the event?
  - How did you react at the time of the event?
  - What is your interpretation of this event?
  - Why was this incident significant to you?
  - What underlying assumptions about your teaching does this critical incident raise for you?
  - Now that you have reflected on this critical incident, would you react any differently if it happened again? Why, why not?
- Farrell and Baecher (2017) outline and discuss 40 different critical incidents related to language teaching. Try to get this book and reflect on as many of these that you think are related to your classroom context:
  - *Creating a Positive Classroom Community*, details four problems of practice related to the important topic of relationship building for positive classroom environments:
    1. Fostering Relationships with Challenging Students
    2. Confronting Cultural Tensions between Students
    3. Establishing the "Teacher Role" with Students
    4. Promoting Collaboration among Students
  - *Curriculum Development*, details four problems of practice related to curriculum development and its place in the life of the novice teacher:
    1. Working with Mandated Curricula
    2. Integrating Content and Language
    3. Aligning Lessons to Standards
    4. Facing a Lack of Resources
  - *Teaching Mixed-Level/Large Classes*, details four problems of practice related to mixed-level proficiency levels and large classes teachers have to teach:

1. Planning for Mixed-level Classes
2. Managing Large Classes
3. Engaging Lower-Proficiency Students
4. Supporting Pre-literate Students
- *Classroom Management*, details four problems of practice related to classroom management issues:
  1. Establishing Routines and Rewards
  2. Developing a Discipline Plan
  3. Managing Time in the Lesson
  4. Determining when to use the First Language in Class
- *Developing Students' Speaking Skills*, details four problems of practice related to teaching speaking:
  1. Tackling students' shyness about speaking English
  2. Handling students' outright refusal to speak English
  3. Teaching speaking rather than practicing speaking
  4. Dealing with pronunciation issues in speaking classes
- *Developing Students' Reading Skills*, details four problems of practice related to teaching reading in L2 classrooms:
  1. Helping students with different alphabetic backgrounds to read in English
  2. Increasing extensive and independent reading
  3. Encouraging students to use reading strategies
  4. Use decoding to improve word identification problems while reading
- *Developing Students' Listening Skills*, details four problems of practice related to teaching listening:
  1. Getting students interested in listening lessons
  2. Improving students' ability to listen for interactional purposes
  3. Helping students understand differences in spoken and written texts
  4. Encouraging extensive and independent listening
- *Developing Students' Writing Skills*, details four problems of practice related to teaching writing:
  1. Guiding students to become peer-editors
  2. Helping students utilize process writing techniques
  3. Developing focused writing lessons
  4. Providing appropriate feedback on written work

- *Addressing Workplace Challenges*, details four problems of practice related to conflict in schools and settings where English is taught:
  1. Working in a team-teaching model
  2. Supporting students with special needs
  3. Confronting the impact of poverty on student learning
  4. Coping with the pressures of testing
- *Professional Development*, details four problems of practice related to teacher professional development:
  1. Working with a mentor teacher
  2. Understanding your teaching context
  3. Establishing your identity as a teacher
  4. Developing your language proficiency

Case Study

Whereas a critical incident (see above) is a retrospective analysis of any unexpected event, dilemma, or specific incident that occurs instantaneously during a lesson, a case study is a more formal reflection on a particular issue or topic that freeze-frames (Schön, 1983) that event or case. The freeze-frame allows a teacher to not only reproduce the event or issue in broader detail, but also to somewhat "relive" it in a more detached manner so that the teacher can learn from the analysis. As Shulman (1992) points out, case study analysis "provides teachers with opportunities to analyze situations and make judgments in the messy world of practice, where principles often appear to conflict with one another, and no simple solution is possible" (p. xiv).

When writing up the details of a case study, it is important to start with a description of the setting, then particulars about the dilemma or issue of the case, followed by an analysis of the consequences of the dilemma or issue and any conclusions used to solve the dilemma or issue. Wassermann (1993) suggests the following three steps be followed in order:

1. *Fact-finding*: During this early stage, teachers place more emphasis on getting as many of the details of the case as possible for later analysis and delay discussing any solutions. Fact-finding thus forces teachers to slow down their thinking and only focus on the facts.
2. *Meaning-making*: After accumulating the information/facts as above, it must be organized into some meaningful cohesive account by making connections between issues that relate and make sense to each

other. One way of organizing the information from the point of view of making sense of it all is to use concept maps to see the complex relationships that may have developed within a case.
3. *Problem-solving*: Teachers are now ready to begin making decisions about how to solve the case and use all the information gathered in the previous two steps.

When making decisions about the case study from stage three above, it should be noted as Jackson (1997, p. 8) points out, that "in the real world of professional practice there are rarely perfect solutions to problems that ESOL teachers confront. Instead, there are usually several possible courses of action, each with strengths and limitations." Thus, teachers should try to generate a broad range of alternatives and consider each one in light of the issue at hand, and when they decide on a particular outcome, they should also point out why the other outcomes were rejected.

All language teachers have accumulated a lot of experiences and knowledge, however, much of this remains with each teacher and is not available as a source of learning and reflection for other teachers. By documenting examples of successful and problematic practices, language teachers can provide a valuable set of records that can be used as a basis for professional development. Analyzing such cases can help language teachers get a better hand on the messy world of real life, ill-structured teaching situations that are present throughout their teaching careers.

Time Out

- Write up a case study about any dilemma or issue of interest that you can use to reflect on and develop yourself as a teacher. The following are examples of case studies that could be used by you as you develop topics for your case study (from Richards & Farrell, 2005, pp. 128–129):
    - Information collected over a period of a semester concerning how two different students (one with high proficiency and one with low proficiency) performed during group activities
    - An account of the problems a teacher experienced during her first few months of teaching
    - An account of how two teachers implemented a team-teaching strategy and the difficulties they encountered

- An account of observation of one high-achieving student and one low-achieving student over a semester in order to compare their patterns of classroom participation
- A teacher's journal account of all of the classroom management problems she had to deal with in a typical school week.
- An account of how a teacher made use of lesson plans over a three week period.
- An account of how two teachers resolved a misunderstanding that occurred between them in relation to the goals of a course
- A description of all the changes a student made in a composition she was working on over a three-week period, from the drafting stage to the final stage.

• After you write-up the details of your case study, use the following questions to help you reflect critically and creatively on this so that you can really stretch your thinking on the issues at hand (from Jackson, 1997, p. 7):
- Why is this case a dilemma?
- Who are the key players?
- What are the main issues/problems?
- What, if anything, should be done to resolve the situation?
- What are the consequences of each solution?
- What would you do if you were the decision maker?
- What did you learn from the case?

• Read the following short case study about how a course coordinator tried to implement changes in an EFL program in Korea (Farrell, 1998, pp. 125–128). The case is summarized in point form and in the words of the author who was the course coordinator; it includes the context, the problem, and a solution.

Context

➢ Small women's university in Seoul, South Korea.
➢ Program had 25 part-time native Korean English instructors.
➢ Syllabus was designed exclusively by the director, as were all the examinations.
➢ Each freshman and sophomore student had to take English classes: conversation, video/audio classes for freshmen, and reading classes (prescribed text) required for the sophomore students.

Problem

- Because I was the first foreign director of the program, the instructors did not know what to expect.
- Previous teacher meetings consisted of giving the instructors their syllabi.
- Needs analysis had never been conducted.
- The instructors had not had any meetings during the semester or year to discuss their classes.
- What developed: different groups of teachers (usually arranged by age) gathered informally and discussed things about their work at lunch or in the teachers' lounge.
- Instructors never participated in other group discussions.
- I tried to establish better collaboration by having more teacher meetings on topics, usually topics I had thought important.
- Everybody came to these meetings, and at first I was pleased.
- However, it soon became apparent that I was doing all of the talking at the meetings, even when we broke up into group discussions.
- When I tried to institute peer observation, I was indirectly told, "This is not the Korean way," or "It will not work." And indeed it did not. The biggest obstacle I faced was that as a director in a Korean situation, I should have been seen as acting more authoritatively (as one professor later remarked).
- I was never given feedback from the teachers during my first year as director; instead they gave feedback to the previous director who in turn told me everything was great.
- I knew better.

Solution/Response

- To solve this dilemma, I tried a few different methods, some of which succeeded and others that were only marginally successful.
- I tried to meet the teachers "by chance," outside my office to see who would be interested to talk about teaching and who might be interested in sharing their views about the program.
- About teaching: teachers could bring lesson plans (their favorite ones) and put them in a drawer. Both old and new teachers could

compare and use them. What really happened was that I put in my lesson plans. Some other teachers did the same, but only a few and the cabinet did not fill up. But I did manage to tap into some of the informal discussions.

- About the program: I started an examination committee. This method seemed to work because the teachers had a vested interest in that their students were going to take these examinations. If Korean teachers have one overriding concern, it is for their students' success.
- Surprise: from this examination committee, I found a group of teachers who were interested in the program and their own teacher development. These five teachers met with me regularly to discuss their classroom situations in more detail. We taped our classes and brought these tapes to our group meetings. We played the tapes and discussed our teaching. These meetings continued throughout the semester.

  o What are some of the main issues that emerged from this case study?
  o What other responses could have been made to the problems encountered?

Teaching Portfolios

Language teachers may wonder what they can do with all the material they have gathered concerning their professional development, and how they can convey what they have learned to others including peers, and supervisors. I have found compiling a teaching portfolio to showcase what I have done in terms of my professional development, and where I intend going in the future as a useful professional development tool. As Evans (1995, p. 11) notes, a portfolio is a "collection of carefully selected or composed professional thoughts, goals and experiences that are threaded with reflection and self-assessment. It represents who you are, what you do, why you do it, where you have been, where you are, where you want to go, and how you plan on getting there."

Richards and Farrell (2005) outline two different types of portfolios: a working portfolio and a showcase portfolio. A working portfolio contains items that show how a teacher has progressed towards meeting a particular goal. For example, a language teacher may demonstrate how he or she has moved towards a more student-centered teaching approach, and he or she can show such evidence (e.g., video of teaching, lesson plans, student comments, student papers) in the portfolio that this goal has been reached. A showcase portfolio contains a collection of items that show the range and depth of skills the teacher possesses at present or an overall picture of the teacher's achievements. Such a portfolio can be used for self-assessment and appraisal, and/or as part of an application for a new teaching position (as I have used successfully in the past) or for promotion (also as I have also used in the past). Thus, teaching portfolios can act as both a "mirror" and a "map." The portfolio can act as a "mirror" because it allows teachers to "see" their development over time. The portfolio can also act as a "map" because it shows your goals and future plans about where you intend to go professionally during your career (Costantino & De Lorenzo, 2002).

In terms of contents, a teaching portfolio might include a statement of teaching philosophy, description of teaching goals, example of lesson plans, materials development, assignments, and examinations as well as audio and videotapes of lessons (see above), student and annual supervisor evaluations, and any other artifacts that showcase your work as a language teacher. The contents of the portfolio should also be accompanied with the teacher's written (or oral) reflection on the contents, and a self-assessment of the collection itself. This can be followed by details of any professional development plans for the future.

Teaching portfolios can be written and/or electronic with the latter more popular these days. A popular type of electronic portfolio was adopted in Europe called the European Portfolio for Student Teachers of Languages (EPOSTL) as a self-assessment tool. The main aims of the EPOSTL are, among others according to Mirici and Hergüner (2015), to encourage pre-service teachers to reflect on their competences and on the underlying knowledge which feeds this competence. This idea can also be expanded to more experienced language teachers where they can also use teaching portfolios as a self-assessment tool. When all of this information is gathered together it begins to create a story of who the learner TESOL teacher has become as a developing language teaching professional.

Time Out

- The following is an example of a teaching portfolio from a teacher in the USA explains why he compiled his showcase portfolio, what he chose to include and why, and what he gained from this process (adapted from Richards & Farrell, 2005):

I have been teaching ESL/EFL/EAP for the past twenty years after having graduated with an MA. Now I have started to compile my teaching portfolio and I decided to include the following items: Resume; Letters of Reference; Copies of Transcripts; Copies of Diplomas; Beliefs about my Teaching; Course Outlines; Student Testimonials; Copies of My Own Curriculum Materials; and Student Evaluations. I chose these eight items as I figured these would be an overall representation of who I am as a teacher. It took me about three months to finally put this portfolio together, but I am really amazed at what I was able to assemble. I did not realize that I had accomplished so much, especially in the past few years. For example, I had not realized the vast number of diverse courses I designed and taught successfully in the past few years. Additionally, I learned a lot from reading my student evaluations. For example, I was surprised to see some of them felt that they were not improving in their speaking and writing ability and that I was not correcting them enough. Apart from that, they all seemed satisfied that I was doing a good job. I understand their attitude toward corrections; it was like they were thinking: "Why can't the teacher give me some magic feedback that will eliminate my writing problems?" I think I have to do a better job of explaining my strategies as a writing teacher. The most challenging aspect of the teaching portfolio for me was writing about my beliefs and values of teaching and learning. I found it very difficult to bring to the surface what I usually do instinctively when I teach. This was a major reflective essay for me, as I had to articulate beliefs that I have but are not always easy to write down on paper. I really enjoyed putting my portfolio together. I was pleasantly surprised at the breadth and depth of what I have accomplished since I started teaching. Even though it was time-consuming, I hope others compile their teaching portfolios too.

  ○ What is your opinion of this portfolio?

- I now encourage you to compile your own showcase (see above) teaching portfolio. Try to compile as many of the following materials that can be a part of any teaching portfolio regardless of the specific purpose for creating it (from Farrell, 2002):
    - Knowledge of subject matter: Documents that relate to your knowledge of the subject matter might include the following artefacts:
        - Highlights of a unit of instruction, reflections on the class and implications for future instruction.
        - Descriptions of courses, or workshops you conducted.
        - A reflective essay about how your knowledge of the subject matter has informed your instructional decisions and how you plan to increase student learning. Do you know what aspects of your course(s) teachers are using/implementing during their first year(s) as teachers?
    - Planning, delivery and assessing instruction: Documents compiled for this section include a statement about your beliefs and values regarding language teaching and learning, what you do in the classroom (lesson plans, video of a class, student works examples), and what others think about your classroom work (supervisor's evaluation, peer observation reports):
        - A reflection of your beliefs about teaching and learning. This outlines your approach to teaching the language.
        - Sample lesson plans.
        - Samples of student work.
        - Samples of students' evaluations'/feedback of your lessons.
        - A videotape and/or audiotape of you teaching a class with a written description of what you were teaching and your reflection of that class.
        - Feedback from a supervisor and/or an administrator.
        - Classroom observation report from a peer teacher.
    - Professionalism: Documents compiled for this section include a statement of your development plans are, and other documents that confirm your standing in the profession (resume, copies of degrees etc.):
        - A current professional development plan. This plan outlines what you plan to achieve professionally in the near future such as attending certain conferences, seminars and inservice

courses that can upgrade one's skills, researching certain topics (action research projects) that can make one a more effective teacher and upgrading one's technical skills (IT).
- ➤ A current resume.
- ➤ A list of membership of professional organizations.
- ➤ A description of any leadership positions held such as head of department, curriculum development unit, and committees.
- ➤ Copies of degrees, certificates, honours, and awards held.

Action Research

Action research as a means of self-reflection and monitoring has gained much popularity in recent forums on professional development as a more rigorous method to focus on specific problematic aspects of practice. Bailey (2001, p. 490) maintains that action research for language teachers is "an approach to collection and interpreting data which involves a clear, repeated cycle of procedures." In other words, language teachers note that a problem exists with some aspect of their teaching, they gather and interpret data about this problem, and they then engage in some kind of planned intervention in order to solve this problem. The solution, as Wallace (1991, pp. 56-57) points out, can have a "specific and immediate outcome which can be directly related to practice in the teacher's own context." Thus, the control and focus of the research remains with the teacher because he or she knows their own classroom best and as such can implement changes more credibly as these changes are related to their needs. As Sagor (1992, pp. 3-4) notes: "The topics, problems, or issues pursued [in academic research] are significant, but not necessarily helpful to teachers on the front line."

Such type of localized action research usually follows a process of teachers first identifying the specific problem at hand, then they do a literature review related to that topic, followed by the collection of information in their lesson related to that problem, analyzing that information, reflecting and then acting on the problem and seeing its result. Burns (1995, 2009) maintains that in action research projects, the data collection methods most commonly used and most appealing to language teachers draw on qualitative and ethnographic methods and techniques. These approaches usually include some combination of the following careful and systematic collection of information about classroom events

Individual Approaches to Teacher Professional Development 49

through interviews, observation, field notes, questionnaires, recordings (audio and video) and transcriptions of lessons.

Richards and Farrell (2005, p. 185) maintain that when planning any action research project, language teachers should keep the following questions in mind.

- *Purpose*: Why am I starting this action research project? Is it to solve a problem that has occurred in my classroom? Or is it something else?
- *Topic*: What issue am I going to investigate? What is going on in my classes at present that is causing me concern?
- *Focus*: How can I narrow down the issue to investigate to make it manageable within a specific time frame? What is the precise question I am going to ask myself?
- *Mode*: How am I going to conduct the research? What data collecting methods will I need and why?
- *Timing*: How much time will it take and how much time do I have?
- *Resources*: What are the resources, both human and material, that I can call upon to help me complete the research? How can my institution help?
- *Product*: What is the likely outcome of the research, as I intend it?
- *Action*: What action will I expect to take as a result of conducting this research? How will I carry out this action?
- *Reporting*: How will I share the finding of this research with other teachers? What forum will I use for this and why?

Time Out

- The following is a report of an action research project conducted by a language teacher that developed from his use of questionnaires, and other methods that initially did not work for him: An Action Research project I worked on taught me a great lesson about this language teaching field. I was researching my own classroom, trying to find problems with the teaching methodology in relation to learner achievement. Getting the students to openly dissect the lessons was proving to be very difficult, I used questionnaires, interviews, general discussions, nothing was working very well. There was a problem with learner achievements but when asked why this was so, no one would open up. I was lost and didn't know what to do. I was not collecting data that could be very useful. Suddenly, after many weeks I realized my

problem. I was not motivating my students in the right way. Previously, I had been telling them how this research was going to be a very helpful exercise for all of us, how we were all going to benefit from it and learn a lot—my learners were all aged between 20–25, and I felt that a bit of intrinsic motivation would work. I decided to bribe them, as a desperate measure with extra 5 marks if they came up with solid and sensible reasons for the problems in the class and that worked. Next, I used Pepsi's—students who would again provide me with the right sort of honest data would get a free drink from the canteen. It was expensive for me but it worked. There was a lot of enthusiasm and energy in the students which resulted in very successful discussions. Try it, it works—use external rewards to motivate them.
  o What is your opinion of this action research project?

- Conduct your own action research project on any topic you are interested in related to your teaching. Below is a list of steps I have used successfully with my own action research projects that you may like to consider following:
  o Identify an issue, interest, or problem.
  o Seek knowledge (e.g., literature review, ask other teachers) to clarify the issue, interest, or problem.
  o Plan an action to learn about the issue or interest or solve the problem.
  o Report on the plan; use feedback to adjust the plan.
  o Implement the action.
  o Observe the action.
  o Report on the action taken and observation of the consequences.
  o Reflect on the observations and the report discussion.
  o Revise the plan.

Language Awareness

This final section of the chapter may seem somewhat odd because language awareness may probably be perceived by many to mean that so-called non-native English speaker teachers (NNESTs) may need to improve proficiency in the language they teach (English). First, I do not like the dichotomy that has developed in the field of TESOL related to so-called native speaker teachers and (or versus) non-native speaker teachers with the former being preferred as "better" language teachers rather than the latter, because of perceived deficiencies in their proficiency levels. I think this is disingenuous to all "qualified" language teachers regardless of their first language, or country of origin. All "qualified" language teachers have different strengths and weaknesses and hence need to engage in their own professional development.

For some language teachers, their individual professional development interests may include gaining more language awareness or more knowledge about the underlying systems of language and linguistics such as syntax, morphology, semantics, pragmatics, phonology, and/or sociolinguistics to name but a few. For other language teachers, their individual professional development interests and needs may include development of their proficiency and use of the target language as they may want to become confident when using it. Indeed, Berry (1990, p. 99) has noted that "certain approaches to language teaching are incompatible with low levels of proficiency in teachers." This would be the case when teachers want to implement a communicative language teaching (CLT) approach where a lot of oral usage of the target language is required, rather than a grammar-translation approach where less oral usage of the target language is required.

Freeman (2017) outlines an English-for-Teaching course in Japan, which focuses on classroom language use of the target language and this approach seems useful for all teachers of English regardless of their levels of proficiency. The teachers begin the course with a self-assessment of their confidence in performing various classroom tasks in English in which the course then presents functional English to carry out these tasks (in short classroom-based scenarios). What this approach does is provide an alternative to the conventional face-to-face training of teachers to overcome their "deficit" in language proficiency thereby further entrenching the idea of native-speakerism. I agree with Freeman (2017, p. 50) when he maintains that "outmoded ideas of fluency in general language use, which ultimately refer back to native-speakerism, need to be replaced with the notion that ELT teachers are "native" to their classrooms." Freeman (2017, p. 50) continues: "This professional definition of nativeness means that teachers know what they want to do in their teaching; they understand the purposes and uses that English needs to accomplish in their classrooms. What they are seeking is the specific language 'for-teaching' to do so." The core of this course is that teachers can progress at their own pace and reports from teachers who took it suggest that they were more confident to teach in English as a result.

Time Out

- How do you think a teacher's language proficiency level in the target language influences his or her teaching style?
- Do you think you need to improve your proficiency in the language you are teaching?
- If yes, what will you do to improve it?

Conclusion

This chapter has outlined and discussed various approaches to professional development for individual language teachers. These approaches include development through self-monitoring through the use of lesson reports, questionnaires and checklists, as well as collecting samples of teaching through audio-recording and video-recording our lessons. The chapter also outlines how teachers can analyze critical incidents and case studies, as well as reflect with teaching portfolios and conduct action research projects. Finally, the chapter alerts teachers to the idea of reflecting on awareness of their own target language use and how this may impact some of the teaching methods they may want to use. The main idea of pursuing professional development as an individual emphasizes the teacher's individual and personal contribution to their own learning and to understanding of their classrooms and uses activities that focus on the development of self-awareness and personal interpretation through such activities as self-monitoring, critical incident and case study analysis, compilation of teaching portfolios, and engaging in action research and reflection on awareness of their own target language use. The next chapter outlines and discusses various approaches to professional development for language teachers that are collaborative but can also include all of the topics covered in this chapter.

3
Approaches to Language Teacher Professional Development: *Collaborative*

Introduction

The previous chapter introduced a variety of methods and procedures available for language teacher development at the individual level that included self-monitoring, analysis of critical incidents and case studies, compiling and reflecting with teaching portfolios, and engaging in action research projects as well as becoming more aware of individual teacher's use of target language you are teaching. This chapter considers approaches to professional development activities that can be carried out at the collaborative level and includes development with *critical friends*, reflecting with and in *team teaching*, and *peer coaching* arrangements, participating in *classroom observations*, and reflecting in *teacher reflection groups*.

Time Out

- What activities have you used in the past for your collaborative professional development?
- Of all the collaborative professional development activities you have participated in, which were most useful for you and why? Which were least useful and why?
- Read the following real example of a collaborative professional development experiences of an English for academic purposes (EAP) teacher in Singapore about her reflections in a critical friendship with this author at the time (from Farrell, 2001): One day Poh and I were talking about reflecting on teaching when she suddenly asked me to be her critical friend. We are both teaching in the same institution: she teaches

academic writing in an Intensive English Program for scholars from The People's Republic of China (PRC) and I am teaching in the English Language Teacher Education program. Poh asked me to observe her classes because she said that she wanted to have an outsider's view of her teaching practices besides her own perspective and that of her students. Poh initiated the process, chose her preferred methods of reflection, selected the lessons to be observed, and decided on the cycle of observation which related to her chosen sequence of a cycle in a process approach to writing. My designated role was to observe lessons, talk with her after the process, read and interpret her journals, and manage the process in general. I observed seven of her classes (each lasting two hours): the first three were pre-writing activity classes, the fourth was a peer-response class, the fifth was for writing and typing the first draft of the essay, while the sixth was for revising the first draft. The seventh class I observed was the first of a new cycle. For this observation Poh asked me to "observe any changes you see from the first cycle." She did not ask me how or what to observe in any other of the classes. After the first classroom observation I could see that Poh was an experienced practitioner in search of self-development. I also realized that she could probably ask and answer many of her own questions about her teaching. The pattern that developed was that I would document my observations within each phase of the cycle. I did not share these observations during the process and was not asked to do so. A striking pattern emerges from this summary: we both had similar comments to make about each class, even though we did not compare notes until after the last class. One example of this pattern concerned classroom interaction. It turned out that both of us had made similar observations and comments about the interaction in her classes. From a reflection point of view, it is interesting that Poh addressed most of the issues I raised without having seen my observation notes. This was not planned, but it seems likely that this delayed reflection (in the form of regular journal writing and the use of e-mail) gave Poh an opportunity to initiate her own changes to her teaching behaviors, based on her reflections. It may be that a teacher needs time to let the experiences of the class actions and emotions sink in before being asked to articulate any reflections. This delay can take the pressure off both "friends" from having to "come up with" some explanation for something they are not ready for.

o What is your opinion of this collaborative arrangement (critical friendship)? Compare your opinion with what you read below.

Critical Friends

It may seem something of an oxymoron to include the word "critical" with the word "friend" given that the former has something of a negative connotation in everyday speech, while the latter has a more positive connotation. However, a critical friend will place emphasis on the "friend" rather than the "critical" and thus encourage each other to develop their practice. In such collaborative arrangements, two teachers meet to examine each other's practice in order to develop together as language teachers. An effective teacher critical friendship entails one teacher enters into a collaborative arrangement with another teacher "in a way which encourages talking with, questioning, and even confronting, the trusted other, in order to examine planning for teaching, implementation, and its evaluation" (Hatton & Smith, 1995, p. 41). In addition, Farrell (2001b) reminds teachers that the word "critical" in such a collaborative friendship arrangement does not, and should not connote any negativity, as is the case in everyday conversation usage. As Farrell (2013, p. 88) has suggested, critical friendships can provide teachers with opportunities to "reflect on and consolidate their philosophical and theoretical understanding of their practices."

Although the usual composition of critical friends is two teachers, sometimes more than two teachers may want to come together and this is called a critical friends group (CFG), and can consist of up to twelve members (Bambino, 2002). As Johnson (2009, p. 101) has noted, CFGs all share some common elements such as "sharing the question or dilemma, inviting questions from the participants, giving and receiving feedback, and promoting self-reflection." Farrell (2014) outlined an example of a CFG in language teaching where three English as a second language (ESL) teachers reflected on their practice over one semester of teaching as critical friends. All three ESL teachers reported that they really enjoyed collaborating with each other because of the isolated nature of the job of teaching. As one of the teachers explained, the critical friends group made her realize the value of colleagues collaborating; she said, "it just started to hit me that as we were taking that we could do more together than this; that's what you need between colleagues to get this kind of thing going" (Farrell, 2014, p. 51).

The collaboration involved in this critical friends group created an overall sense of empowerment for each of its members than if they had pursued professional development on an individual basis (Farrell, 2014),

In an interesting application of a video-mediated critical friendship, Gonzalez Smith (2019) used the following framework to structure a video-mediated dialogue with her language teacher candidates that I believe can also be used with experienced language teachers wishing to enter into such a friendship. It consists of five stages: *catching up, holding hands, stirring the pot, shoulder to lean on*, and *pep talk*. The process begins with "catching up" where the "friend" asks introductory questions to establish the context of the lesson that the teacher is viewing on video. Questions such as, "What was your ESL instructional goal?" "Why did you record this?" "What did you analyze?" can be used here. This is followed by "holding hands" which occurs after repeated viewing of the lesson on video to focus attention on patterns that emerge in the lesson. Questions such as, "What pattern(s) do you see?" "What do you notice?" "What does this (pattern) mean/suggest?" can be considered. Next comes "stirring the pot," where the "friend" notes any event that the teacher may have missed, and asks some probing questions about this such as, "Let's watch that part of your video again." "What is happening here?" This is then followed by "shoulder to lean on" where the "friend" offers more emotional support to the teacher who may be experiencing feelings of dissonance if he or she thinks something unexpected (and probably unwelcome) has occurred in the lesson. Finally, there is a "pep talk" where the "friend" encourages the teacher to consider alternative approaches to teaching or professional development. I believe this is a useful framework to follow and critical friends can adapt it to their own particular context in any manner they feel useful. As Francis (1995, p. 234) has noted, "critical friends can stimulate, clarify, and extend thinking ... and feel accountable for their own growth and their peers."

Time Out

- Smith's (2019) five stage framework in a video-mediated critical friendship are outlined above and begin with an introductory "catching up" stage that includes introductory prompts the critical friend uses to understand the teacher's classroom context, expectations they had about the lesson, focus of the video recording and analysis, and the ESL instructional goal (lens) used to analyze the video recording. Review the

following dialogue between the critical friend and the teacher and give your opinion on how this stage frames the dialogue that is about to take place:
    o *Critical friend*: What was the ESL instructional goal you chose for this lesson?
    o *Teacher*: My goal was for ESL students to act out vocabulary words for comprehension.
    o *Critical friend*: Why did you select this goal?
    o *Teacher:* I feel that if I allow ESL students to act out new vocabulary, then they will know what the new word means because they are doing it.
    o *Critical friend*: I see, so did you pick this goal with a particular ESL student in mind?
    o *Teacher*: I initially picked it for the whole class, but then, I noticed the goal was more so for one ESL student in my class; his vocabulary really needs support [points at screen].
    o *Critical friend*: I see.
    o *Teacher*: Yeah, So I decided to place the camera on the side of the classroom where he [ESL student] was sitting so I could focus on him.
- Read and comment on the following critical friendship between this author and an Australian English as a foreign language (EFL) teacher in Korea that lasted for a period of sixteen weeks (from Farrell, 2007). This example only reports on the reflections of the EFL teacher in the critical friendship dyad. The initial goal of the critical friendship was to talk about teaching in general and the teacher's teaching (Greg) a set of specific classes in a private company in particular and all at the teacher's request. Greg also kept a teaching journal and wrote whenever he wanted to. Greg was teaching an English conversation class which was part of a private company's on-going education program. The objective of the course was to increase the students' (who were all company employees) English conversational ability. Greg invited the critical friend to visit his classes and observe with the use of a video camera (both negotiated this and agreed it would be good for the reflection process. No specific role was discussed for the critical friend except to manage the observation process of his teaching and to try to stimulate discussion of the teacher's teaching after observed classes. The discussions after each observed lesson usually started with the teacher evaluating his

lesson either positively or negatively. He then tried to interpret the students' interactions and/or problems he perceived that they had encountered. For example, in one meeting, he started with a negative evaluation of his lesson. He said that he was disappointed with the class. He continued: "I must work harder on the lead into my introduction, but still I am unsatisfied, I had wanted them to talk more. I was not happy with Y.S., speaking a lot of Korean. A good lesson for me is when students are talking together; today they were not talking, so it was not a good lesson." On one later occasion he asked the critical friend for suggestions on how to check what his students had learned in each class. The critical friend suggested he use a short questionnaire that he had used in his own classes that asked four short questions as follows: What do you think you learned today? What was easy for you? What was difficult for you and why? What did you enjoy? He decided to use the questionnaire at the end of his following class near the end of the reflection process. In his teaching journal he wrote that the students gave less than flattering answers: "Two [out of a class of seven] did not understand the first question, and one answered he did not enjoy anything, and said nothing was interesting." Even though he was surprised with these answers, the process of asking his students for their perceptions caused him to reflect on his teaching in general; "I haven't looked at my teaching. I haven't been looking at my class and my teaching closely, only vague and theoretical." As a result, in the final discussion, he said he would try to change: "I am trying to develop a new teaching method because I don't want to continue the same old way. I have to work harder."

Team Teaching

Team teaching is a similar arrangement to critical friends outlined above, as it involves two (or more) teachers collaborating to teach the same lesson to a class. An important benefit of team teaching is that it promotes collegiality among teachers in a school because it enables them to learn a great deal about each other and develop a closer professional and personal relationship.

This is mainly because the "team" shares responsibility for lessons; for example they share responsibility for planning the class (or course), for teaching the class (or course), as well as for any follow-up work associated with the class such as evaluation and assessment. The main concept of teams is that they cooperate as equals throughout the process but may also have different levels of experience with particular skills or activities, so some elements may involve some coaching from both teachers. As Eisen (2000, p. 9) points out, "no two teams are exactly alike because they operate along a continuum representing countless variations in goals, team membership, and members' relationships." Each team can collaborate in different ways according to Sandholtz (2000) on this continuum, for example, in a relaxed "sharing" of responsibilities between the two, or joint planning with only one teacher teaching the lesson, or another possibility that includes joint planning, both teachers teaching and evaluating the lesson.

It is this latter team-teaching collaboration that I emphasize in this section where both teachers take responsibility for planning, teaching and evaluating a series of lessons. In such an arrangement, according to Richards and Farrell (2005), learners also benefit from having two teachers plan and teach their lessons because they can also get the target language input from two different users of the language, as well as two different teaching styles and different personal contacts between learners and teachers. Some teams may assign different roles for each teacher within each lesson in order to provide a change in lesson pace or direction so that the students will not get bored or used to one teacher. While one teacher is teaching, the other teacher can observe or assist and generally help out in various different ways that would be impossible for a single teacher to manage (e.g., monitoring group work). In addition, the members of the team can share their expertise and alternative ideas, techniques, and methods about how to deal with different aspects of teaching, thus gaining different perspectives on teaching and learning. As Shannon and Meath-Lang (1992, p. 131) note, successful teams recognize the "gifts, skills and expertise of the partner without feeling denigrated, or in any way less skilful." In other words, the teachers in the team do not evaluate each other, rather they observe and assist each other and provide constructive feedback that all lead to effective professional development. That said, for such teams to work best, mutual trust and respect that requires both teachers to have confidence in each other's abilities must be present so that team teaching can be successful (Bailey, Curtis, & Nunan, 1992). Indeed, after each team-taught lesson, both teachers should review how it went and what the students have learned as well as what both teachers learned about their own teaching and development.

Richards and Farrell (2005) maintain that when setting up team teaching arrangements, the following factors should be considered for successful implementation. The purpose of such an arrangement should be clearly decided before it commences. For example, is such an arrangement for the purpose of helping novice teachers develop their teaching skills, and/or to establish a greater sense of collegiality within the school, and/or to provide a language specialist as one member of the team who has greater expertise than the other member (e.g., see Stewart, Sagliano & Sagliano (2002) below), and/or to change the usual teaching routines within the school? Teams will want to know how much time this arrangement will take, how disagreements between members will be solved and by whom, and what will happen if the students like one or none of the teachers. Thus, at a basic level, the members of the team should have a clear understanding of what the goals are and how it all works before they begin. In addition, after each class or each week of classes, teachers can meet to discuss the success of each lesson, and evaluate how this approach is working, what was learned from it, and whether it is worth continuing.

In English language teaching contexts, team-teaching has been introduced in certain countries where one teacher is a so-called native speaker of the target language (e.g., English) and the other is a non-native speaker teacher of the target language. Such a native speaker/non-native speaker co-teaching arrangement (Park, 2014) has also acted as a stimulus for target language improvement in many countries where English is not widely used, for example, South Korea (Heo & Mann, 2015). For the most part such native speaker/non-native speaker co-teaching arrangements have had positive outcomes as Sturman, (1992) noted in the context of Japan where native and non-native teachers teamed up to teach English as a foreign language. What was most impressive was that the students felt that their English language skills improved as a result of these teams and that they had enjoyed the whole experience. Such collaborations can provide an effective means of professional development for both teachers as they discuss their teaching methods and techniques in a non-evaluative environment where both can appreciate alternative approaches to teaching the same lesson.

Time Out

- Stewart, Sagliano, and Sagliano (2002) discovered that successfully implementing a team-teaching arrangement in an English-medium four-year university in Japan where partners were equals demands a lot of time, patience, and honest reflection by the teachers and administrators. Read the following summary of their experience and comment on it.

o   The context is an English-medium four-year university in Japan with a liberal arts program. The program incorporates a sheltered immersion approach using pairs of language and content teachers to lead classes. This program is institutionalized in the first two years, and students in it develop English proficiency as they learn content disciplines in the humanities and social sciences. This interdisciplinary team-teaching situation has been implemented institution wide. The make-up of the faculty is divided evenly between language and content disciplines. More than eighty percent of the faculty are foreign, and all speak English.

o   *Process*: For newcomers, the process begins with an orientation to the college's mission and teaching philosophy. This includes workshops on ways to make interdisciplinary team-teaching work. Teachers choose partners by making a ranked selection of desired co-teachers prior to each term. Administrators then set the teams by matching first and second choices. Some pairs must be assigned. Each teaching pair negotiates their own procedures for developing and teaching a course. Normally the instructor of the academic discipline will suggest content for the course. Once appropriate learning objectives and content have been negotiated, teams set out to jointly create materials that meet both content and language objectives for the course. As equal partners, co-teachers jointly create materials, teach, and determine grades. Courses are self-contained with instructors working simultaneously in the classroom. The instructional time is a collaborative effort. They trade off the lead and supporting teaching roles.

o   *Outcomes*: College policy has shaped how team teaching has evolved. Both instructors must be present in the classroom at all times. Furthermore, each instructor is guaranteed equal input into the computation of final course grades. Except for these obligations, the language and content partners are free to arrange the partnership in a mutually acceptable manner. Early on in this experiment, many teams were most comfortable with variations on the adjunct model of team teaching. That is, although they were in the same classroom together, they segregated their teaching time. Teaching "linked"

components to the same course allowed instructors to exercise freedom in lesson planning, materials' design, and classroom instruction. As more experience and confidence was gained, some teaching teams began to adopt a more fully collaborative approach to interdisciplinary team teaching. They tried to blend instruction in language and content as seamlessly as possible.
- o *Insights*: Successful implementation of team-teaching demands time, patience, honest reflection, re-evaluation and response by faculty and administrators. Every teacher should continuously be developing their pedagogy. Administrators should schedule time and channel activities into a program of continuous professional development. To be effective, institutions need to require participation and must provide incentives for involvement in regular workshops. Veteran team teachers should mentor newcomers and talk frankly about their experiences. Guidelines should be provided to team teachers to ensure they are asking the right questions. Ideally, administrators should actively team teach to better understand the commitments involved. Instructors need time to meet before and/or after lessons. Teachers also need appropriate spaces where they can hold meetings undisturbed.
- Struman (1992, p. 169) suggests that the team consider "The principle of flexible equality" whereby teachers with different personalities acknowledge these differences and not try to avoid or bury them. Instead, the teachers can define their roles and responsibilities that are most suitable for their own individual needs and situations. Set up a team-teaching situation in your school with another teacher (or teachers) and discuss the roles within the team-teaching collaboration as well as planning, teaching and evaluating the process.
- When evaluating the overall success of a team-teaching approach, Richards and Farrell (2005) suggest that the views of students and participating teachers should be sought. After your team-teaching program consider asking questions to your students such as:
  - o Do you think your English has improved through team teaching? In what ways?
  - o Are you more interested in learning English when your classes are taught this way?
  - o How do these classes differ from other classes you have?
  - o Would you like to continue studying English this way?

- Teachers can be surveyed about their perceptions with questions such as:
  - What are the advantages of team teaching?
  - What are the disadvantages of team teaching?
  - How do you think it affects the students' language learning?
  - Do you think your students enjoyed this mode of teaching?
  - What suggestions would you like to make to improve the existing team teaching program?
  - Would you like to continue with this way of teaching English?

Peer Coaching

Peer coaching is a process where two teachers collaborate to help one or both teachers improve some aspect of their teaching. As Robbins (1991, p. 1) notes, in a peer coaching relationship, two teachers come together to "reflect on current practices, expand, refine, and build new skills, share ideas; teach one another; conduct classroom research; or solve problems in the workplace." Although similar in many ways to critical friends and team teaching as outlined in the sections above, peer coaching is somewhat different than both because it places one teacher in the position of "coach" and the other in the position of "learner" for the particular skill that is being "coached." However, it is different from the usual coaching connotation in sports, for example, where the coach remains in charge of a team for the whole season "telling" the players what to do in a more managerial, rather than collaborative arrangement (I also realize that many coaches may be collaborative) because they have sole responsibility for the success or failure of the team. Hence the use of the term "peer" and so, peer coaching is best defined as "the process where teams of teachers regularly observe one another and provide support, companionship, feedback, and assistance" (Valencia & Killion, 1988, p. 170).

Furthermore, in a peer coaching arrangement there is no evaluation, and no real supervising. The process involves collaboration in which one teacher wants another peer teacher to observe his/her class in order to obtain feedback on one specific aspect of teaching or learning in order to learn more about this aspect, and perhaps improve his or her level of instruction. Gottesman (2000, p. 8) recommends that such feedback in a peer coaching arrangement should be non-judgmental and be influenced by the motto for peer coaching: "No Praise, No Blame." As Gottesman (2000, p. 8) points out, statements from the peer coach should be "specific in nature, about items the teacher can control, solicited rather than imposed, descriptive rather than evaluative, tactful, well timed, checked for clarity and simplicity, dealing with behaviors rather than personalities (of either teacher or students), not personality-driven, and well organized."

Peer coaching has the following characteristics: two teachers decide on a collaborative relationship; the two plan a series of opportunities to explore teaching collaboratively; one adopts the role of coach or "critical friend" (see above); they undertake a joint project or activity that involves collaborative learning; and the coach provides feedback and suggestions; it is ultimately up to the teacher what to implement from the coaching experience (Richards & Farrell, 2005). In addition, Richards and Farrell (2005) suggest that there are different types of peer coaching arrangements where the coach can take on different roles such as *technical coach* where a teacher seeks the assistance of another teacher who is experienced and more knowledgeable in order to learn new teaching methods/techniques. This can be especially helpful for the professional development of more inexperienced teachers as they try to develop new knowledge and skills through the lens of a more experienced peer teacher as he or she "coaches" the peer by providing constructive feedback in a supportive environment. Another role can be to act as a *collegial coach* where two teachers (one of them may have more knowledge of the teaching method than the other, and so would take a coaching role) may simply want to confirm their views on teaching or refine their existing teaching practices. Johnson (2009, p. 102) calls this role "mirroring," where the coach observes and provides feedback for the teacher to analyze or make sense of himself or herself. Yet another role of coach is called a *challenge coach*, where two teachers focus on a problem that has arisen in one of their classes in some aspect of teaching, and thus invites a trusted peer to come observe the class in order to help identify the cause of the problem, give specific suggestions and work together to find a solution.

The teacher who is being "coached" also has a cooperative role to play in a peer coaching relationship. From the very beginning it should be pointed out that the person in the role of teacher is not a weaker peer in any manner; he or she is a really open-minded professional interested in finding new ways to teach a particular skill and thus provide even more opportunities for his or her students to learn. Gottesman (2000, p. 37) suggests the following useful guide for participants in a peer coaching relationship:

Collaborative Approaches to Teacher Professional Development

- Be committed to peer coaching as a way of analyzing and improving instruction.
- Be willing to develop and use a common language of collaboration in order to discuss the total teaching act without praise or blame.
- Be willing to enter into a peer coaching relationship (e.g., by requesting a classroom observation visit and to observe as a coach if so asked).
- Be open-minded and willing to look for better ways of conducting classroom business.
- Act as a colleague and as a professional.

Whatever type of peer coaching arrangement language teachers enter into for their professional development needs, they can benefit from the new opportunities of trying out new teaching strategies and methods as well as develop more of a sense of collegiality between peers.

Time Out

- The following is an example of an American EAP teacher who used an informal peer coaching arrangement while teaching in Malaysia in order to develop and implement materials for an integrated EAP skills class—reading, writing, and listening (adapted from Richards & Farrell, 2005). Do you think this peer coaching arrangement worked for the EAP teacher? If yes, why? If no, why not?
    o Together with the curriculum coordinator (who actually proposed peer coaching at a meeting), I and one other teacher first wrote materials for an integrated skills module consisting of a reading and a writing section. For the reading section I was in charge of developing certain materials that focused on helping students to develop their skills on reading academic topics. When I finished this, we had the problem of how to implement the materials. So, as a peer coach I helped the other teacher by offering suggestions for using the materials in her classes while she was teaching. Sometimes I demonstrated how I would use the materials and she also came to my classes and saw how I used the materials with my students. We found the whole peer coaching relationship to be very helpful in making optimal use of the new materials in all our classes because we wanted to ensure uniform implementation of the new materials in all the classes. Now both of us had the same ideas about imple-

mentation so we entered into other peer coaching relationships with all the other teachers who were involved with these modules.
- Read the following account of a community of peer coaches and support that Robert J. Dickey (and presented in his words), set up in South Korea because the COVID-19 pandemic was having such a huge impact on the language teachers there as they struggled to pivot suddenly to online teaching. What is your opinion of such a peer support group in such an online platform as Facebook?
    o COVID-19 turned classroom teaching upside down, and some of the most experienced classroom teachers had the greatest difficulties in the new "remote teaching" environment. Other teachers with more online technologies skills and intuition support leaped forward to help us all navigate essential and supporting tools. Facebook discussions by a few teachers in Korea led to the creation of a specialty Facebook group "Teaching synchronously online using Zoom in Korea" in early March 2020. It has grown by leaps and bounds, now with nearly 600 members (Sept 2021). Why? Because of its peer coaching approach and supportive environment. As the name implies, most of the discussions are about teaching with Zoom, particularly teaching English in Korea. The description states it best, *This is a place to share ideas*. Almost everyone was a novice with Zoom in the first weeks, some "technophiles" put more time into discovering the tool and shared their insights. Periodically small groups will join in a Zoom room to explore and experiment with features. Sessions and text-based discussions included basic and advanced features of Zoom, and how these differ depending on your type of account: free personal, free campus-email registered, paid personal, and campus or corporate paid account. Also, how external functions, activities, and technologies can be used alongside Zoom, such as chatbots, Padlet, etc. In some cases, these replace less-effective Zoom functionalities, in other cases they augment Zoom. Even those of us less in love with technologies found resources to share, and asked questions that raised the awareness of all. Zoom has continued to develop, albeit with some hiccups, and these changes and additions, temporary glitches, are pointed out as they arise. Sometimes we publicize announcements from Zoom. Other times we discover new challenges in the heat of the lesson! External issues that impact teaching online, paralleling with

recorded classes or face-to-face classroom instruction, collection of assignments through other online systems (e.g., Moodle), and life in general are also discussed in the group. All very collegial and supportive, few disagreements (though alternative perspectives are sometimes shared). Cartoons, words of encouragement, etc. are just as valued, whether in an original post or just a comment following words of frustration. Additionally, we exchange materials that can be shared with students about using and living with Zoom. And occasionally mentions of scholarship related to online remote video teaching. Unsurprisingly, it was amazingly busy the first weeks back in Spring of 2020. Most of us are far more comfortable in Zoom today than when we first entered that world. Still, the group lives on.

- Farrell and Jacobs (2020) make the following suggestions as to how teachers can act as coaches to foster language teacher development that includes the following: informal chats about their teaching in the form of anecdotes about what is happening in their classroom; collaborating to design materials; observing each other's lessons; co-teaching lessons and observing each other's approach and teaching style; and videotaping lessons and watching them together. Set up a peer coaching arrangement similar to the above outline or a modified outline to suit your needs and document the outcome.
- In any peer coaching arrangement, Richards and Farrell (2005) point out that it is important for both the teacher and the coach to step back from the relationship in order to reflect on what happened and thus should seek answers to the following questions:
    o Were the roles of the teacher and the coach clearly defined before the process began?
    o Was a culture of trust established during the process?
    o Was the feedback specific and only related to the topic requested by the teacher?
    o What kind of language was used in the feedback session? Was it judgmental and/or evaluative? If so, how can this be avoided in the future?
    o Was the peer coaching process helpful for the teacher (e.g., if it involved classroom observations, did this lead to more effective teaching?)?
    o Is the process taking up too much time?

Peer Observations

As mentioned in the previous chapter, language teachers can individually self-monitor their practice using audio and video recordings, check lists, surveys and questionnaires. However, language teachers can also help each other develop collaboratively by engaging in peer observations and obtain even more awareness of not only what they do, but also what others are doing in their classrooms. Peer observations, according to Richards and Farrell (2005), provide an opportunity for both teachers to see how someone else deals with many of the same issues they face each day. Such a collaborative arrangement also encourages collegiality within a school and/or district as peers share ideas and expertise, as well provide information and feedback to each other that would not be possible through individual self-monitoring.

As such, peer observations should not be evaluative (i.e., with the use of predesigned checklists which can be threatening because we do not know who designed them or why); rather, they should be developmental and non-judgmental descriptions (verbal or written) of what actually is happening in a lesson (Gebhard, 2006). When classroom observations are carried out non-judgmentally with a peer, they can lead not only to more collegiality among teachers, but also more self-knowledge about the type of teaching strategies other teachers use so that all teachers can have a better understanding of teaching and ultimately to gain better control over it. Indeed, non-evaluative observation within the context of professional development is often welcomed by teachers, as the following teachers' comments reveal (from Richards, 1998):

- It revealed more detailed information on student performance during specific aspects of the lesson than I could have generated on my own.
- It revealed unexpected information about interaction between students during a lesson.
- It helped me develop a better working relationship with a colleague.
- It has taught me how much I can learn from my colleagues.
- It made me more aware of the limited range of teaching strategies that I have been using.
- I realized that I need to develop better time management strategies.
- I have learned the value of evaluating myself. Also, now I know more about my strengths as a teacher as well.

Richards and Lockhart (1995, pp. 24–26) offer the following useful guidelines for effective peer observations where they suggest that in order for the process to be viewed as positive, the observer's function should just be to gather information and not to be involved in anything else including any evaluation. In terms of general principles, they maintain that the observation should have a particular focus so that the observer can collect information pertaining to that focus that is useful for the teacher. Next, the observer should use specific procedures to make their task more effective while at the same time not become involved in any part of the lesson. In terms of procedures used to carry out peer observations, they suggest there should be a pre-observation meeting where the two teachers discuss the type of class to be observed (students, materials, lesson plan), and this followed by a discussion of the particular focus for the observation (see time out below for more on this). Then, the teachers should decide on what procedures the observer should use such as a checklist of some kind, a written narrative, or some other method for taking notes during the observation. After the observation has been completed, Richards and Lockhart (1995) suggest that both teachers engage in a post-observation session where the observer reports on the information he or she collected during the observed lesson. In addition, classroom observations can also be phased-into a peer coaching arrangement (see section above for more on peer coaching) similar to a similar four-step sequence as above of pre-observation discussion, actual classroom visit, post-visit discussion, and general review of the process. For the peer coaching classroom observation arrangement, a more inexperienced language teacher may ask an experienced teacher to come to his/her class for a limited period of time and follow the four-step sequence as above.

Such a non-evaluative peer observation collaboration arrangement, with observation as its main component that also involves discussion and reflection with peers, can produce a real and deep understanding of the events of a lesson that were observed. This collaborative process can help language teachers learn more about what other teachers think and what they do related to teaching and learning a second or foreign language, while at the same time, each teacher takes more responsibility for this or her professional development.

Time Out

- As mentioned above, Richards and Lockhart (1995) suggest that peers engaging in peer classroom observations identify a focus for such observations and offer the following examples you can choose from to focus your observations (or you can add more if these do not meet your needs):
    o *Organization of the lesson*: the entry, structuring, and closure of the lesson.
    o *Teacher's time management*: allotment of time to different activities during the lesson.
    o *Students' performance on tasks*: the strategies, procedures, and interaction patterns employed by students in completing a task.
    o *Time-on-task*: the extent to which students were actively engaged during a task.
    o *Teacher questions and student responses*: the types of questions teachers asked during a lesson and the way students responded.
    o *Students' performance during pair work*: the way students completed a pair work task, the responses they made during the task, and the type of language they used.
    o *Classroom interaction*: teacher-student and student-student interaction patterns during a lesson.
    o *Group work*: students' use of LI versus L2 during group work, students' time-on-task during group work, and the dynamics of group activities.
- Four ESL teachers in a university language school were interested in engaging in classroom observations to consider their wait-time after asking questions during their lessons (from Farrell & Mon, unpublished manuscript). Priscilla, a female ESL teacher and Steve, a male ESL teacher, both have four years teaching experience. The other two participants possessed more than five years of experience teaching in an ESL context. Molly, a female experienced ESL teacher, had approximately eight years of teaching experience. While Gunther, a male experienced ESL teacher, had a little over six years of teaching experience (all names mentioned are pseudonyms) Four one-hour classroom observations were conducted. During the classroom observations, the observer sat at the back of the room, where she would not disrupt the students. A tape recorder was used to record the classes observed. The observer took notes to describe the teachers' actions

during the classes. The classroom observations formed the basis for discussion with each teacher after each observed class about what they did and why. All classroom observations were recorded and transcribed. The main focus of these observations in this case study was how long they waited for their students to answer after they asked a question or their wait-time. Before being observed, all four teachers felt that an appropriately long teacher wait-time was important in order for students to process the question and formulate a response. The indicated average teacher wait-time length varied from teacher to teacher, but all agreed that it should be longer than five seconds with Pricilla thinking she waits 30 seconds, Steve between five and 15 seconds, Molly up to 60 seconds and Gunter five or more seconds.

Table 3.1 *Average wait-time (sec)*

	Priscilla Average Wait-time (sec)	Steve Average Wait-time (sec)	Molly Average Wait-time (sec)	Gunther Average Wait-time (sec)
Observation 1	1.11	1.61	1.04	0.4
Observation 2	1.56	1.70	0.22	1.06
Observation 3	1.13	1.39	0.25	1.17
Observation 4	1.11	1.60	1.04	0.4
Overall Average	**1.23**	**1.58**	**0.64**	**0.76**

As Table 3.1 indicates Priscilla's overall teacher wait-time average was approximately 1.23 seconds. Steve's overall teacher wait-time average was approximately 1.58 seconds. Molly's overall teacher wait-time average was approximately 0.64 seconds. Gunther's overall teacher wait-time average was approximately 0.76 seconds. Although the teacher wait-time varied slightly from teacher to teacher, however, each teacher's wait-time was approximately 1 second. Table 11 compares the teachers' perceived wait-time or what they thought their wait-time was before they were observed teaching and their actual wait-time when observed teaching.

Table 3.2 *Comparison of teachers' perceived wait-time and observed wait-time*

	Perceived Teacher Wait-time (sec)	Observed Teacher Avg Wait-time (sec)
Priscilla	30	1.23
Steve	5-15	1.58
Molly	60	0.64
Gunther	5+	0.76

All teachers expressed the importance of teacher wait-time. For example, Molly stated, "If you're working with some of the Asian cultures, it takes them a little bit longer to process and then to have the confidence to speak...so I wait as long as it takes them to speak." Similarly, Steve stated, "you definitely need to give students time to think about the answer." Priscilla indicated, "If it's a complex question, I will tell them they need to think long about this one before they answer." Likewise, Gunther indicated, "the classes I'm teaching this term...my wait-time needs to be about 30 seconds." From these follow-up interview statements; teachers are well aware that a long teacher wait time is necessary for students to process the question and think when formulating an answer. However, the results from Table 11 indicate a great disparity between the teachers' perceptions about their teacher wait-time and their observed average wait-time. Although there were instances where teachers exceeded the recommended teacher wait-time of 3-5 seconds, the average teacher wait-times for all teachers was approximately one second. This average teacher wait-time of one second is well below the recommended wait-time and is remarkably lower than wait-times indicated by the participants. It is also interesting to note that both novice teachers had the longest wait times.

- o Why do you think there is divergence between the teachers' beliefs regarding teacher wait-time and their observed teacher wait-time practices?
- o Why do you think the novice teachers' (Priscilla and Steve) wait-time tended to be longer than the more experienced teachers (Molly and Gunther)?
- o Do you think the length of teacher wait-time has any significant effect on student participation?

- Observation checklists are ubiquitous, and most language teachers must use them at some point in their careers. What is your opinion of the following classroom observation checklist designed by an ESL teacher for a writing class? Would you change anything? If yes, why? If not, why not? After reviewing this checklist, design your own checklists for observing your lessons.

Language Objectives:

Materials:

Teaching Approach:

Evaluation System: 1 = below average; 2 = average; 3 = good, 4 = very good; 5 = excellent; N/A = not applicable

| *Lesson Plan* | 1 | 2 | 3 | 4 | 5 | N/A |

Clear objectives
Realistic aims
Expected difficulties

Presentation Stage

| *Lesson* | 1 | 2 | 3 | 4 | 5 | N/A |

Organization
Awareness of students needs
Pace of the stage
Students response
Achievement of stage objective
Timing

| *Materials/Activities* | 1 | 2 | 3 | 4 | 5 | N/A |

Variety
Appropriacy
Integration
Brainstorming

| *Classroom Management* | 1 | 2 | 3 | 4 | 5 | N/A |

Use of visual aids
Use of board

Pacing/Staging
Interaction with students
Setting up activities/feedback

Practice Stage

Lesson	1	2	3	4	5	N/A

Organization
Awareness of students needs
Pace of the stage
Student response
Achievement of stage objective
Timing

Materials/Activities	1	2	3	4	5	N/A

Variety
Appropriacy
Integration

Classroom Management	1	2	3	4	5	N/A

Use of visual aids
Use of board
Pacing/Staging
Interaction with students
Setting up activities/feedback

Production Stage

Lesson	1	2	3	4	5	N/A

Organization
Awareness of students needs
Pace of the stage
Student response
Achievement of stage objective
Timing

Materials/Activities	1	2	3	4	5	N/A

Variety
Appropriacy
Integration

| Classroom Management | 1 | 2 | 3 | 4 | 5 | N/A |

Use of visual aids
Use of board
Pacing/Staging
Interaction with students
Setting up activities/feedback

| *Teacher* | 1 | 2 | 3 | 4 | 5 | N/A |

Control of lesson
Presentation/Modelling
Explanations/Definitions
Correction Techniques
Dealing with questions
Giving instructions
Teacher speaking time
Student speaking time
Set up of activities
Development of material
Body language
Patience
Empathy with students

Observer Comments:

Teacher Comments:

- Set up your own peer observation arrangement. Richards and Farrell (2005, p. 93) suggest the following four guidelines that may be useful for you to consider when implementing this process:
  1. Select a colleague to work with. This may be a teacher who is teaching the same course or using the same textbook as you, or you could observe a teacher teaching a different kind of class, depending on mutual interest.
  2. Each teacher takes turns at teaching and observing as follows: Arrange for a pre-observation orientation session. Before each observation, meet to discuss the nature of the class to be

observed, the kind of material being taught, the teacher's approach to teaching, the kinds of students in the class, typical patterns of interaction and class participation, and any problems expected. The aim of these discussions is for the observer to understand the kind of issues the teacher is facing and to learn more about the class and what their particular circumstances or problems are. The teacher who is teaching the lesson should also identify a focus for the observation at this stage and set a task for the observer to carry out. The observer's role is to collect information for the teacher that he or she would not normally be able to collect alone. It is important to stress that this task should not involve any form of evaluation.
3. Decide on observation procedures to be used and arrange a schedule for the observations. During the observation complete the observation using the procedures that were agreed on.
4. Arrange a post-observation session. Meet as soon as possible after the lesson. The observer reports on the information collected and discusses it with the teacher.

Teacher Development Groups

The final collaborative arrangement for language teachers outlined in this chapter is teacher development groups where a group of teachers come together to discuss and reflect on their practice. Teacher development groups can provide a forum for teachers to encourage each other, examine their practices, and receive feedback, and also provide emotional support and empathy for each other during the process (Farrell, 2014). For the most part, teachers teach behind closed doors in isolation (and all this even more accentuated with the sudden move to online teaching as I write this book in 2021–2022 during the COVID-19 pandemic) without much interaction or support from other teachers. As Oprandy, Golden, and Shiomi (1999, p. 152), point out, teacher development groups provide a means "to others wishing to break out of the shells of isolation separating teachers from their colleagues as well as from teacher educators."

Head and Taylor (1997, p. 91) define a teacher development group as "any form of co-operative and ongoing arrangement between two or more teachers to work together on their own personal and professional development." Teacher development groups can come together for different professional development purposes such as to reflect on their teaching, which can be especially helpful if everyone in the group is teaching the same course. Thus, they can decide to meet regularly to discuss what activities, materials and methods each member uses and evaluate these as a group. They can also decide to try out new teaching methods in different classes and report their experiences to the group. Groups can also develop their own materials and/or bring in materials they use for teaching the various skills and discuss these with the group. Groups can also engage in peer observations (as outlined above) and discuss these observations with each other during group meetings. Groups can also view recordings of other teachers outside the group teaching and discuss any applications of what they observe to their own teaching. In addition, groups can consider if they want to present any action research projects at seminars and workshops either within their institutions if they are all from the same institution, or alternatively they can consider publishing their projects in local, national, and/or international journals.

Setting up such a teacher development group, however, is not easy and teachers should consider and negotiate the following issues before they begin: the *type* of group, different *roles* within the group, what *topics* they are interested in discussing, and how they will *evaluate* the success of the group. In terms of the *type of group* teachers may want to form, Farrell (2007), for example, has outlined three main types of teacher development groups: *peer groups* can be set up within one school such as all the English language teachers in the school. Teacher development groups can be set up at the district level, called *district level groups*, where peer networking can operate outside the school and within a school district and where teachers can set up a central coordinating committee that integrates activities and communicates with the teachers. *Virtual groups* of language teachers can of course be set up anytime as they can easily communicate and "interact" on the Internet. Many such groups have become very popular during the COVID-19 pandemic (e.g see the group outlined in the Time Out above that Robert J. Dickey set up in South Korea because of the COVID-19 pandemic).

In addition, each teacher development group will be composed of members with different roles especially in terms of who controls, either officially or by default, the group. Thus, groups may want to consider different types in terms of members' roles: a *power-with* group where collaboration is emphasized, and members do not impose their interests, topics, or values on one another. Kriesberg (1992) maintains that a *power-with* type of teacher group empowers its members because members find ways to satisfy their desires and to fulfill their interests without imposing these on each other. The alternative type of group is a *power-over* group characterized by a hierarchical view of roles where particular members assume or are given command and control. This sometimes occurs in a top-down mandated professional development scenario where the institution may want to keep some kind of control over the group members in terms of topics covered, and decision-making abilities. However, as Kriesberg (1992, p. 47) cautions, power-over relationships "cuts off human communication and creates barriers to human empathy and understanding." Thus, I am not advocating for any "power-over" group roles or membership. In a "power-with" group, members can first brainstorm a theme and/or topic(s) democratically as a group, and these can be narrowed down later and depending on the direction the discussions and interactions take them. This negotiation of the narrowing down of themes/topics allows all participants to focus their attention on issues that have personal meaning for each of them, but not at the expense of other group members. When a particular topic is temporarily exhausted, then the group can start another cycle of brainstorming for a topic of interest in the same manner as above. After a teacher development group concludes its period of reflection it is important that all group participants evaluate the process and if it has led to overall professional development of its members. Participants can reflect on whether they achieved their individual and group goals, their individual and the group accomplishments and factors that can be considered if they or others want to set up another teacher development group.

A teacher development group that is built on trust can provide a safe place where language teachers can discuss and reflect on their practice. When language teachers come together in such a group, they can break feelings of isolation and collaborate on different aspects of their practice and plan and carry out activities already outlined in the sections above such as peer coaching, team teaching, and classroom observations. Teacher groups, as Lieberman and Grolnick (1998, p. 723) point out, play a major role in "providing opportunities for teachers to validate both teacher knowledge and teacher inquiry."

Time Out

- The following is a case study of the experiences of three experienced female English as a second language (ESL) teachers in Canada (for more details, see Farrell, 2014). The genesis of the teacher group was somewhat unusual, in that I was approached by the three participants and asked if I would be willing to facilitate all three with their professional development as a group. As one of the teacher's said: "I've plateaued...gone a little stale." My role was discussed, and we agreed that I would facilitate their group discussions and, as a non-participant-observer in the classroom observations. The teachers, all very experienced ESL teachers with advanced degrees, and all from the same school, met intensively for one semester with weekly group meetings and observations as well as follow-up meetings during the second semester and some in the second year as well. Comment on what they talked about and how successful you think this teacher reflection group was.
    o The most frequent category covers comments the teachers made about their school *administration*. In general, most of the three teachers' comments focused negatively on the school administration, but positively about their interactions with other ESL teacher colleagues. For example, when they talked about their school's administration, they suggested that the administration did not really know what an ESL teacher's many duties and roles were within the school, and that they sensed that there was a real disconnect between administration and the ESL teachers in the school. As a result, all three teachers agreed that they felt somewhat under-appreciated by the administration. They also felt a special pressure as ESL teachers that other teachers in the institution may not have felt, that of student retention because all were well aware of the institution's desire to move the international students into other programs in the institution as soon as possible after "successfully" completing their ESL courses.
    All three teachers said that they enjoyed being in the classroom teaching and being around students in general, both inside and outside the classroom, and saw this as the most satisfying and rewarding part of their professional lives thus far. Although positive about their learners they did have an issue with the type of relationships they have established with their students, not only

inside the classroom but also outside the classroom and school. All three teachers maintained that when teachers can identify with their students beyond the classroom, it tends to make teaching in class easier and more effective, but at the same time it also takes up a lot of their free-time and energy and that they sometimes had a problem balancing these. Therefore, they all wondered about where they should draw a line between their professional and private lives regarding interacting with their students outside class.

So all three mid-career ESL teachers seemed to be frustrated with their administration but had positive feelings and interactions towards their colleagues and their learners. The three teachers seemed to feel that they have had an impact on their students' learning and achievements both inside the class (language learning) and outside the classroom (successful acculturation to Canadian culture), and they said that this was realized while reflecting in their teacher discussion group. The period of reflection for all three mid-career ESL teachers seemed to help them not only articulate their frustrations regarding their perception that the administration did not understand their roles and duties but also to articulate these roles and duties in terms of their interactions with their colleagues and their learners.

- Belbin (1993) has identified nine group role types listed below. Try to form your own teacher development group with between five and eight members and then consider the roles below for your members:
    o *Coordinator* or *facilitator*: member who makes a good chairperson and ensures that everyone in the group has an opportunity for input
    o *Shaper*: member who drives the group forward
    o *Planter*: member who provides the creativity
    o *Implementer*: member who gets things done
    o *Monitor evaluator*: member who ensures that all options are considered
    o *Team worker*: member who helps cement the group together
    o *Resource investigator*: member who develops outside contacts
    o *Complete/finisher*: member who finishes things off
    o *Expert*: member who provides specific areas of knowledge

Conclusion

This chapter has outlined and discussed various approaches to professional development activities that can be carried out at the collaborative level. These include collaborative teacher development through critical friends, team teaching, peer coaching, peer observations, and teacher development groups. When teachers collaborate through critical friends, team teaching, peer coaching, peer observations, and teacher development groups, they become a true community of professionals where members interact with each other for the purposes of "developing particular shared practices, routines, rituals, artifacts, symbols, conventions, stories, and histories" (Wenger, 1998, p. 6). As Brandt (2005, p. 21) notes: "Teacher isolation is a salient problem for all teachers" and one way to fight against such isolation is to collaborate with other teachers so teachers do not have to feel that they are in the classroom by themselves. The next chapter addresses the important topic of teacher development needs.

4
Teacher Development Needs

Introduction

The previous two chapters have outlined and discussed how language teachers can engage in professional development activities from an individual perspective (see Chapter 2) and also from a collaborative perspective (see Chapter 3). The main point in both chapters is, as Johnson (2000, p. 1) has pointed out, professional development is seen as "a reflective process, a situated experience, and a theorizing opportunity" for all language teachers. This chapter continues the discussion on professional development and focuses on the various and different needs of language teachers depending on their levels of experience. The chapter outlines and discusses the professional development needs of novice language teachers as well as the needs of more experienced teachers.

Novice Teacher Needs

There is no doubt that all learner teachers enter initial teacher education programs in order to learn how to teach. However, and as was pointed out in Chapter 1, there are a lot of inconsistencies and some doubts about the contents they are presented with during these programs, and as Calderhead and Shorrock (1997, p. 8) point out, most novice teachers in their first few years in the classroom "experience difficulties in learning to teach." Among the various difficulties faced by novice teachers in their first years include a "reality/culture shock" (Caspersen & Raaen, 2014) they will experience as they transition from their teacher education programs to the "reality" of a real classroom, and also the "culture shock" of having to adapt to a new context. As a result, Calderhead and Shorrock (1997) point out, novice teachers will need a lot of support and professional development opportunities need to be greatly expanded after their initial teacher education programs.

Unfortunately, similar findings as those above for novice teachers in general education studies have also been reported of the experiences of novice language teacher woes (Artigliere & Baecher, 2017; Farrell, 2016, 2017a), with many also left to cope on their own without much guidance or support (Higginbotham, 2019). During their first year(s), novice language teachers come to realize that they may not have been adequately prepared for how to deal with two different and complex roles: teaching effectively and learning to teach (Peacock, 2009). Indeed, many may also have discovered that they have been set up in their pre-service courses (and teaching practice) for a teaching approach that does not work in real classrooms, or the school culture may prohibit implementation of these "new" approaches (Shin, 2012). In addition, Farrell (2021) cautioned that most of what is presented in language teacher education programs may be washed away by the first-year experiences of becoming a novice teacher, and that a lot of the blame falls with language teacher education programs because they are not delivering relevant content that novice language teachers can implement in real classroom settings.

Many novice language teachers report that when they commence teaching in their first year, their expectations of applying what they have learned in teacher education courses are being quickly overcome by the reality of teaching in real classrooms because the knowledge that they received in teacher education programs is too theoretical at the expense of practice (Farr & Riordan, 2017). However, when novice language teachers are plunged into the real world of classrooms where the contents of their education program generally followed a vague "learn-the-theory-and-then-apply-it model" approach that forces them into developing quick-fixes through a process of what Dewey (1904, p. vii) called "blind experimentation" in order to survive their first years.

Nevertheless, the field of language teacher education pedagogy has been "very slow" to recognize this issue (Wright, 2010, p. 281). Moreover, many language teacher preparation programs have limited information about how their graduates are faring in their first years of teaching, or what early career language teachers' work lives involve, or even if they remain in the profession beyond their first years (Higginbotham, 2019). In addition, it is still a fact that within language teacher education as a profession, we still do not know what content knowledge is appropriate to provide in language teacher education (Richards, 2014). As a result, it seems that the language teaching profession finds itself in a bit of a quandary: on the one hand we have teacher educators providing the knowledge (both content and pedagogical) they consider necessary for learner language teachers to become effective teachers throughout their careers. Yet, on the other, we also have research evidence that language teachers are struggling when trying to implement what they have learned in their teacher education once they begin teaching in their first years (e.g., Farrell, 2019c). For example, Farrell (2019c, p. 1) reported the following message he received by e-mail from a well "qualified" experienced teacher who felt a lot of frustration with her initial language teacher education experiences:

> I have been in ESL/EFL for over a decade. I did a MA in Linguistics with an emphasis in TESL since my only qualifications while working overseas were a BA in Linguistics and a 200-hour TESL certificate. I feel that my training has failed me for the most part. With TESL being part of the linguistics program (not applied linguistics), the majority of what I studied in my program was research based. Therefore, I've had next to no practical classroom-ready type training.

Although some time ago, Faez and Vaelo (2012) pointed out that language teacher education programs should be reconfigured in order to work out how the program content could be aligned more closely with the *needs* of novice language teachers, until recently not much has changed (Farrell, 2019c). As Farrell (2019c, p. 1) remarked, this shows that "something is [still] not working in the field of second language teacher education." In reaction to this conundrum Farrell (2021) has recently attempted to reconfigure language teacher education by developing a "novice-service" approach that includes initial teacher education (and teaching practice) as well as continued contact beyond the initial program into the early career years of teaching. Farrell (2021) has noted that what usually happens in traditional approaches to teacher education is that struggling early career teachers fall through the gap between pre-service education and later professional development opportunities because of the lack of any professional development support during these crucial early years. Farrell's (2021) novice-service approach is based on two main premises: that reflection is important to incorporate in language teacher education programs, and that teacher education is only the beginning of a process of a novice teacher's professional development journey that should also include the first five years. This can be achieved, he suggested, through continued collaborative interactions between language teacher educator-mentors, novice language teachers, and other interested stakeholders in this important early career period.

Farrell (2021) suggests that learner teachers' professional development begins in teacher education programs where they are introduced to reflective practice activities and tools that they can use throughout their teaching careers, but especially in their novice years. In such a manner they can become more adaptive professionals during their novice years as they reflect on, evaluate and adapt their own practices to their individual needs. Indeed, some time ago, Wright (2010, p. 267) acknowledged that the goal of language teacher education should be to produce "reflective teachers, in a process which involves socio-cognitive demands to introspect and collaborate with others, and which acknowledges previous learning and life experience as a starting point for new learning."

More recently, some language teacher educators have indeed begun to reconsider their teacher education programs by encouraging reflective practice activities for learner language teachers (Mann & Walsh, 2017). The previous two chapters provide examples of individual teacher professional development through such reflective practice activities as *self-monitoring*, *critical incident* and *case study* analysis, reflection with *teaching portfolios*, and engaging in *action research*, and development of individual teacher's *language awareness* (see Chapter 2). In addition, reflective approaches to professional development activities that can be carried out at the collaborative level such as *critical friendships, team teaching, peer coaching, peer observations*, and *teacher development groups* are also covered (see Chapter 3). All of these can, and should, be incorporated into language teacher education programs so that learner language teachers are trained at an early stage of their development to be able to meet whatever demands they are faced with in their novice years. As Yost (2006, p. 61) has noted, "in order for novice teachers to become successful, they require the [reflective] tools necessary for coping with challenges they encounter."

When learner language teachers graduate from their teacher education programs, Farrell (2021) has noted that, for the most part, they are abandoned by that program with no further contact with their graduates. Research in general education (e.g., Olsen & Anderson, 2007) has reported that many early career teachers have reported that they have "plateaued" and are "stagnating," and have an overall feeling of disillusionment with teaching as a career/profession, and this even after only one- or two-years teaching. This is worrying because novice teachers entering the profession are said to bring with them enthusiasm, idealism and recent, newer training initiatives from their teacher education programs and this can only improve the teaching profession (OECD, 2018). However, and astonishingly, research has revealed that nearly half of all beginning teachers will leave the profession within their first five years (Ingersoll, 2015).

Thus, language teachers in their first years will need regular professional development opportunities in order to be able to thrive and not just survive their first years. Such professional development continues from their initial teacher education programs and carries on throughout the first five years of a novice teacher's career (Farrell, 2021). As Cirocki, Madyarov, and Baecher (2019, p. 2) point out, "teacher learning is an ongoing, reflective and constructive process. It begins during university degree programs, or certificate courses, and continues in and outside the classroom throughout teachers' careers." Novice language teachers will require continued mentoring and support from their language teacher educator/supervisors, cooperating teachers, school appointed mentor teachers and peers. Consequently, the old traditional pre-service teacher education programs that have an entrance/exit notion where on exit (i.e., graduating from the program) novice language teachers have no further contact, and left to their own devices to survive in their early career teaching years in the real world of classroom teaching, should be abolished. As Farrell (2021) notes, if we consider language teacher educators as mentors during the teacher education program, then these same teacher educator/mentors should continue to act as "reflective-colleagues" for novice language teachers throughout their first years as they are being socialized into a new community of practice (Wenger, 1998). Such a "novice-service" approach to language teacher education, according to Farrell (2021), will prepare language teachers for the reality of what they will face in real classrooms because they are encouraged to take a reflective approach to teacher learning that begins in initial teacher education programs and continues throughout the early career teaching years. This approach also encourages continued contact and collaboration throughout this period between graduating novice language teachers and their teacher educator/mentors.

Time Out

- Look at the five different orientations to teacher education below proposed by Calderhead and Shorrock (1997) and consider if any represent your initial language teacher education program experiences?
    - *Academic orientation*: the focus is on subject mastery with personal academics (through liberal arts education) giving a teacher professional strength.
    - *Practical orientation*: the focus is on teaching methods and mastery of practical classroom techniques of the teacher through the apprenticeship model of preparation.
    - *Technical orientation*: the focus is on a competence-based approach where teachers' behavioral skills are acquired through practices that include micro-teaching experiences.
    - *Personal orientation*: the focus is on development of interpersonal relationships in the classroom through humanistic techniques (from psychology) and developed through experimentation and discovery of personal strengths.
    - *Critical inquiry orientation*: the focus here is through the prism of "schooling as a process of social reform," and the promotion of democratic values to reduce social inequities through the development of critical reflective practices in teachers as agents of social change.
- Describe your initial language teacher education program.
- What faculty (e.g., humanities, social science, education) was/is your program situated in?
- What courses did/do you take and why?
- What was the ratio of theory focused courses to practical focused courses in your program?
- Which aspects of your language teacher preparation program did/do you consider as valuable?
- What aspects of your language teacher preparation program did/do you consider as not valuable?
- Did/Do you perceive any theory/practice gap in the language teacher education program?
- What do you think are the needs of novice language teachers?

Experienced Teacher Needs

Most practicing language teachers will undergo some kind of in-service education program after they graduate from their initial teacher education programs, and such programs will of course, vary from country to country, district to district, and school to school. As outlined in Chapters 2 and 3, language teachers have a multitude of reflective activities that they can engage in as part of their professional development. Such professional development opportunities can be initiated by the teachers themselves, or by their school, district, region, and/or ministry of education and carried out individually, pairs and/or in groups with or without the use of technology. As I have already outlined and discussed many of these professional development activities in the preceding chapters, and these all meet the needs of experienced teachers to guide them in their reflections on their practice, I will thus focus on one very popular method of professional development not covered thus far in the book, that of workshops.

Workshops are one of the commonest forms of professional development activities for language teachers and are usually led by a person who is an expert in the area of focus and designed to provide an opportunity to acquire specific knowledge and skills that they can later apply in the classroom (Richards & Farrell, 2005). Workshops can provide several benefits for the professional development of language teachers that include (adapted from Richards & Farrell, 2005):

- *Provide Expert Input*: Experts are familiar with their particular topic and language teachers often need the help of any expert in order to familiarize themselves with these topics. Thus, a workshop can provide an opportunity for an expert to share knowledge and experience with teachers in a comfortable learning environment.
- *Offer Practical Classroom Applications:* A workshop is usually intended to enhance teachers' practical skills by providing new ideas, strategies, techniques and materials that can be used in their classrooms, rather than a theoretical knowledge of these.
- *Raise Teachers' Motivation and Collegiality*: Workshops can offer a forum where teachers can share issues with peers either in the same school, or from different schools. These discussions can serve to renew teachers' enthusiasm for teaching as well as develop collegiality.

- *Support Innovations*: Workshops can be used to prepare teachers for the implementation of curricular changes within a school or district.

In addition, Richards and Farrell (2005) suggest whomever (schools or individual teachers) is planning to implement workshops they should consider that they choose an appropriate topic, a limited number of participants, a suitable workshop leader/expert, and an evaluation at the end. Regarding picking a suitable topic, my experience suggests that it is best to consider topics that will have a practical rather than theoretical application and be one which participants have an interest in developing in their own teaching. Thus, it is probably best to limit the number of participants to those whose interests align to that topic. In addition, the workshop facilitator/ expert in that topic can provide new knowledge on that topic and better interact and provide feedback with a smaller number of participants. The workshop facilitator/expert should be skilled at organizing group-based learning, have good time management skills, and be able to pitch it at the right level for the audience at hand. At the end of the workshop, any evaluation should answer if the original goals of the workshop were achieved and then details about how the workshop was executed such as suitability of content covered, presented skills, teacher participation and planned follow-ups.

The general purpose of many of these top-down organized workshops is usually to promote school focused issues, but they do not provide much relevance to the needs or interests of individual participants. Thus, it is important to also obtain *their* perspective/voice about what *they* are interested in developing. With this in mind, Reed and Chappell (2021) surveyed 92 practicing language teachers in Australia about their professional development (PD) needs, and how satisfied they are with their own PD. According to Reed and Chappell (2021) most of these teachers had experienced a modified version of top-down management-run traditional approach to their professional development and mostly through taking workshops (see above). Although there were mixed responses from the respondents related to their satisfaction or dissatisfaction with their professional development experiences, the study generated some key practical recommendations for both teachers and managers to *jointly* develop a holistic professional development program, one which would meet managers and teachers' needs. These eight recommendations proposed by Reed and Chappell (2021) include:

1. *Involve teachers in PD planning, especially through teacher-led committees.* When teachers are consulted about their professional development by management, they become more invested in the process as they feel more ownership of the process. This can be facilitated by developing a collaborative committee within the school to jointly develop the PD program.
2. *Provide mechanisms for regular teacher feedback on the PD program.* When only management evaluate the success or failure of a PD program, then they only consider if *their* needs have been met. Thus, including the teacher participants where they can contribute their honest feedback (without penalty or punishment) in the overall evaluation of a PD program is essential if the program is going to have any impact on the institution and especially what the teachers incorporate from that PD session. In other words, management should make the whole evaluation process as transparent as possible.
3. *Initiate individual PD programs negotiated between teacher and manager, where the manager facilitates the developing autonomy of the teacher.* Reed and Chappell (2021) discovered that the most satisfied teachers with their PD program who reported in their survey were those who collaborated with their managers as they discussed how their individual needs could be aligned with the institution's needs. The word "support" arose a lot in their survey results as the teachers appreciated any support for their needs from the institution, especially when they displayed interest in the teachers' development. The teachers also reported that the most successful PD programs in their estimation were ones that followed a learning cycle of well stage activities followed by evaluation and reflection of the process as a whole. In other words, the most successful PD programs were deliberately planned well in advance and reflected on after.
4. *Set a PD expectation with teachers, with flexible options on how to meet goals.* Sometimes when institutions set up PD programs in advance, they are fairly set as experts have been invited and teachers have been allotted time to attend. How many teachers have begun to dread the inevitable "PD Days" the last Friday of each month because these are compulsory PD activities for the teachers without much flexibility? Reed and Chappell (2021) noted that the teachers they surveyed found such compulsory attendance demotivating and preferred more flexibility in choosing and directing their own process of PD that could

also include taking some online study options. Such flexibility they suggested, would better meet their own PD goals.

5. *Support teacher access to PD through funding, time and energy.* One of the main complaints of many experienced teachers undertaking professional development is that they usually have to fund most of their own self-initiated programs because their school management will not provide funding or support such as providing release time to travel outside the school for such development programs. Teachers are much more motivated when the institution provides such support including funding and release time to attend outside PD events that further their individual development needs.

6. *Preference PD options that are collaborative and teacher-led, including action research and communities of practice.* Indeed, as outlined in the first three chapters of this book, successful PD experiences are usually long-term, individual and/or collaborative approaches that are context sensitive to individual teachers' needs. The teachers in Reed and Chappell's (2021) survey noted again that reflection in the form of action research and teacher reflection groups are more useful for the teachers' professional development than lecture-style seminars provided by management. They also note a plethora of other activities that can be used for collaborative many of which are outlined in Chapters 1 and 2 such as self-reflection, analysis of critical incidents and case study, reflection with teaching portfolios, and development of individual teacher's language awareness as well as critical friends, team teaching, peer coaching, and classroom observations.

7. *Embed ongoing PD into all aspects of practice throughout the institution.* Job-embedded professional development is just that, "embedded" into the day-to-day work of a teacher. It can be formal and informal and includes, but is not limited to, discussion with others, peer coaching, team-teaching, mentoring, teacher reflection groups, action research, compiling teaching portfolios, peer observations and more. The teachers in the survey reported that when PD was part of an "ecosystem" then individual teachers engaged in activities considered themselves part of a whole approach where the institution encouraged a culture of PD. Thus, professional development is viewed as a continuous process rather than a one-off event.

8. *Value and promote teacher leadership through mentoring.* When teachers have experienced their own professional development activities

throughout their careers as supported by their institutions, they can give back by becoming coaches and mentors for their less experienced colleagues and thus everyone wins: the teachers and the institution. All schools are staffed by many teachers with a multitude of valuable experiences for the most part that go unnoticed by management. However, when schools provide opportunities for these teachers to share their wealth of experiences with their colleagues, they become even more motivated to develop themselves and the program. The teachers reported in the survey that when managers encouraged them to step out of their comfort zones, they had a whole new perspective on their job as a teacher. Indeed, most teachers said that they enjoyed attending events organized by their fellow teachers.

Time Out

- What kind of workshops have you experienced throughout your teaching career?
- How would you evaluate the success of these workshops? Did they meet your needs or those of your school/institution?
- What is your opinion of the following three-hour workshop (Designed by Dr. George Jacobs) on cooperative learning, and would you like to attend? If yes, why? If no, why not?

Outline of Workshop:
1. Introduction of workshop facilitator, including his contact information—phone, email, website (which has many pages on cooperative learning) for follow-up. His qualifications and enthusiasm concerning the topic.
2. Acknowledgement of sources of ideas to be presented, with websites.
3. Overview of what will be presented: Advantages of groups, problems with groups, a definition of cooperative learning (CL), CL techniques.
4. Overview of how ideas will be presented: Participants will learn about cooperative learning by working in cooperative learning groups. They will first experience three short, simple to use CL techniques as the facilitator's students and then work together to apply those techniques to their own students.

5. Participants in pairs use a CL technique to think of potential advantages of group activities. Facilitator calls on a few participants to share what their partner said.
6. The facilitator presents his own list of potential advantages of groups, including evidence from research on cognitive and affective benefits. As he does so, he explains four CL principles, using the first CL technique to illustrate the principles and teaching participants a mnemonic device to help remember them.
7. The facilitator gives a few examples of how that CL technique could be used in the classroom.
8. Participants work in pairs to develop a lesson with that technique which they can use in the next week. A lesson planning template—including a place to write the date when the lesson will be used—is provided to promote thinking.
9. Each pair tries out their lesson, with the other pair in their foursome acting as their students.
10. The facilitator introduces another CL technique. Participants use this technique to discuss problems that may arise when group activities are used.
11. The facilitator asks a few participants to share a problem described by their partners, and then he goes through a list of 10 problems that can arise when groups are used.
12. Steps 7–9 are repeated to help participants use this second CL technique with their students. Additionally, the facilitator leads participants to understand how the four previously explained CL principles are embodied in that CL technique.
13. The facilitator explains a third CL technique including its relation to the four CL principles. Participants use this technique in their groups to identify one of the previously discussed problems that they feel is a particular impediment to their use of group activities.
14. Participants use the same CL technique to generate ways of addressing the problem which their group identified.
15. The facilitator calls a number and group members with that number travel to another group to describe their group's problem and their ideas for solving it. Members of the other group provide feedback.
16. Travelers return and report on the feedback received.
17. Steps 7–9 are repeated with this third CL technique.

18. The facilitator gives a definition of CL, indicating its connection to the problem-solving that participants did in Steps 14–16.
19. The facilitator concludes by elaborating on what CL is and is not, emphasizing that CL involves more than just asking students to work in groups. He also stresses that in tandem with promoting learning, CL can also promote a more harmonious environment in the classroom, the school, and, hopefully, beyond.
20. The facilitator welcomes questions, comments, and disagreements. He asks teachers to please really use the lessons they planned and to report back on that at the next session. Finally, the facilitator thanks participants for their active engagement in the workshop and asks them to thank their group mates for helping them learn.

- What are your professional development needs?
- What do you think of the seven recommendations (detailed above) from Reed and Chappell's (2021) recent survey?
- Where do you want to go in your future career as a language teacher? How will you get there?
- Do you see any gaps in your qualifications or do you see a need for a further qualification to meet the requirements of a new job or position or the like?

Conclusion

This chapter outlined and discussed the professional development needs of novice teachers as well as the needs of more experienced teachers. It is noted that all along the teaching career cycle language teachers will have different developmental needs. Teacher development is always ongoing and incomplete and so we should listen to all language teachers' voices about their perceived needs for professional development opportunities throughout their careers. If language teachers are to be fully invested in their own professional development that fulfills their needs, they need to be able to set their own agenda and it must be on their own terms if they are to fully benefit from the process. The chapter that follows offers some ideas both schools/institutions and individual teachers can consider when implementing professional development programs.

5
Implementing and Sustaining Professional Development

Introduction

Most language teachers will engage in some sort of professional development throughout their teaching careers because they want to remain relevant in an ever-changing profession. As mentioned earlier, such development is not necessarily a result of not being trained or educated correctly at the pre-service level, but a response to the fact that not everything a language teacher needs to know can be provided in initial teacher education programs (Richards & Farrell, 2005). How each school and each teacher implement and sustain their professional development, will be different as mentioned in previous chapters. This chapter outlines and discusses how professional development can be *implemented* and *sustained* from both the *institutional perspective*, and the *individual perspective*.

Implementing Professional Development: *Institutional Perspective*

When institutions implement professional development programs, not only the institution benefits but also the teachers and students in that institution benefit. Joyce (1991, p. 8) has identified five dimensions of institutional improvement which professional development can contribute to:

- *Collegiality*: creating a culture through developing cohesive and professional relationships between staff (and the wider community), in which "broad" vision-directed improvements as well as day-to-day operations are valued.

- *Research*: familiarizing staff with research findings into school improvement, teaching effectiveness etc, which can support "in-house" development.
- *Site-specific information*: enabling and encouraging staff to collect and analyze data on students, schools and effects of change –both as part of a formal evaluation and informally.
- *Curriculum initiatives*: collaborating with others to introduce change in their own subject areas and on a cross-curricular base.
- *Instructional initiatives*: enabling staff to develop their teaching skills and strategies.

In addition, this will have an enormous benefit on student learning within the school because confident teachers (i.e., those who willingly take part in institutionally developed professional development initiatives) can better communicate their teaching methods in their lessons so that they provide an overall positive class atmosphere where optimum opportunities are provided for their students to learn.

To successfully implement professional development program initiatives, institutions should try to develop a culture of support for professional development initiatives in the institution, provide sufficient time for the program, and evaluate the results of the program. Of course, most institutions will consider their own needs first, which upper management will decide in advance. However, this can also be a starting point for the school to develop a culture of support within, especially if the teachers are consulted about their individual needs as well. Institutions can administer questionnaires to their teachers inquiring about these and can also arrange staff meetings to identify such needs. In fact, if institutions include their teachers in their planning process, they can cover everyone's needs. As Díaz-Maggioli (2003, p. 4) has pointed out, "programs which involve participants in the planning, organization, management, delivery and evaluation of all actions in which they are expected to participate have more chances of success than those planned using a top-down approach, where administrators make decisions in lieu of teachers."

In order to establish a culture of support in any school there must be collaboration between the administration and the teachers, and this will entail that management/leadership must reach out to teachers and try to involve them in all aspects of the professional development plans. This will involve organizing meetings with the teachers or teacher representatives and trying to find some common ground when planning and establishing the professional development programs, as well as detailing how the institution will provide specific support for these to succeed. The details of these collaborations will vary depending on the culture of the school, the district, and the country in which they take place. Eraut (1995, p. 250) suggests that in planning teacher development activities, institutions should consider the following:

- Change should be managed and phased so as not to put impossible demands on any one person at any time. Teacher development also needs to be planned over a period of time to keep its demands at a realistic level.
- Each professional development activity has to be resourced and supported at a level that gives it a reasonable chance of achieving its purpose. Distributing resources over too many separate activities is likely to result in none of them being effective.
- Negotiation should take place, preferably with each individual teacher, about the proper balance between the teacher's personal needs and the needs of the school. A teacher's professional development plan should normally incorporate elements of both.

Another essential component for a successful institutionally directed professional development program is the provision for sufficient time to make it all work. Indeed, time is the perennially cited reason for the failure of institutionally developed professional development programs (Abdal-Haqq, 1996). As Abdal-Haqq (1996, p. 1) has noted, "teachers, researchers and policy-makers consistently indicate the greatest challenge to implementing effective professional development is lack of time." Indeed, some institutions deliver professional development programs with the expectation that the teachers immediately implement what they have learned. However, it takes time to discuss, understand, reflect, and consider the personal relevance of any new ideas or initiatives before they can be implemented, yet many institutions overlook this teacher need for time. Thus, institutions will need to reconsider the idea of time as a crucial and integral part of their overall development programs. Abdal-Haqq (1996) outlines five essential types of time that institutions can generate for language teachers for their professional development

1. Freed up time using teaching assistants, college interns, parents, and administrators to cover classes; regularly scheduled early release days
2. Restructured or rescheduled time lengthening school day on four days, with early release on day five.
3. Better-used time using regular staff or district meetings for planning and professional growth rather than for informational or administrative purposes.
4. Common time scheduling common planning periods for colleagues having similar assignments.
5. Purchased time establishing a substitute bank of 30–40 days per year, which teachers can tap when they participate in committee work or professional development activities.

In addition to encouraging a culture of support and providing sufficient time for professional programs to succeed, each institution will also want to consider what "success" will look like by evaluating what has been learned once the programs have been delivered. Institutions will want to consider if such programs were worth their investment, and detail what was achieved for their institution as well as for their teachers. Kirkpatrick (1988) developed four levels of assessing professional development activities that can be useful for both institutions (and individual teachers) to consider when evaluating the professional development programs:

1. *Reaction*: How do people feel during and immediately after the experience?
2. *Learning*: How much have they learned in terms of knowledge, skills and attitudes?
3. *Performance*: What are they doing differently now as a result of the learning experience?
4. *Organizational Results*: What additional benefits has the organization gained?

This evaluation can be carried out formally or informally, but the reason will be the same: to discover if the program succeeded and at what level, and if any improvements will be necessary for the delivery of future professional development programs in the institution. In addition, and to further the collaborative initiative between the administration and teachers, each institution can provide forums for teacher participants to present their reactions, what they learned, what they did and what their perceptions of the results were (by basically answering Kirkpatrick's four level analysis outlined above). The analysis can be written (e.g., a report), oral (e.g., lunchtime brown bag talks), an institution developed newsletter, and/or institution organized seminars further exploring the focus of the initial professional development activities.

Time Out

- Does the institution in which you work encourage a culture of support for the professional development of their teachers?
- How can the institution in which you work develop a culture of support that encourages teacher professional development?
- As outlined above, Joyce (1991) identifies five dimensions of institutional improvement which teacher development can contribute to: *collegiality*: *research*; *site-specific information*: *curriculum initiatives*: *instructional initiatives*. Which of these are most important and have you ever experienced anywhere you have worked? Can you add more that you think are important?
- Does the institution where you work provide sufficient time for professional development?
- What kind of time would be most important for them to provide in your opinion?
- What is your opinion of Abdal-Haqq's (1996) five types of time that can be created for language teachers in professional development?
- How can institutions evaluate the success of their professional development programs?
- Does your institution include you and the other teachers when determining the success of their professional development programs?
- Does your institution provide any forum for the dissemination of the results of their mandated professional development programs?
- Would you be willing to provide brown bad lunch talks and/or seminars or workshops to help them disseminate their results?

Implementing Professional Development: *Individual Teacher's Perspective*

Richards and Farrell (2005) offer the following useful guidelines that reflect professional development from an individual teacher's perspective.

1. The first guideline is to decide what *you* would like to learn about *your* teaching. As mentioned in the previous chapters, even though you have graduated from your initial teacher education program, your professional development continues throughout your teaching career. The first step in planning for your ongoing professional development is to determine what your short term and longer-term goals are. Only you will be able to decide these goals and specific topics you are interested in developing based on your current level of experience.
2. The second is to identify a strategy to explore the topic you are interested in. This book has introduced several different ways of facilitating your professional development either individually (Chapter 2) and/or collaboratively (Chapter 3). You can ask yourself which of the activities seems to be best suited to clarifying the issues you want to explore and to helping you achieve your goals? Richards and Farrell (2005) recommend starting with a simple activity such as self-monitoring (Chapter 2) or peer observation (Chapter 3) in order to develop some preliminary ideas about the topic you are interested in. Later you can decide if you want to follow up your initial investigation with other activities, such as peer coaching or action research.
3. The third guideline they suggest is to talk to other peers who have taken part in a professional development activity. Try to meet and talk to other teachers who have taken part in teacher development activities of the kind you wish to try out. Online discussions can also be an excellent way of getting in touch with other teachers who share your interests and concerns. For example, you can find out what their experience of different reflective activities such as what journal writing or team teaching was like for them: how they went about it, what they learned from it, and what recommendations they would give to someone who wished to carry out a similar activity.
4. The fourth guideline is to decide what kind of support you will need. Many of the activities discussed in this book (especially Chapters 2 and 3) do not need much support (except allocation of time perhaps—see above) from a manager. However, some activities outlined in Chapter 3, such as peer observation, team teaching, and peer coaching, will benefit from some kind institutional assistance so that they are effective. Thus, and as outlined above, teachers and the institution can discuss the goals of such an activity and negotiate suitable support that that help make such professional development initiatives successful.

5. Their fifth guideline to consider is to try to select a colleague or colleagues to work with if you want to take a collaborative approach to your professional development (Chapter 3). This means you will need to find a colleague or colleagues you can trust to work with you as you investigate an issue of interest to all involved. This relationship can be in the form of a critical friendship, team teaching, peer coaching, or a teacher development group (see Chapter 3 for more on these).
6. When all of the above has been decided, teachers will need to set realistic goals and establish a time frame, the sixth guideline to follow. As noted above, time is one of the most imposing problems for teachers wishing to engage in professional development opportunities, so you must set realistic time goals for the activities you choose as you may need to carry them out a few times before they are fine-tuned to your aims.
7. This can also include evaluating (Richards & Farrell, 2005, seventh guideline) what you have learned by engaging in professional opportunities such as your perceived level of improvement in a teaching skill or how you modified some other approach in any way.

Time Out

- Go through Richards and Farrell's (2005) guidelines that reflect professional development from an individual teacher's perspective and fill out the details based on your professional development needs:
    1. Decide what you would like to learn about your teaching and about the field.
    2. Identify a strategy to explore the topic you are interested in
    3. Talk to people who have taken part in a professional development activity
    4. Select a colleague or colleagues to work with.
    5. Set realistic goals and establish a time frame.
    6. Decide what kind of support you will need.
    7. Evaluate what you have learned and share the results with others
- Choosing which professional development issue and activity to pursue can impose pressures of its own. Which of the following would concern you as you go about your development?
    o Do you feel that you have nothing to say or that the issue and activity you want to do is of little significance?
    o Do you feel daunted by the difficulties of juggling all your responsibilities, professional and personal?

- o Do you feel that you are being a little bit selfish, to pursue an area of interest which inevitably is going to involve sacrifices by yourself and others?
- o Do you have any other fears or worries about pursuing your professional development?

Sustaining Professional Development Through Practitioner Research

So far in this book I have outlined and discussed various approaches and activities that both individual teachers and institutions can consider for pursuing professional development opportunities. I have also posed many questions to you in the Time Outs in the previous chapters that encourage you to consider particular aspects of your practice that you may want to develop. Now in this section, I would like to outline how you can sustain your professional development even further throughout your career by undertaking your own practitioner research. For too long, and especially with the language teaching field, many curriculum changes and a vast array of teaching methods and approaches have been imposed *on* teachers because they are seen as mere technicians delivering a product (language) to clients (students) for the purposes of profit. Indeed, English as a second or foreign language learning has always been seen as a business for schools rather than an educational endeavor that can help students' lives. Within this business view, language teachers have been ignored because they are there only to implement predesigned teaching methods that can be easily tested, and their artistry and intuitive processes were (and still are in many contexts) even considered as a hindrance. Thus, language teachers lacked ownership, and as a result many also lacked self-worth and teacher agency to direct their own professional growth.

However, as I have already noted in this book, I consider teaching to be a profession, and self-determination and autonomy are key aspects or hallmarks of teacher professionalism. As Hoyle (1974, p. 315) has noted, "professionalism refers to the strategies and rhetoric employed by members of an occupation in seeking to improve status, salary and conditions, and professionality refers to the knowledge, skills and procedures employed by teachers in the process of teaching." In addition, Hoyle and Wallace (2007, p. 19) maintain that any "meaningful conception of professionalism must reflect the *reality* of daily practices." For our purposes this would entail individual teachers engaging in their own professional development so that they can improve their own status and working conditions through conducting their own practitioner research.

Teacher research is defined as "all forms of practitioner enquiry that involve systematic, intentional, and self-critical inquiry about one's work" (Cochran-Smith & Lytle, 1999, p. 22). When language teachers engage in their own teacher research, they can further develop their theoretical and practical knowledge that is based on their particular interest and needs. As Sachs (1999, p. 41) argues, teacher research can "act as a significant source of teacher and academic professional renewal and development because learning stands at the core of this renewal through the production and circulation of new knowledge about practice." Unfortunately, within the field of language teaching, research that is conducted by academic researchers who are removed from classrooms tends to be more highly valued, rather than classroom research done by researcher-practitioners who acknowledge real-world English language teaching problems (McKinley, 2019). Unfortunately, this academic focus has led to the publication of research findings from decontextualized studies which do not reflect the messiness of the real world of teaching language, nor the complex issues that teachers deal with in their daily classroom practices.

Hence, I encourage you to undertake practitioner research as part of your professional development because it is more grounded in *your* classroom context and more related to your teaching needs. Borg (2013) points out that conducting such research promotes teacher autonomy (e.g., by boosting teachers' criticality so they depend less on educators and/or "external" authorities), develops teacher empowerment (e.g., by getting involved in processes of social change), and improves teacher well-being (e.g., reducing feelings of professional inadequacy). To these Farrell (2016b) adds the following benefits: language teachers can learn about, with and from their learners; improve classroom dynamics via collaboration on research with their learners (e.g., by involving learners in various stages of the research project); and positively influence other language teachers' practices by sharing their own work. As Freeman (1998, p. 6) has pointed out, teachers are best suited to carry out research in their own classrooms because they are "more insiders to their settings than researchers whose work lives are elsewhere."

How should language teachers approach research and what methods should they use are also important questions to consider? First, and as was pointed out earlier in this book, teachers should select approaches and methods based on their needs and within their unique contexts. Generally, most conducting research can be conceived as a process whereby teachers first pose a question, or problem, then collect data related to that problem, analyze the data, and interpret the results all related to *their* practice (Nunan & Bailey, 2009). Fueyo and Koorland (1997, p. 337) explain the process as follows:

> Teachers as researchers ask questions and systematically find answers. They observe and monitor themselves and their students while participating in the teaching and learning process. They question instructional practices and student outcomes. They make date-based decisions, validating their practice. They implement change.

As series editor and developer of language teacher research in the TESOL USA organization some years ago (see Farrell, 2017), I was honored to launch TESOL's *Language Teacher Research* series that consisted of six volumes each outlining how practicing language teachers conducted teacher research in six different continents: Asia, Africa, Europe, the Middle East, New Zealand/Australia, and Africa. A total of 68 studies published in the six volumes document how language teachers systematically reflected on a wide range of topics related to their teaching. A common theme across the six continents was how language teachers can improve student performance in various aspects of language learning. In addition, the majority of the teacher-researchers used some kind of qualitative research methods as their preferred mode of data collection. Perhaps you can locate the volume for the continent you are teaching in at present and review the studies and consider which ones you may want to replicate for your own needs.

When engaging in any practitioner research, teachers will see that teaching and classroom research really go together. As Stewart (2013, p. 32) has pointed out, "Teaching raises the questions for investigation and the classroom provides the setting." Engaging in such classroom-based research empowers individual language teachers as Stewart (2013) also notes, while in pursuit of their professional development. As a result, language teachers can become generators of their own theory, rather than being constant consumers of academic controlled research as noted above and everyone in

Implementing and Sustaining Professional Development   **105**

the language teaching profession as a whole, including our students, benefits.

Time Out

- As mentioned above, TESOL's *Language Teacher Research* Series used the same template outlined below to conduct TESOL teacher research in six different continents.
  - *Statement of the issue.* This includes a brief description of the context and the participants. Why was this issue (this does not have to be a problem) important to you? Identify and express what you see as important to the situated nature of your work.
  - *Brief review of the literature relating to the issue researched.* Please only include previous research considered directly relevant to the issue.
  - *Procedures or responses the researcher made to the issue.* What was the procedure or response taken, why this procedure or response, and where did it come from? How was it implemented? For example, if interviews were used, were they structured or unstructured? What were the questions asked? Please give as many details as possible here as other teachers may want to replicate your research in different contexts.
  - *Result.* What was the outcome? Give details and discuss the results.
  - *Reflection.* A statement that articulates answers to the question, "So what?" What will you do now and in the future? What action will you take as a result of your findings? If you have already acted on your findings, what did you do? What have you learned as a result of the whole process? For example, what have you learned about your teaching? What have you learned about doing research? Also, at this point, the issue of the situated nature of the work should be revisited: why you think the issue is specific to your context.
- Follow the same chapter template outlined above conduct your own TESOL teacher research either replicating some of the studies above or by conducting research on your own topic.
- Discuss your language teacher research plans with a colleague for which of the six books in the LTR volume would be most useful for you to help you to conduct research. The books are:
  - Borg, S. (Ed.). (2006). *Language teacher research in Europe*. Alexandria, VA: TESOL.

- Burns, A., & Burton, J. (Eds.) (2008). *Language teacher research in Australia & New Zealand*. Alexandria, VA: TESOL.
- Coombe, C., & Barlow, L. (Eds.) (2007). *Language teacher research in the Middle East*. Alexandria, VA: TESOL.
- Farrell, T.S.C. (Ed.) (2006c). *Language teacher research in Asia*. Alexandria, VA: TESOL.
- Makela, L. (Ed.) (2009). *Language teacher research in Africa*. Alexandria, VA: TESOL.
- McGarrell, H. M. (Ed.) (2007). *Language teacher research in the Americas*. Alexandria, VA: TESOL.

Sustaining Teaching and Development in an Online World

I am writing this book as the COVID-19 pandemic ravages the world in different ways, and for language teachers (and language schools and students) it has meant that we have been suddenly "forced" to move to teaching online, and many of us with little or no prior training. Many language teachers had already developed their tried and trusted instructional approaches, built up over whole careers while teaching our students face-to-face. We were able to provide prompt feedback and "read" our students' body language to see if they look interested, or bored. In face-to-face learning our students could interact in real time with each other and because they have their classmates next to them, they could motivate and encourage each other as well as clarify any questions they may have about the lesson content. Then this all ended suddenly for many in March of 2020 when the pandemic struck, and everyone was required to adapt fast to a new virtual world. Yes, online teaching and learning is not new, but before the pandemic it was presented as a supplement or complement to our classes, but not as a replacement. Teachers, students, and language schools, without much time to prepare, had to scramble to adapt their traditional face-to-face instruction and learning to make them suitable for this new "face-to-screen" online delivery mode.

What teachers took for granted in traditional instruction such as teaching methods, lesson activities, time spent on tasks, student responses, feedback, student paralinguistic cues, assignments, and assessment all have changed and have become more of a demanding task for both teachers and students. Other online issues that have also caused trouble for everyone are related to technology such as computers, internet platforms, programs, student presence on/off camera, preparation time, time at sitting at screen to name but a few. Thus, the onset of COVID-19 and online teaching has greatly increased language teachers' stress because the changes have shattered all the usual classroom teaching boundaries: physically, temporally, and psychologically (MacIntyre, Gregersen, & Mercer, 2020).

No language teacher education or development program could have truly prepared any teacher (or student) for this sudden and emotionally stressful transition. Under these demanding COVID-19 conditions, it becomes even more important for language teachers to engage in their own professional development through reflective practice so that they can gain a better understanding of teaching online and their associated adaptation challenges. For example, in a recent case study in Costa Rica of four English as a foreign language (EFL) teachers' sudden move to online teaching modes, Farrell (2021b) noted that all four teachers struggled to adapt their methods, approaches, activities, planning, interactions, and classroom management techniques to an online environment. The four language teachers discovered the hard way that there was no longer an opportunity for the class to function as a social group. This is because with a switch to on-line teaching, much of the emotional and social support for learning disappears. Their learners are all studying remotely in front of their laptops while the teacher's presence is primarily via videoconferencing tools such as Zoom. The textbook no longer functions as a source of pair and group-based activities and requires considerable adaptation and supplementation; activities take more time to accomplish and can induce frustration and boredom on the part of teachers and students, and the teacher is no longer able to provide the kind of individual support, guidance, and feedback students have come to expect. Indeed, there are technical problems encountered with the technology and little logical support from the institution that can lead to both frustration and anger. There are the same pressures associated with assessment and the institution now assumes responsibility for assessment excluding what would normally have been part of the teacher's responsibility. In addition, because this move happened without warning or preparation and training, heightened emotional stresses were triggered, and teachers had to develop their own coping strategies in order to be able to adapt themselves to online language teaching.

So important implications for sustaining professional development of language teachers in such an online world emerge from this case study that can be considered by stakeholders in all contexts. One immediate implication is that when planning for online delivery modes, there should be no attempts to replicate traditional face-to-face lessons because delivery formats, platforms, and tools available are different in both, in addition to the differences in interaction, assessments and evaluations necessary for online instruction. Another implication is that language teacher education and development programs should instruct teachers the skills necessary to better integrate more digital tools into their teaching practices such as how to check non-verbal cues online, gauge their student responses online, set up and monitor breakout groups where students collaborate online, as well as provide effective feedback throughout online lessons.

The COVID-19 pandemic is still sweeping the world at time of writing, and no doubt this terrible disease has disrupted your life personally and professionally. Professionally we have all had to make a difficult transition from our usual "face-to-face" teaching to sudden "face-to-screen" teaching platforms. Indeed, another result of the pandemic is that many language teachers have also been forced to seek professional development opportunities online given that most conferences have gone virtual. However, Ballıdağ and Dikilitaş (2021) point out that language teacher educators and institutional leaders who plan to encourage language teachers to engage in online professional development should consider providing more time and space for them to freely select and engage in self-selected online activities, as well as the ability to negotiate individual (digital) resources that they might need to boost their motivation. They should also plan various forms of support which they might need in the case of self-paced individual learning, as well as organize an institutionally assisted social environment in which such teachers can be appreciated and recognized while they pursue online professional development opportunities. Ballıdağ and Dikilitaş (2021) maintain that online professional development which is characterized by bottom-up, self-initiated and self-paced can lead to more meaningful teacher learning and development.

Time Out

- What new knowledge and skills would you like to acquire in order to effectively deliver on-line lessons?
- What kinds of on-line professional development activities would be most useful for you to learn?

- How can institutions provide support for your on-line professional development?
- What are the benefits and limitations of engaging in online professional development activities?
- Although it has been stated in some circles that online professional development programs offer a more convenient approach for many language teachers to adopt, some studies have noted that a series pitfall is that there is also a high drop out rate of such learners mostly because of time, technology problems, lack of support, and lack of motivation issues. How would you protect yourself from dropping out from such online professional development programs for any reason?

Conclusion

This chapter has outlined and discussed how professional development can be implemented from both an individual and an institutional perspective. The chapter also discussed how such professional development opportunities can be sustained when language teachers engage in their own practitioner research throughout their careers. In addition, given the new (COVID-19) world order the chapter noted that most language teachers now find themselves teaching online, and so it becomes even more important for them to engage in their own reflective practice related to their adaptation challenges to this online world. In addition, the chapter pointed out that since more traditional forms of professional development opportunities (such as workshops and attending conferences) have ended and moved to virtual formats, language teachers are now forced to go online looking for professional development opportunities, many of which will require more institutional support. The final chapter outlines ten different scenarios of professional development for your reflection.

6
Ten Professional Development Scenarios for Reflection

Introduction

Chapters 2 and 3 provided examples of reflective practices for individual language teachers through *self-monitoring*, analysis of *critical incidents* and *case study*, reflection with *teaching portfolios*, and *action research*, and development of individual teacher's *language awareness* (see Chapter 2), and also reflective approaches to professional development activities that can be carried out at the collaborative level that includes development through *critical friends, team teaching, peer coaching, peer observations,* and *teacher development groups* (see Chapter 3).

As the title suggests, this book reflects my insights into language teacher development and draws on some 40 years of my experiences in North America, the Asia Pacific region, and Europe while working with wonderful language teachers. I have conducted numerous talks, led seminars and workshops as well as written many books and papers on these topics. In this chapter I have compiled various scenarios mostly related to the teacher development activities outlined in Chapter 2 and Chapter 3 that are based on real examples of practicing language teachers worldwide. The teachers' names are not used, and so I refer to the "teacher" or "teachers" as a generic way to protect their identities. Time Outs continue in this chapter at the end of each scenario so you can consider your reaction to each one. I now present ten different teacher development scenarios (in no particular order) that you can consider for your own professional development reflections.

Scenario 1

A group of English as a Foreign Language (EFL) teachers in Spain came together to engage in professional development because all four noticed that their students were not speaking enough English during their classes and worse still, some consistently spoke Spanish during their classes. So, they met to discuss what they could do about this issue and so they decided to meet as a group once a week for a few weeks to discuss this problem while at the same time write a journal entry to each other also once a week. During one meeting one of the teachers revealed to the group that she was now becoming even more concerned with the situation in her class because her students have gone silent nearly totally and do not even speak in Spanish after she told them to stop using Spanish in English class. So, they all (as a group) decided to make a general plan to observe each other's classes for a period of two weeks. After this period, they came up with the following suggestions: (1) the teacher should not fill in any silence in their classes and to let the students fill in any gaps in silence in English themselves. (2) The teacher could scaffold more during the class by providing starter answers to questions in English, and (3) the teacher can introduce more structured topics during the class so that the students would not feel intimidated when speaking English. Over time, they all incorporated these suggestions into their classes and as a result, their students began to speak more English during the classes. The teachers realized the power of collaboration and the importance of seeking professional development opportunities throughout their careers.

Time Out

- Comment on the example from the group of teachers.
- What do you do if your students use their L1 in your language lessons?
- What do you do if your students do not speak much in the target language in your language lessons?

Scenario 2

Van, a novice ESL teacher in Canada, has encountered some difficulties establishing discipline and control in his classes this semester. Van has tried to win the students over by being as friendly as possible to them both inside and outside class. However, the class always seems to be too noisy and many of the students seem to be continuously talking to each other even when he is trying to teach some aspect of English. Van sensed that some of the students did not have much confidence in him as a teacher because he was a novice, and suspected they were trying to make fun of him, but he was not sure about his own teaching methods. Van decided to get help from a more experienced colleague, Jessica, by asking her to come observe his classes for a while. When Jessica came in to observe, Van noticed a change in his class atmosphere as many of them knew that Jessica was an experienced teacher in that school. They began to listen better to Van during these classes and Jessica also suggested he establish a policy of giving students 20% of their end of term grade based on their classroom participation and cooperation. When Jessica had stopped observing, Van noticed that the students continued to listen better and were generally more cooperative during his classes. Van was happy he sought help from his colleagues before his classes become more difficult to handle and he was very happy with the advice Jessica had given him regarding the grading of student participation as this seemed to work with his students. He has decided from now on to seek more guidance from his more experienced colleagues rather than to try to solve his own problems in an isolated manner.

Time Out

- Comment on the example from Van and Jessica.
- Have you felt a similar insecurity as a novice teacher? If yes, how did you cope?
- Have you ever asked a more experienced colleague for advice?
- How do you grade student participation in your language lessons?

Scenario 3

Minjung, an EFL teacher, decided to reflect on her beliefs about teaching English conversation classes in South Korea. She decided to first write everything in a journal about her classes for one month. She wrote her thoughts before each class and directly after each class and after monitoring her classes in this way over the first four weeks she noticed a pattern developing in the journal entries. Minjung noticed that many of his students were not responding well to the various speaking activities she introduced during these classes. When she examined the activities that she used for these classes, Minjung realized that they were all taken from the textbook which was prescribed by the course coordinator. So, Minjung, although she knew she was "breaking the rules," she decided to change the activities and to not use any from the textbook. Minjung designed activities that encouraged her students to speak rather than read because she believed

Ten Professional Development Scenarios for Reflection 113

this was the best approach to develop Korean students' oral communication skills. Minjung reread one of her journal entries at that time: "A good lesson for me is when students are talking together; today was better because I changed the activities, and the students began to talk more in class." Some of the activities that Minjung designed involved the students acting out different roles in particular role-playing situations and Minjung noticed that these were the most popular with the students, so she decided not to correct many language mistakes during the role plays but to note the common ones made and then to address them at the end of each class. As Minjung noted in her journal, this seemed to work best for her and for her students. Minjung began to gain more confidence as an EFL teacher as the months went because she continued to monitor her all her classes including her grammar and writing classes but this time, she also made audio recordings of the classes and each week she played them back and tried to note whatever patterns she saw developing in any particular class.

Time Out

- Comment on the example from Minjung.
- Do you design your own language lesson activities, or do you follow the textbook?
- How do you think writing regularly helped Minjung develop as an EFL teacher?

Scenario 4

Rosita, an EFL teacher in Malaysia, decided to write about her reflections on how she approached corrections in her English classes. She decided on this topic because one of her students told her that he was concerned that she was not correcting his mistakes enough, not only in speaking classes but also in writing classes. Rosita decided to write everything she did when she corrected the students in her speaking classes as soon as she could after it, and at the same time she audio recorded the class so she could later transcribe the parts where she corrected the students. This way Rosita would have some concrete evidence about her correction techniques (or lack of them as she wrote in her journal). After a month of writing about her correction techniques and listening to the relevant parts where she gave corrections in classes, Rosita noted that the student was correct in that she did not correct many spoken errors in the speaking classes. However, in her writing classes, Rosita noted that she corrected every error she could find and used a red pen to highlight these errors. She then wrote about her beliefs and approaches to teaching speaking and writing and discovered that she wanted to promote fluency in her speaking classes and accuracy in her writing classes. This coincided with her lack of corrections in her speaking classes to encourage fluency and the opposite in her writing classes to encourage accuracy. Rosita wondered if these two beliefs and approaches were at odds with each other and decided to share these beliefs with her colleagues. Some agreed with them, and some did not, but as Rosita soon realized, she would have to make up her own mind about her beliefs and practices regarding how she would correct student errors in her speaking and writing classes. Rosita also noted in her journal that she should better explain how she approaches corrections to her students and why she followed these approaches. Rosita discovered that writing in a journal allowed her to step back for a moment and "stop" to think about this topic. So, Rosita continued writing a teaching journal about various aspects of her work after this experience.

Time Out

- Comment on the example from Rosita.
- How do you deal with spoken and written errors in your language lessons?
- How does writing in a journal allow teachers to "stop and think" about issues?

Scenario 5

Yoko, Hitomi, and Sachiko, three female Japanese EFL teachers in different institutions in Japan, decided to meet regularly to discuss their teaching after they attended a talk on teacher development at an international language learning and teaching conference in Japan. They were especially interested in videotaping their English language classes and then watching these videotapes together in order to discuss what they observed. As they were all teaching in the Tokyo area, and within two or three subway stops, they decided that they could observe each other teach for one whole semester. However, they had a few issues to discuss before the peer observations and videotaping could take place. These were: Who would tape the classes? Answer: Hitomi. Can the observers talk to the students?

Answer: No. Who would act as facilitator for the discussions after the viewing? Answer: Yoko because she has the most experience teaching English (five years); Hitomi had three years teaching experience and Yoko had two years teaching experience. Who would set the agenda for the discussions? Answer: They decided that each teacher would set the agenda when they were viewing their particular videotape of the lesson. How many lessons would they observe and tape? Answer: three for each teacher during the twelve-week semester. They also decided not to discuss each class until they had finished all three rounds of observations for all three teachers. What aspects of their teaching would they focus on for discussions? Answer: As this was their first time to observe each other teach and for them to be videotaped, and that it was unusual for teachers in Japan to share their teaching and classrooms, they decided to look at general aspects of their teaching and to look for patterns in their teaching and that of the other teachers. If they discovered anything else, they could focus on that later. After their initial nervousness of being taped, especially for Yoko as she was the most inexperienced teacher—"The taping made me nervous. I felt I was performing for the camera"—each teacher settled down to teach their classes as they would normally do and went through the three rounds of classroom observations and videotaping smoothly. They then met to discuss the tapes and decided to devote separate meetings to discuss each set of videotapes of one teacher's class. They learned many things about their teaching as a result of the videotapes and the group discussions about their lessons.

Time Out

- Comment on the example from Yoko, Hitomi, and Sachiko.
- In what ways can observations help teachers develop?
- In what ways can observations make teachers nervous?

Scenario 6

Jielin, an English teacher in a Chinese university English language program, was assigned a writing class to teach, and so she decided to do an action research project on grammar corrections for her students' written work. Jielin always wondered how she had done this in the past, so she decided to just continue doing what she had always done when reading and correcting grammar issues in her students' essays from the beginning of this semester.

After four weeks she collected all her students' written work and her written corrections and noted what she had done. Then she interviewed all her students to ask them about their perceptions of how she corrected grammar in their written work. She noted that she usually corrected all their grammar mistakes in their written work and that the students said they liked this. However, she also noted that they continued to make the same mistakes even though she had corrected them in previous assignments. Jielin decided to read up in the literature of grammar teaching and writing about what the so-called experts think about grammar correction in written work. She discovered that many suggest teachers do not correct all the grammar mistakes, but rather focus on particular mistakes that students can learn from. So, Jielin made a plan to only focus on selected grammar mistakes in her students' writing and not to correct all of them as she had done before. Jielin explained to her students that she would be making these changes to her correction techniques and why she was doing it. Then after another four weeks she looked at all her students' written work and noticed a slight change in that some students were beginning to make fewer grammar mistakes. However, when Jielin interviewed her students, many said they were not happy she was not correcting all the mistakes and wondered if they were being instructed in the correct manner. Jielin then showed them the progress they were making, but some continued to doubt.

Time Out

- Comment on the example from Jielin.
- Do you ever focus your corrections on a few items in your students' written assignment? What would be the advantages and disadvantages of this?
- In what ways can action research help teachers reflect?

Scenario 7

Anna and Carmen are both Australian EFL teachers teaching in a private institute in Taiwan. They each teach four classes but team-teach one of them. For that class, they plan the class together. They divide up the activities in each unit of their textbook deciding who will teach which exercises and which exercises they will present together. They plan each of their lessons to determine their roles within the lesson. They are both present for every lesson and share the teaching time. They both enjoy their team-taught lessons and feel that both they and their learners benefit from them. The following example shows how Anna and Carmen planned an intermediate level reading class:

Lesson Objectives:

To teach the students to skim to find the main idea of a passage

Prior Knowledge:

Students have learnt how to locate information by reading and finding the main sentence of each paragraph. This lesson is to practice increasing their reading speed within scanning and skimming for information.

Materials:

Reading materials—a passage from their textbook on Sports plus supplementary materials
Overhead projector

Lesson Plan:

Stage I: Opening (5 to 10 minutes): Introduction to the topic—sport. Anna activates students' background knowledge on sports and asks students to suggest as many different kinds of sport as they can within three minutes. Anna asks students to rank their favorite sports in order of importance. As the students call out their answers Carmen writes them on the board.
Stage II: Anna distributes a handout on the sports schedule from the newspaper and a worksheet. Carmen asks the students to read it quickly and answer the true/false questions about it within three minutes. Carmen goes over the answers. At this stage of the lesson Carmen wants to focus on the concept of skimming for general gist with authentic materials.
Stage III: Carmen discusses skimming to get the general meaning or gist of a passage. Anna asks students to turn to a text on Sport in the textbook. Anna asks the students to read and answer the true/false questions within 5–7 minutes. Anna asks students for answers and writes them on the board.
Stage IV: Closing: Carmen summarizes the importance of reading a passage quickly first in order to get the gist. Carmen gives homework of reading the

next day's newspaper front page story and writing down in four sentences the gist of the story.

Follow-up: Carmen and Anna meet briefly after class in order to evaluate the lesson they just taught.

Post Lesson Discussion

Carmen and Anna discussed their lesson in the staff room immediately after class. They decided to look at what they thought went well and what they were unsure about. Both were pleased at the way the students were able to follow their instructions and directions. Anna, however, felt that Carmen's instructions for the skimming phase of the lesson were a bit fast as some of the students near her did not do what was required of them until they asked Anna for clarification. Carmen had not realized this. They also realized that the changeover from Carmen to Anna to use the text in Stage III did not go smoothly. So, they decided to make two changes for the next team-teaching session: (1) to back up oral instructions with written instructions on the whiteboard in future so there would be fewer misunderstandings. (2) Decide on one of them to take responsibility for each stage with the other teacher acting as a resource person like distributing handouts or writing answers on the board (as happened in Stage II). This way, they hoped the students would not become confused about who was teaching them and who to answer when asked questions. Overall, though, they were very pleased that way the lesson went and looked forward to the next session.

Time Out

- Comment on the example from Anna and Carmen.
- In what ways can team-teaching help teachers?
- In what ways can critical friendships help teachers?

Scenario 8

Three teachers of English language in Australia decided to come together as a group to explore strategies for teaching reading. Most of the students in the school came from a non-English speaking home environment and had below average English language proficiency, especially in writing. After approaching the school principal, John, to ask for school support, the group decided they would go ahead with such a collaborative relationship with one of them acting as a kind of coach to the other two so that they could clarify certain issues regarding their teaching of reading. John was delighted that they had volunteered to enter into such a collaborative relationship, so he decided that he would help them both personally and administratively. First, John agreed that when one teacher was observing the other teachers, he would find other teachers and pay them to teach all their classes. John also made time for them in their teaching schedules so that they would be able to meet at least one time a week as a group to discuss their progress. All three teachers decided on the schedule they would follow during the semester and gave this to John so he could prepare for it and help them succeed as a teacher development group. The group decided to record all of their group discussions, write regular journals, and then write up their results to present to their colleagues at the end of the semester. This arrangement seemed to benefit both the teachers in the teacher development group and the school, who has a supportive principal, as other groups of teachers volunteered to come together when they heard the group present their findings at the end of the semester. John set up a time at the end of the semester when the three teachers could present their findings to all the other teachers in the school.

Time Out

- Comment on the example from the three teachers.
- Comment on how the principal may have facilitated the teachers' professional development when teaching reading lessons.
- How would you set up such a similar group for your professional development?
- In what ways can teacher reflection groups help teachers develop?

Scenario 9

Larry, an instructor in an Intensive English Program in the USA, teaches academic writing and advanced listening. He has kept records of his teaching for several years but never really put it all together for anyone to see, not to mention himself. For example, he has many files with such items as old course outlines, teaching materials, and lesson plans and even some examples of workshops he gave over time. Now he has a chance of getting another job as a senior teacher within the intensive program he is teaching in, but they require him to present them with a teaching portfolio in advance of the interview. Larry has heard about teaching portfolios before but never put one together before. So, he started to gather all his documents together in one place. He collected all his student evaluations, lesson plans, course outlines, examinations, teaching materials and activities, and examples of workshops he gave and updated his CV. He was amazed when he saw all these in one place for the first time as he had had no idea that he had done so much in the past. He decided to write a reflective journal on this compilation—its meaning for Larry and what his future professional development plans were—and added it to his teaching portfolio. He also added a written account of two classroom observations made by peers the previous year and a reflective essay about his approach to teaching and his own teacher development. After he reviewed his teaching portfolio, Larry could reflect on his accomplishments over his career to himself and also with his interviewers for his new job.

Time Out

- Comment on the example from Larry.
- What would you include in your teaching portfolio?
- In what ways can teaching portfolios help teachers reflect?

Scenario 10

A group of three nonnative English speaking EFL teachers in Turkey, Axiel, Subeda, and Fazel, came together as a group to develop their English language proficiency levels. Each teacher had not been able to reflect on their particular use of English while they were teaching and wondered if they were using correct English in classroom situations. They first decided to read up on appropriate classroom language and discovered some specific examples of classroom discourse that include speech acts and functions such as:

- *Requesting, ordering, and giving rules.*
- *Establishing attention.*
- *Questioning.*
- *Repeating and reporting what has been said.*
- *Giving instructions.*
- *Giving and refusing permission.*
- *Warning and giving advice.*
- *Giving reasons and explaining.*

They also considered ideas of classroom language and her observations that teachers check their language use during the lesson as follows:

- *Getting organized: seating, books, blackboard.*
- *Checking attendance.*
- *The beginning of the lesson.*
- *Introducing different stages of the lesson.*
- *Dividing the class up: choral, individual and teams.*
- *Interruptions: late comers, things lost.*
- *Control and discipline.*
- *Ending the lesson or a stage in the lesson.*

So, the group decided to not only observe each other's teaching and reflect on their use of language outlined above but also to video record each class so they could all watch the replays together. They used the first observation to work out such issues as where the peer observers should sit (they decided at each corner in the back of the room), if they should write during the observations (they decided yes), and if they should interact with the students during the class (they decided no). After this first observation all three felt less threatened by the peer observation process. The group then decided that each peer would write down the exact type of language the teacher used during the different stages of the lesson and compare notes after the observation. They also decided to video each class at this time now that the students seemed to be used to observers in the class. After they got their students' permission to do this, they placed the camera at the top of the room facing the students and left it there. After this, they set aside time to replay each video of each class to make sure they were seeing what they observed and to find out if they left out anything. Later however, they realized that this would be too much work for each observer, so they decided to break up the observation process and to let each teacher watch his or her individual lesson alone and to report back to the group. For example, Axiel decided to look at all the instructions she gave during class and the type of language she used while giving these instructions. Subeda decided to examine her use of group work during her oral English classes and the type of language she used to set up and monitor groups, while Fazel decided to investigate how (the methods and results) she started and ended each class and the type of language she used to do this. They did this for two rounds of observations (and videotaping while reviewing each video individually) and then they met as a group to share their observations and discuss what they would do as a result of the findings. This latter meeting lasted for three hours and only resulted in each teacher giving an account of the classroom observations. They realized that they would have to have another meeting to evaluate and interpret these findings, and that after each teacher had a chance to digest what their peers had said. This next meeting produced interpretations by each group member and each teacher decided to make certain changes as a result of the meeting discussions.

Time Out

- Comment on the example from Axiel, Subeda, and Fazel.
- Why is it important for teachers (especially non-native speaker teachers) to have good language proficiency levels in the target language?
- Have you ever considered developing your proficiency in the target language you teach? If yes, how did you develop this? If no, why not?

Conclusion

This final chapter has presented ten different scenarios of language teachers engaging in professional development opportunities. These are real examples (with names changed) of wonderful language teachers in action as they try to become the best that they can be for their students. Although I have written and presented many different professional development activities for you to consider in this book, there is no "correct" method or activity that is suitable for all teachers. The "best" activity is the one that works for you in your context that can further your professional development so that you can continue to provide wonderful learning opportunities for your students. I wish you all the best of luck as you pursue professional development opportunities throughout your teaching careers.

References

Abdal-Haqq, I. (1996). *Making time for teacher professional development*. ERIC Digest. Washington, DC: ERIC Clearinghouse on Teaching and Teacher Education.

Artigliere, M., & Baecher, L (2017). *Sink or swim: aligning training with classroom reality in ESL co*-teaching. In T.S.C. Farrell (Ed.), *TESOL voices: Insider accounts of classroom life—preservice teacher education*. Alexander, VA: TESOL Press.

Bailey, K.M. (2001). Action research, teacher research, and classroom research in language teaching. In M. Celce-Murcia (Ed.), *Teaching English as a second or foreign language* (3rd ed.) (pp. 489–498). Boston: Heinle & Heinle.

Bailey, K.M., & Nunan, D. (Eds.). (1996). *Voices from the language classroom: Qualitative research on language education*. New York: Cambridge University Press.

Bailey, K.M., Curtis, A., & Nunan, D. (2001). *Pursuing professional development: The self as source*. Boston: Heinle & Heinle.

Ballıdağ, S., & Dikilitaş, K. (2021). Preparatory school teachers' self-directed online professional development. *Iranian Journal of Language Teaching Research, 9*, 3, 25–38.

Bambino, D. (2002). Critical friends. *Educational Leadership, 59*(6), 25–27.

Belbin, R.M. (1993). *Team roles at work*. London: Butterworth-Heinemann.

Berliner, D.C. (1987). Ways of thinking about students and classrooms by more and less experienced teachers. In J. Calderhead (Ed.), *Exploring teachers' thinking* (pp. 60–83). London: Cassell.

Berry, R. (1990). The role of language improvement in in-service teacher training: Killing two birds with one stone. *System, 18*, 97–105.

Borg, S. (2013). *Teacher research in language teaching: A critical review*. New York: Cambridge University Press.

Brandt, S.L. (2005). A life preserver for the "sink or swim" years: An investigation of new teacher obstacles and the impact of a peer support group. Dissertation Abstracts International, 3443A. (UMI No. 3201434).

Brookfield, S.D. (1990). *The skillful teacher*. San Francisco: Jossey Bass.

Burns, A. (1995). Teacher-researchers: Perspectives on teacher action research and curriculum renewal. In A. Burns & S. Hood (Eds.), *Teachers' voices: exploring course design in a changing curriculum* (pp. 3-29). Sydney: NCELTR, Macquarie University.

Calderhead, J., & Shorrock, S. (1997). *Understanding teacher education*. London: The Falmer Press.

Caspersen, J., & Raaen, D. (2014). Novice teachers and how they cope. *Teachers and Teaching: Theory and Practice, 20*, 2, 189-211.

Chung, E. (2021). Eleven factors contributing to the effectiveness of dialogic reflection: Understanding professional development from the teacher's perspective. *Pedagogies*. Advance online publication. https://doi.org/10.1080/1554480X.2021.2013234

Cirocki, A., Madyarov, I., & Baecher, L. (Eds.). (2019). *Current perspectives on the TESOL practicum: Cases from around the globe*. Cham: Springer.

Clarke, D.J., & Hollingsworth, H. (2002). Elaborating a model of teacher professional growth. *Teaching and Teacher Education, 18*, 8, 947-967.

Cochran-Smith, M., & Lytle, S.L. (1999). Relationships of knowledge and practice: Teacher learning in communities. *Review of Research in Education, 24*, 249-305.

Costantino, P.M., & De Lorenzo, M.N. (2002). *Developing a professional teacher portfolio: A guide for success*. Boston, MA: Allyn & Bacon.

Dewey, J. (1904). The relation of theory to practice in education. In C.A. McMurry (Ed.), *The third yearbook of the National Society for the Scientific Study of Education. Part I.* (pp. 9-30). Chicago, IL: The University of Chicago Press.

Díaz-Maggioli, G. (2003). Professional development for language teachers. ERIC Digest EDO-FL, 03-03.

Dunne, F., Nave, B., & Lewis, A. (2000). Critical friends: Teachers helping to improve student learning. *Phi Delta Kappa International Research Bulletin (CEDR), 28*, 9-12.

Eisen, M.J. (2000). The many faces of team teaching and learning: an overview. *New Directions for Adult and Continuing Education, 87*, 5-14.

Eraut, M. (1995). Developing professional knowledge within a client-centered orientation. In T.R. Guskey & M. Huberman (Eds.), *Professional development in education* (pp. 227-252). New York: Teacher's College, Columbia University.

References

Evans, S.M. (1995). *Professional portfolios: Documenting and presenting performance excellence.* Virginia Beach, VA: Teacher's Little Secrets.

Faez, F., & Valeo, A. (2012). TESOL teacher education: Novice teacher perceptions of their preparedness and efficacy in the classroom. *TESOL Quarterly, 46*(3), 450–471.

Farr, F., & Riordan, E. (2017). *Prospective and practising teachers discuss the theory-practice divide through blogs and E-portfolios.* In T.S.C. Farrell (Ed.), *TESOL Voices: Insider accounts of classroom life—preservice teacher education.* Alexander, VA: TESOL Press.

Farrell, T.S.C. (2001). Critical friendships: colleagues helping each other develop. *ELT Journal, 55,* 368–374.

Farrell, T.S.C. (2002). Reflecting on teacher professional development with teaching portfolios. *Guidelines, 24,* 4–8.

Farrell, T.S.C. (2006). (Ed.). *Language teacher research* (6-volume series). Alexandria, VA: TESOL, Inc.

Farrell, T.S.C. (2007). *Reflective language teaching: From research to practice.* London: Continuum Press.

Farrell, T.S.C. (2012). *Reflective writing for language teachers.* London: Equinox.

Farrell, T.S.C. (2013). Critical incident analysis through narrative reflective practice: A case study. *Iranian Journal of Language Teaching Research, 1*(1), 79–89.

Farrell, T.S.C. (2014). *Reflective practice in ESL teacher development groups: From practices to principles.* Basingstoke: Palgrave Macmillan.

Farrell, T.S.C. (2015). *Promoting teacher reflection in second language education: A framework for TESOL professionals.* New York: Routledge.

Farrell, T.S.C. (2016a). *From trainee to teacher: Reflective practice for novice teachers.* London, UK: Equinox.

Farrell, T.S.C. (2016b). Teacher-researchers in action. Teachers research! *ELT Journal, 70*(3), 352–355.

Farrell, T.S.C. (Ed.). (2017). *TESOL Voices: Insider accounts of classroom life—Preservice teacher education.* Alexandria, VA: TESOL Press.

Farrell, T.S.C. (2018). *Research in reflective practice in TESOL.* New York: Routledge.

Farrell, T.S.C. (2019a). *Reflection as action in ELT.* Alexandria, VA: TESOL International publications.

Farrell, T.S.C. (2019b). *Reflective practice in ELT.* London, UK: Equinox.

Farrell, T.S.C. (2019c). "My training has failed me": Inconvenient truths about second language teacher education (SLTE). *TESL-EJ, 22*(4), 1–16.

Farrell, T.S.C. (2021a). *TESOL teacher education: A reflective approach.* Edinburgh: Edinburgh University Press.

Farrell, T.S.C. (2021b). "COVID-19 challenged me to re-create my teaching entirely": Adaptation challenges of four novice EFL teachers of moving from "face-to-face" To "face-to-screen" Teaching. *Iranian Journal of Language Teaching Research, 9*(3), 119–132.

Farrell, T.S.C., & Baecher, L (2017). *Reflecting on critical incidents in language education.* London: Bloomsbury.

Farrell, T.S.C., & Jacobs, G. (2020). *Essentials for successful English language teaching* (2nd ed.). London: Bloomsbury.

Feiman-Nemser, S., & Floden, R.E. (1986). The cultures of teaching. In M. C. Whittrock (Ed.), *Handbook of research on teaching* (3rd ed.) (pp. 505–526). London: Collier-Macmillan.

Fessler, R., & Christensen, J.C. (1992). *The teacher career cycle: Understanding and guiding the professional development of teachers.* Boston, MA: Allyn and Bacon.

Francis, D. (1995). The reflective journal: A window to preservice teachers' knowledge. *Teaching and Teacher Education, 11*, 229–241.

Freeman, D. (1982). Observing teachers: three approaches to in-service training and development. *TESOL Quarterly* 16(1), 21–28.

Freeman, D. (1989). Teaching training, development, and decision making: a model of teaching and related strategies for language teacher education. *TESOL Quarterly, 23*, 27–45.

Freeman, D. (1998). *Doing teacher-research: From inquiry to understanding.* New York: Heinle and Heinle.

Freeman, D. (2016). *Educating second language teachers.* Oxford: Oxford University Press.

Freeman, D. (2017). The case for teachers' classroom English proficiency. *RELC Journal, 48* (1), 31–52.

Freeman, D., & Richards, J.C. (1993). Conceptions of teaching and the education of second language teachers. *TESOL Quarterly, 27*, 193–216.

Fueyo, V, & Koorland, M. (1997). Teacher as researcher: A synonym for professionalism. *Journal of Teacher Education, 48* (5), 336–344.

Garton, S., & Richards, K. (Eds). (2008). *Professional encounters in TESOL: Discourses of teachers in teaching.* Basingstoke: Palgrave Macmillan.

Gebhard, J.G. (2006). *Teaching English as a foreign or second language: A teacher self-development and methodology guide* (2nd ed.). Ann Arbor, MI: The University of Michigan Press.

Gonzalez Smith, M. (2019). A video-mediated critical friendship reflection framework for ESL teacher education. *TESL-EJ, 23*(1), 1–19.

Gordon, R., Kane, T., & Staiger, D. (2006). *Identifying effective teachers using performance on the job*. Hamilton Project discussion paper. Washington, DC: Brookings Institution.

Gottesman, B. (2000). *Peer coaching for educators* (2nd ed.). London: The Scarecrow Press.

Green, G. (2002). *Training and development*. Oxford: Capstone Publishing.

Guskey, T. R. (2000). *Evaluating professional development*. Thousand Oaks, CA: Corwin Press.

Hatton, N., & Smith, D. (1995). Reflection in teacher education: Towards definition and implementation. *Teaching and Teacher Education, 11* (1), 33–49.

Head, K., & Taylor, P. (1997). *Readings in teacher development*. Oxford: Heinemann.

Heo, J., & Mann, S. (2015). Exploring team teaching and team teachers in Korean primary schools. *English Language Teacher Education and Development, 17*, 13–21.

Higginbotham, C. (2019). Professional development: Life or death after pre-service training? *ELT Journal, 73*(4), 1–13.

Hoyle, E. (1974). Professionality, professionalism and control in teaching, *London Educational Review, 3*(2), 13–19.

Hoyle, E., & Wallace, M. (2007) Educational reform: An ironic perspective, *Educational Management, Administration & Leadership, 35*(1), 9–25.

Huberman, M. (1989). On teachers' careers: Once over lightly, with a broad brush. *International Journal of Educational Research, 13*(4), 347–362.

Huberman, M. (1993). *The lives of teachers*. New York: Teacher College Press.

Huberman, M. (1995). Professional careers and professional development. In T.R. Guskey & M. Huberman (Eds.), *Professional development in education: New paradigms and practices*. New York: Teachers College Press.

Ingersoll, R. (2015, March 30). Revolving door of teachers costs schools billions every year. *NRP*. Retrieved from https://www.npr.org/

sections/ed/2015/03/30/395322012/the-hidden-costs-of-teacher-turnover
Jackson, J. (1997). Cases in TESOL teacher education: Creating a forum for reflection. *TESL Canada Journal*, *14*(2), 1–16.
Johnson, K. (Ed.). (2000). *Teacher education*. Alexandria, VA: TESOL.
Johnson, K. (2009). *Second language teacher education: A sociocultural perspective*. New York: Routledge.
Joyce, B. (1991). The doors to school improvement. *Educational Leadership*, *48*(8), 59–68.
Kelchtermans, G. (1993). Getting the story, understanding the lives. From career stories to teachers' professional development. *Teaching and Teacher Education*, *9*, 443–456.
Killion, J., & Williams, C. (2009). Online professional development. *Multimedia & Internet@Schools*, *16*(4), 8.
Kirkpatrick, D.L. (1998). *Evaluating training programs: The four levels*. San Francisco, CA: Berrett-Koehler.
Kriesnerg, S. (1992). *Transforming power: Domination, empowerment, and education*. New York: SUNY Press.
Kumaravadivelu, B. (2003). *Beyond methods: Macrostrategies for language teaching*. New Haven, CT: Yale University Press.
Lange, D. (1990). A blueprint for a teacher development programme. In J.C. Richards & D. Nunan (Eds.), *Second language teacher education* (pp. 245–268). Cambridge: Cambridge University Press.
Leung, C. (2009). Second language teacher professionalism. In A. Burns & J.C. Richards (Eds.), *Cambridge guide to second language teacher education* (pp. 49–58). Cambridge: Cambridge University Press.
MacIntyre, P.D., Gregersen, T., & Mercer, S. (2020). Language teachers' coping strategies during the Covid-19 conversion to online teaching: Correlations with stress, wellbeing and negative emotions. *System*, *94*, 102–352.
Malderez, A., & Bodoczky, C. (1999). *Mentor courses. A resource book for trainer-trainers*. Cambridge: Cambridge University Press.
Mann, S. (2005). The language teacher's development. *Language Teaching*, *38*, 103–118.
Mann, S., & Walsh, S. (2017). *Reflective practice in English language teaching: Research-based principles and practices*. New York: Routledge.
McKinley, J. (2019). Evolving the TESOL teaching-research nexus. *TESOL Quarterly*, *53*(3), 875–884.

Meister, D.G., & Ahrens, P. (2011). Resisting plateauing: Four veteran teachers' stories. *Teaching and Teacher Education, 27*(4), 770–778.

Milstein, M.M. (1989). Plateauing as an occupational phenomenon among teachers and administrators. Paper presented at the annual meeting of the American Educational Research Association, San Francisco, CA (*ERIC Document Reproduction Service No. ED 306 675*).

Mirici, I.H., & Hergüner, S. (2015). A digital European self-assessment tool for student teachers of foreign languages: The EPOSTL. *Turkish Online Journal of Educational Technology, 14*(1), 1–10.

Nunan, D., & Bailey, K.M. (2009). *Exploring second language classroom research*. Boston, MA: Heinle.

Olsen, B., & Anderson, L. (2007). Courses of action: A qualitative investigation into urban teacher retention and career development. *Urban Education, 42*, 5–29.

Oprandy, R., Golden, L., & Shiomi, K. (1999). Teachers talking about teaching: Collaborative conversations about an elementary ESL class. In J. Gebhard & R. Oprandy (Eds.), *Language teaching awareness* (pp. 149–171). Cambridge: Cambridge University Press.

Organization for Economic Co-operation and Development (OECD). (2018). *Early career teachers: Pioneers triggering innovation or compliant professionals?* OECD Education Working Paper No. 190. Paris: OECD Publishing.

Park, J.E. (2014). English co-teaching and teacher collaboration: A microinteractional perspective. *System, 44*, 34–44.

Peacock, M. (2009). The evaluation of foreign language teacher education programmes. *Language Teaching Research, 13*, 259–278.

Reed, M., & Chappell, P. (2021). Teachers driving their own professional development: Theory and practice. *English Australia Journal*, 37(1), 5–26.

Richards, J.C., & Lockhard, C. (1995). *Reflective teaching*. New York: Cambridge University Press.

Richards, J.C. (1998). *Teaching in action*. Alexandria, VA: TESOL.

Richards, J.C. (2010). Competence and performance in language teaching. *RELC Journal, 41*, 2, 101–122.

Richards, J.C. (2014). *Key issues in language teaching*. Cambridge: Cambridge University Press.

Richards, J.C., & Farrell, T.S.C. (2005). *Professional development for language teachers*. New York: Cambridge University Press.

Richards, J.C., & Farrell, T.S.C. (2011). *Practice teaching*. New York: Cambridge University Press.

Robbins, P. (1991). *How to plan and implement a peer coaching program*. Alexandra, VA: *ASCD*.

Sachs, J. (1999). Using teacher research as a basis for professional renewal. *Journal of Inservice Education, 25*, 1, 39–53.

Sagor, R. (1992). *How to conduct collaborative action research*. Alexandria, VA: Association for Supervision and Curriculum Development.

Sandholtz, J.H. (2000). Interdisciplinary team teaching as a form of professional development. *Teacher Education Quarterly, 27*(3), 39–54.

Schön, D.A. (1983). *The reflective practitioner: How professionals think in action*. New York: Basic Books.

Schön, D.A. (1987). *Educating the reflective practitioner*. San Francisco, CA: Jossey-Bass.

Senior, R. (2006). *The experience of language teaching*. New York: Cambridge University Press.

Shannon, N.B., & Meath-Lang, B. (1992). Collaborative language teaching: A co-investigation. In D. Nunan (ed.), *Collaborative language learning and teaching* (pp. 120–140). Cambridge: Cambridge University Press.

Shin, S. (2012). "It cannot be done alone": The socialization of novice English teachers in South Korea. *TESOL Quarterly, 46* (3), 542–567.

Shulman, J. (Ed.). (1992). *Case methods in teacher education*. New York: Teachers College Press.

Stewart, T. (2013). *Classroom research for language teachers*. Alexandria, VA: TESOL, Inc.

Stewart, T., Sagliano, M., & Sagliano, J. (2002). Merging expertise: Promoting partnerships between language and content specialists. In J. Crandall & D. Kaufman (Eds.), *Content-based language instruction*. Alexandria, VA: TESOL, Inc.

Struman, P. (1992). Team teaching: A case study from Japan. In D. Nunan (Ed.), *Collaborative language learning and teaching* (pp. 141–161). Cambridge: Cambridge University Press.

Tang, E. L-Y., Lee, J.C., & Chun, C.K. (2012). Development of teaching beliefs and the focus of change in the process of pre-service ESL teacher education. *Australian Journal of Teacher Education, 37*(5), 90–107.

Thiel, T. (1999). Reflections on critical incidents. *Prospect, 14*(1), 44–52.

Towndrow, P. (2004). Reflections of an on-line tutor *ELT Journal 58*, 174–182.

Tripp, D. (1993). *Critical incidents in teaching: Developing professional judgement*. London: Routledge.
Underhill, A. (1999). Continuous teacher development. *IATEFL Issues, 149*, 14–18.
Valencia, S.W., & Killion, J.P. (1988). Overcoming obstacles to teacher change: Direction from school-based efforts. *Journal of Staff Development, 9*, 2–8.
Wajnryb, R. (1992). *Classroom observation tasks. A resource book for language teachers and trainers*. Cambridge: Cambridge University Press.
Wallace, M.J. (1991). *Teacher training: A reflective approach*. Cambridge: Cambridge University Press.
Walsh, S. (2013*). Classroom discourse and teacher development*. Edinburgh: Edinburgh University Press.
Wassermann, S. (1993). *Getting down to cases: Learning to teach with case studies*. New York: Teachers College Press.
Wenger, E. (1998). *Communities of practice: Learning, meaning, and identity*. Cambridge: Cambridge University Press.
Woods, D. (1996). *Teacher cognition in language teaching*. Cambridge: Cambridge University Press.
Wright, T. (2010). Second language teacher education: Review of recent research on practice. *Language Teaching 43*(3), 259–296.
Yost, D.S. (2006). Reflection and self-efficacy: Enhancing the retention of qualified teachers from a teacher education perspective. *Teacher Education Quarterly, 33*(4), 59–74.
Zahorik, J. (1986). Acquiring teaching skills. *Journal of Teacher Education, 27*(2), 21–25.
Zeichner, K.M. (1983). Alternative paradigms of teacher education. *Journal of Teacher Education, 34*, 3–9.
Zwozdiak-Myers, P. (2012). *The teacher's reflective practice handbook. Becoming an extended professional through capturing Evidence-informed Practice*. London and New York: Routledge.

Index

action research, 7, 20, 24, 37, 48-49, 51
administration, 13, 20, 79, 80, 96, 98
case study, 37, 40-44, 51, 71, 79, 85, 91, 107
critical friends, 55-58, 63, 64, 81, 85, 91, 101, 118
critical incidents, 2, 14, 19, 33-40
evaluation, 69, 73, 89, 90, 96, 98
goal
 development, 15
 training, 16
individual development, 91
language improvement, 60
language awareness, 24, 50-51, 85, 91
language teaching
 effectiveness of, 5-7
 view of, 3, 7
NNEST, 51
online
 delivery modes, 108
 discussions, 100
 professional development, 91, 108
 reflection, 21
 teaching, 55, 66-67, 76, 106, 107
 teaching development, 106-109
peer coaching, 32, 63-67, 69, 91, 100

peer observations. 68-76, 85, 91, 114
portfolios. *See* teaching portfolios
professional development
 collaborative, 53
 dialogue in, 21, 22
 implementing, 75, 95-102
 individual teacher's perspective, 15, 25
 institutional perspective, 95-99
 sustaining, 102-109
 writing in, 19-21
reflective practice, 16-18
scenarios for reflection, 110
self-monitoring, 24, 26-33, 51, 68, 85, 100
practitioner research, 102-106
teacher
 career cycles, 1, 10-14
 development groups, 76-80, 85
 native-speaking vs. nonnative-speaking, 51
 plateauing, 1, 12, 13, 23
teacher needs
 experienced teachers, 88-94
 novice teachers, 82-87
teaching portfolios, 44-48, 51, 85, 91, 120
team teaching, 32, 40, 42, 53, 58-63, 118

www.ingramcontent.com/pod-product-compliance
Lightning Source LLC
Chambersburg PA
CBHW071736080526
44588CB00013B/2058

CHANGE
is not a
Scary Word

10
Influencers
Leading the Way

Created by Donna Campisi with stories
from 10 inspiring Change Influencers

Paula Johnson   Marie Kimber

Malka Silver   Donna Campisi

Carmen Taylor   Sean Nicholas O'Leary

Chris Christoff   Naomi Holland

Nikki Ellis   Jo McKenzie

First published by Busybird Publishing 2020

Copyright © 2020 Remains with the individual authors

ISBN

978-1-922465-25-2

This work is copyright. Apart from any use permitted under the Copyright Act 1968, no part of this publication may be reproduced, stored in a retrieval system or transmitted in any form or by any means, electronic, mechanical, photocopying, recording or otherwise, without the prior written permission of the individual authors.

Cover design: Busybird Publishing

Layout and typesetting: Busybird Publishing

Busybird Publishing
2/118 Para Road
Montmorency, Victoria
Australia 3094
www.busybird.com.au

Dedication

To those who know they need to make a change but feel stuck.

To those who have had the rug pulled out from under them by circumstances beyond their choosing, and for the people supporting them who may not even know how or what to do but have the strength to simply sit and be by their side.

To those who are at a crossroads in life where they keep asking the question 'There's got to be more to life than this?'

May these stories inspire you to grow beyond your comfort zone and to move towards a life that you always dreamed about – because you can!

Contents

Introduction		1
CHAPTER ONE Malka Silver		5
CHAPTER TWO Chris Christoff		17
CHAPTER THREE Nikki Ellis		33
CHAPTER FOUR Marie Kimber		49
CHAPTER FIVE Naomi Holland		63
CHAPTER SIX Carmen Taylor		79
CHAPTER SEVEN Jo McKenzie		93
CHAPTER EIGHT Paula Johnson		105
CHAPTER NINE Sean Nicholas O'Leary		119
CHAPTER TEN Donna Campisi		131
Afterword		145
Acknowledgements		147

Introduction

Change is a positive thing, but it can feel scary and exciting, too! Great things, ideas, situations, solutions, and opportunities have come from change!

In February 2020, I thought about all the excitement around me; the joy we all felt about a new year and decade, which often means new goals, ideas, excitement, unknowns. Everyone is enthusiastic, it's contagious! It's exciting!

But then something happens! Exciting dreams are often just left as that, simply a dream left in your mind. We get distracted or prioritise other things that seem more important than our initial aims (although secretly our dreams are more important in our mind). Maybe we have to face fears or have doubts about the changes we need to make to reach that place we first set our heart on…

An example: January is the highest in sales with new clients at a gym. People aim high with great goals, wanting to change their appearance, health, and fitness level. They want to feel good about themselves, gain confidence, and be a good role model to others. But then it's less important by April, and sadly the change never happens.

Why? Their passion was so strong in January! Is it the time or work involved? The lifestyle? The mindset? Allowing other things take more importance? Facing fears? Is it too much of a challenge, or changes are not happening fast enough?

Do we stay in our comfort zone, even if it isn't beneficial?

In February, I gathered a group of Change Influencers together – 10 inspiring leaders who made changes in their lives – to share their stories and insights. I approached these awesome influencers as they've inspired me personally, knowing they faced fears, barriers, doubts, and confrontations that can easily influence the direction people take.

And then, only a month after reaching out to my chosen authors, the world was forced to change drastically! Covid-19 hit us all. We were ALL taken away from our comfort zone. But I knew it was not a time to stop! This was a time where people needed support, help, inspiration, ideas, solutions, and opportunities that come from change.

In these chapters the leaders share their life before facing their challenge to change, their current story, and the effects of the change they created. Some changes were by choice, and others from circumstances out of their control, but all chose how they handled change in a positive way.

Their change stories include surviving near-death experience and how they changed their life after they recovered. Lifestyle and physical body transformations, and self-development, to inspire others to live their best life with less stress. Redefining the importance of acceptance and how to deal with challenges. Confronting physical pain and the continued torment, while helping others reach their goals. Left alone with young children to raise, to making the choice to be strong and follow a dream as a successful business owner. Facing a critical diagnosis, while changing an attitude to live. Living a restrictive upbringing, pushing through barriers, including a mental health condition, to follow a big dream. Feeling trapped in a stressful job, effecting physical, social, emotional, and mental health, to turning their life around choosing freedom, happiness, and wellbeing. Deciding to focus on positives rather than the imperfections to turn one's life around.

You will discover why and how they changed, who or what influenced them, when they noticed the change, and why they

Introduction

encourage you to make the change. They share the benefits they gained from change, and their tips for you to change your game, too.

I'm excited to bring you this collaborative book with my chosen awesome authors of change. 10 influencers leading the way, sharing their stories and insights to encourage you that change can be positive.

Enjoy!

Donna Campisi

Speaker, Author, Adventurer, and Podcaster.

CHAPTER ONE

Change occurs when I step out of my comfort zone, and I am rewarded with immense growth.

Malka Silver

My story of change commenced at a time when my mental state was low, combined with circumstances that might or might not have been in my control.

I was born in Bayreuth, Germany, to a beautiful couple who sadly were physically, mentally, and emotionally fractured, but had a mental strength and character that was full of a desperate need to enjoy every facet of life. They worked incredibly hard and played just as hard, so I believed that this was what normality looked like. Both my parents were Holocaust survivors. Their families, friends, schoolmates and neighbours, had all been murdered by the Nazis and their collaborators.

Growing up, my parents tried to shield my brother and me, thinking they were protecting us from any knowledge or concept of death. We also had no idea what or who our grandparents were until our early teens. At 12 I discovered the shocking truth that both my parents were Holocaust survivors and that our small precious family unit was my father's second family; his first wife and baby daughter had been murdered in Treblinka Death Camp. During that time of my life, I started experiencing horrific nightmares, occurring nightly and lasting for years.

I got married in Melbourne, Australia at the tender age of 18 to the love of my life, Sam, who was then a mature young man of 20. In our 54 year (and counting) marriage we've experienced many vast and interesting changes. At 22, I was already a mother of two children under the age of 2. During those early days of our marriage, there were times where money was scarce and we only had sufficient capital to feed our babies. They were tough times as we were living from paycheque to paycheque.

When my son was 2 and his sister was 6 months old, I lost my incredible mother to ovarian cancer. She was only 49 years young. This situation plunged me into a deep well of depression which took every fibre of my being to shake off. As I look back at this time in my life, I realise that this was not my first bout of depression. Physically and emotionally, my life was a rollercoaster of highs and lows.

Sam and I both enjoyed participating in different forms of sports. Sam played semi-professional soccer and then graduated to B-grade pennant squash, and I loved getting up at 5.00am to do an hour of aerobics before work. I would alternately take my two children horse riding in the stunning countryside of Broadford every second Saturday, together with a work colleague of mine.

Then came the shock that I was over three months pregnant. Amidst working full time, scraping to pay bills, and trying to survive, I gave birth to a beautiful baby boy. The difficult question had been voiced to maybe abort due to hardship. This was not an option for me, I discovered.

Two of my friends who had also had babies around the same time decided to create a mother's group. We met once a week to just vent, laugh at ourselves, and sometimes discuss any issues we were experiencing. Before our meeting on this particular morning, I stepped into my shower. As I washed myself, I found a lump under my left armpit that had not been there the morning before. So, when we settled our babies, we commenced our normal schmoozing and I mentioned that I had just found a lump.

To my surprise and relief, I learnt that both my friends also had found a lump on their bodies. We all decided to make doctor appointments, thinking it had to be a blocked milk duct. For both my friends, that prognosis turned out to be correct, yet my doctor was unsure so she sent me to a surgeon, Dr John Dawson at Box Hill Hospital. He decreed that it was definitely a milk duct and suggested that I keep an eye on it and make a monthly appointment till the time I stopped breastfeeding.

Due to many difficulties I was unable to breastfeed my older two babies, so I desperately wanted to feed this little one, and he took to breastfeeding like a duck to water. Every month after checking me out, Dr Dawson would reiterate that this lump could not be cancer, as it moved and it hurt. His knowledge was that cancer did not move and it was painless.

I was thrilled that I could continue to breastfeed, yet Sam was increasingly uncomfortable about the lump. When I had found the lump it was the size of a five-cent coin, but by the time our little man was eight months old it had grown to the size of a twenty-cent piece. I had a gut feeling that something wasn't right, but I ignored this primal feeling as my specialist kept reassuring me that it was nothing but a blocked milk duct, and he should know. That is when Sam stepped in. He firmly begged me to tell my surgeon that I wanted the lump removed. Unbeknownst to me, as I was on route to Box Hill Hospital, Sam rang and threatened my surgeon – if he didn't demand that I stop feeding and arrange to remove the lump, Sam would come down personally and *fix him up*.

When I sat down at my appointment my surgeon suggested, very meekly, that it was time to see if the lump disappeared after I stop breastfeeding. His opinion that six months was a good innings. He also tried to syringe out any fluid from the lump, without success. I was then booked in the following month to Hartwell Private Hospital for a biopsy.

On Monday 12 November 1979, after a four-hour biopsy operation, my husband watched as my surgeon walked towards him after leaving me still lying on the operating table, and proceeded to profusely apologise; the lump was cancerous.

Sam told me many years later that he had been so shocked and angered that he literally manhandled the surgeon. He lifted him up by his collar and informed him in no uncertain terms, 'That's my life on that table, and you better make absolutely sure that you remove everything that doesn't belong, or you will have me to answer to.' I was shocked but humbled at the same time.

On Tuesday 13 November I had a radical left breast mastectomy. The operation also lasted four hours.

After I returned from theatre I was so cold that my beautiful nurse pinched every blanket she could get her hands on for me. At around 2.00am I was covered with sixteen blankets and was still freezing. This nurse was beside herself with worry, so she climbed under the covers and lay on top of me. By morning I was not cold anymore.

Later the report showed that I had Stage 3 breast cancer.

My whole world collapsed all around me. At that time nobody ever spoke about any cancers, as cancer was then seen as a death sentence. You'd hear someone whisper something like, 'She has the big C.'

You truly do discover who your true friends are, and it inevitably isn't the ones you thought. Some people seriously believed that cancer was contagious and they disappeared out of my life forever. Some didn't know what they should say or how they should act, so I consciously became their example. When they came in tentatively to visit me with a frown on their face, I would smile and make a joke, and it would break the ice. It's not what you say, but how you act and react that people copy.

My neighbour was so terrified to catch cancer from me. I was a week out of hospital, my baby was screaming, and the council help had just left for the day. My children were still en route home from school, a dear friend taxiing them home. I was unable to lift my son out of his cot so I rang my neighbour and basically begged her to come over, just to take him out of the cot and put him into my arms until the children got home. She spewed out a multitude of excuses why she could not do this, yet in the end she did by literally running in, picking him up, and dumping him into my arms as she ran out as fast as her little legs could carry her. Prior to my operation, we had had a very cordial relationship and our children spent a great deal of their playtime together.

My parents were horrified that I would let friends and family know of my affliction. It was not the done thing; you kept it under lock and key and soldiered on. So, when the discussion came around what story I would impart on my two children, my reply was that I would tell them the truth. My parents were appalled but I told them that I had never kept anything from my children and was not about to start now. I even explained that both my children have always had showers with me or their father, and that was not about to change either.

My first day home from hospital was on my eldest son's 10th birthday and it was so very special. Just before bed, his younger sister, who was a couple of weeks off 8, asked to see my stitches. She stood in front of me and counted the stitches, totally in awe, yet her older brother ran into his room, shut the door, and cried his little heart out. After an hour or so he emerged from his room with a plastered smile, red eyes, and a red runny nose and informed me that, 'Everything is going to be alright.'

My daughter, who is now a nurse, stated proudly to me, 'Don't worry, Mummy. It will grow back.'

'No, it won't grow back,' I said, 'but that is fine with me, as long as we all are healthy and happy.'

The first morning that my surgeon came to see me after the operation, I asked him, 'How long do I have to live?' I was terrified as I had a new baby and two other children who needed me.

His answer was calming. 'I can promise you that you will see the sun rise tomorrow, but I can't give any other assurances, either to you or to me.'

After the surgeon left, my nurse informed me that my parents had been waiting a long while to see me. I went to pieces and she sat on the bed next to me and held me till I cried myself dry. What was I to tell my daddy? Eight years earlier he lost his beautiful wife to cancer and now his daughter had it.

I sat in bed recalling how hard my beautiful mother had fought this insidious disease so bravely, yet she ultimately lost her battle. This is when my mental and physical shift came to me.

A bolt of lightning hit me square between the eyes as I realised that I only had two choices: I could either lay down and die, or fight with every fibre of my being.

At that precise moment I stopped thinking, breathing, and living in the negative. I had a goal: I was NOT going to lose this battle, no matter what.

I made a vow only to myself, and no one else was privy to it. I was going to walk my three babies down the aisle to their intendeds, with Sam, of course. I made a conscious decision not to tell a living soul, because I didn't want someone to unintentionally shoot me down.

My choice of how I was going to achieve this was simple. I had to change the way I looked at life. I had to be positive, and most importantly, I had to surround myself with positive people. I was in and out of chronic depression, and I was 100% convinced that any visiting family or friends had to be at least smiling outwardly. None of this 'you poor thing.' I had blinkers on. Uplifting conversation and nothing less would be tolerated.

I worried about my poor dad who had lost so much in his life. I put down an ultimatum to him that very first morning. After my hour of crying, my father and stepmother were shown into my room and I had to gently inform them that I had breast cancer and that if he wanted to visit me, he had to have a smile on his face. This courageous man came twice a day, every day, with punnets of berries and a smile plastered on his face. Those sky-blue eyes of his could not hide his pain and anguish.

When I met my incredible oncologist the first time, Dr Graeme Brodie at Prince Henry Hospital, I made a very conscious decision not to absorb any of the statistics of survival and death that he spewed out. All I focused on was my three precious babies who I needed, even more than they needed me.

That twelve months of chemotherapy was gruesome, gruelling, and I truly cannot recall that year. But Sam informs me that he remembers every moment. My father drove me to every treatment appointment that year. I recall when after one of my appointments it started to drizzle. Dad made me wait inside the front door of the hospital while he collected his car, then he came to get me with an umbrella so I wouldn't get wet. He was a gentle man, and for him chivalry had not died.

From that day on, I concentrated on achieving a happier, healthier mental attitude, even when my depression reared its ugly head.

My stand-alone influences throughout my life were my parents. They were both fighters and survivors of the most horrific period in history. From not even a change of clothing, let alone food, they crawled their way out of the ashes and built a life together. They owned their own home, raised and educated two children, and everything else that goes with this territory. Through all the heartache and pain they smiled, laughed, and occasionally allowed themselves the luxury of memory and tears. I'm sure they experienced many nightmares, but they hid their pain and wore it with incredible strength, like a shield of steel.

If you do the same thing over and over again, you will achieve the same results. So, if you wish for a different result, change what you're doing. I only let myself see myself healthy and happy. I changed my eating habits. Instead of ten or fourteen cups of coffee a day, I drank boiling hot water and lemon, before it became trendy. I stopped eating meat because I had never liked meat, but my mother used to force it down my throat.

I remember waking up one morning and another bolt of light exploded in my head. 'I am an adult now, so I can do what I want.'

I took control of my life. I did everything that the doctors instructed, and a few extra changes that I decided would be an advantage to me and my family.

I started back at the gym five days a week, a 6.00am class that went for an hour. We had to be there on time as only a certain number could do the class, so I was up every morning at 5.00am and got home around 8.00am to get the kids ready for school, as Sam was already at work. I was incredibly fit and healthy.

Our Great Dane, Sasha, was a soothing comfort to me, as she always was for the entire family.

I arranged for Sam, myself, and our teenage son to attend a weekend training course on mind power, called Alpha Dynamics. For me it wasn't a revelation, because going into the lower levels of your imagination is something I've always done subconsciously. But it did refine and teach me invaluable tools to use.

When family or friends came to visit me I always asked if they had any questions to ask me, qualified with, 'I will answer any question that I know about my breast cancer so you will experience it through me second-hand as I don't wish anyone to go through it firsthand.'

I believe that life sets you tests and mine was this. I wish I had never contracted breast cancer, but by saying this, I am humbled that I had this horrid experience as it taught me my greatest lesson of life. I am so grateful to learn that life is a precious gift that we should enjoy every single day. Even the bad and ugly days are our blessings, as they help us to grow.

I still have bouts of depression but I work through them as they arise. I know that the sun will shine and I will be all right, eventually. I don't ever contemplate suicide anymore, as I know that life is too valuable and the blackness will dissipate soon.

One of the biggest lessons I learned from this period is that I love being of service to others. When news got out that I had had breast cancer, I was sought after by many friends, husbands or mothers, to speak to their loved ones who were beginning their own cancer journey. I am humbled to say that I have helped many women. Some have got back to me years later to thank me, as they believed that I saved their lives. But I was only the guide who helped them do their own saving.

A friend rang me just prior to Christmas, 1989, and asked if I could go and see two women in two different hospitals and speak to them. I was ecstatic to be asked. The one I knew was a daughter of one of my parents' good friends, and was a psychologist. I went in to see her. She was a sheer mess due to the breast cancer, but she was a total basket case due to her disastrous marriage. She refused to get rid of the prick (he was sleeping around), but her excuse was that she loved him and couldn't live without him. I tried many times to be of help, but she gave up the ghost and was dead within twelve months. Such a vibrant, beautiful person who counselled others was unable to see past her love.

The second young lady was in her early thirties and had three children. She was devastated that she was going to die because in her eyes, cancer meant death. I visited her a number of times and it was always the same thing. She would be lying in bed crying that she was going to die, but her husband would yell at the top of his voice with such love, pain, and unwavering support that she was going to live. By the third such visit, I was exasperated and at my wits' end as how I could make her see that it wasn't a death sentence. She looked at me and said again for the millionth time, 'I'm going to die and my babies won't have a mother.'

I saw red and blurted out, 'Yes, you are going to die. But not today, so get out of bed and start living. You have a mother who is worried sick for you and doing all the housework. A husband who loves you so much that he is willing to fight your fight. But he can't, because it's your fight and he will be there to support you. You have three babies who need their mother, so get out of bed and fight with every breath you have.' Then I said, 'Goodbye, and good luck. I can't do this anymore.'

Ten years later, I received a call to have a coffee with her. She said that thanks to me she pulled her finger out and started living. I was thrilled and humbled by her words.

Life throws us lots of curveballs. Sometimes we drop the ball because we are distracted to what could be the worst-case scenario. I am so grateful that this hideous disease helped me see how precious life is and that the fight is worth the effort.

On 4 November 2014, I walked the last of my babies, who is now a strapping young man and father of two daughters, down the aisle to his beautiful bride. I achieved my goal and emotionally stood up at his wedding reception, thanking my three children for being my motivation to achieve my mammoth dream and goal.

On 12 November 2019, I celebrated being in remission for 40 years.

In order to change, I believe:

- *You need to want it more than life itself. That's when it will become clear which path you need to take to make change happen.*

- *If you say you can't or if you say you can, you will be right. Change can be daunting, but it's worth the ride.*

About Malka

Malka Silver is a survivor who has fought health and life battles, yet she is still smiling.

Born in Germany to victims of the Holocaust, and spending her early years in Israel, her family immigrated to Australia in 1955.

Diagnosed with Stage 3 breast cancer at 30 years of age, in November 2019 Malka celebrated 40 years in remission. She contributes her courage and strength to her parents, who instilled in her love, integrity, passion, and conviction.

Malka studied Fine Arts at RMIT and has sold her artwork internationally. She paints, does life drawing, craft, tapestries, keynote speaking, and now writes. She also loves to travel; at the time of writing her chapter she is traveling with her husband, Sam, around Australia for twelve months.

Her greatest achievements include being a wife, mother of three and Buba of seven.

Malka is also a passionate volunteer guide at the Jewish Holocaust Centre in Melbourne, a custodian of her father's memory, inspiring author of her father's memoir L'Chaim, which translates to 'To Life', and soon the author of her stepmother's book.

Malka encourages many by sharing her story of courage and strength, and attitude of gratitude as an empowering keynote speaker.

Malka Silver can be contacted at

malka@silvers.net.au

CHAPTER TWO

Could you work 100-hour weeks for one year?
Don't.

Chris Christoff

100 hours out of 168 hours in a week left about nine hours per day for everything else, and two of those were taken up with commuting.

As a child I was very shy and spent years working on myself, and I still do. I lacked self-confidence and belief in my abilities, despite reaching very senior positions in the organisations I worked in. I was loyal to those organisations and gave them priority over everything else in my life.

The bed of roses and then came the thorns

I was invited into an organisation to fix its IT department and the infrastructure. The company was looking to win more contracts and was heavily IT-dependent. For a long time things went well. I rebuilt the IT department, we started upgrading the technology, and there was a very collaborative mood in the organisation. We got to the point where we were winning most contracts, but we were not resourcing appropriately. As we progressed, the culture became toxic, dominated by fear of making any mistakes, the constant threat of firing, blame and back-biting, poor practices, and a 'profit before people' mentality.

Staff turnover was high, and we won a couple of contracts we were not resourced for. With poor software on the client side and requirements for 100% uptime on our side, things got very difficult. There was zero margin for error, and staff spent thousands of hours babysitting poor, but critical, software, while attempting to write software that worked. IT infrastructure upgrades could only be done very late at night as the company serviced many different time zones.

I would drive home in the wee hours of the night after very long days physically shaking at the wheel. My health declined, I wasn't sleeping, the stress inordinate. In the car I had imaginary conversations with my dad who had passed away several years earlier. My wife and kids never saw me, and this put a lot of pressure on our relationship. I spent two Christmases sitting in a boardroom writing tender responses, one time with pleurisy, coughing, feverish, and feeling like someone had stuck a knife in my back.

In those situations you can't think straight and you make poor decisions, making the climate worse. In my head I was arguing, 'What am I doing here? Why am I killing myself for this?' Then one day it came to a head. I had a stand-up argument with the boss and decided it was time to leave. The situation was untenable. Yes, I wanted to be loyal and protect my staff, but I could no longer do that inside the organisation. I was a wreck.

Then I did something totally out of character. Something rash, impulsive, spur of the moment. Usually I analyse decisions to death. Coming from an engineering background, and operating from a fear-based mentality, I analysed everything. Not this time. I resigned that day.

When I walked out of the building something I had never experienced happened. I felt 10ft tall and as if I was walking on air. I had this all-consuming sense of euphoria. I had no job and no income, but I didn't care.

I realised that my corporate loyalty was driven by fear — fear of failing, fear of losing my job. No successes, and there were many, really made any difference to this underlying belief system.

I pointed the analysis tool back on myself

I had a side interest in property, and I managed to wangle an extension on a loan facility and renovated two houses over the next three months. During that time, I analysed my life, what I did well, my successes, what I did poorly, and my failures. There were plenty of all of them. I realised that what happens next is up to me, that I am capable, I do have skills, and I have resilience.

I was loyal to my colleagues, and this paid off for me. Through my contacts I was invited to apply for a contract for an IT project management role, managing aspects of the IT rollout for a globally significant event, the G20 meeting in Australia. I left the interview thinking this job is mine and it was. I worked long hours in this role, but nothing like the previous role. In the interview I was told that as the meeting deadline got closer the working hours would ramp up. My response was, 'I just spent a year working 100-hour weeks. I can handle it.' They agreed.

This was a fantastic project with some great leadership. In the last month, while preparing the Brisbane Convention and Exhibition Centre (and a number of other venues) I walked 340km. This started as a silly competition with a couple of police officers tasked with patrolling the BCEC to see who walked the farthest in a week. I left the step counting app on my phone running for the whole time I was there – 340km.

I have since done a number of successful project management gigs, all obtained through my contacts, because others saw the value I could bring. I returned that loyalty by helping several staff out of that toxic organisation into better organisations and to move through their careers. I worked with one young lady who was damaged by her experience in that organisation. She engaged me as a goal achievement coach, and we set goals for her dream job and started the process. She moved into another organisation and has since moved again, stepping into better roles each time – each a step closer to her dream job.

I continued the analysis of my life, documenting the successes and failures, then thought about writing a book. One trigger for this was reading the book *The Secret*, which I hated. It made me angry that they taught that things would be delivered to your door by sitting on the couch at home and visualising them. I am a great fan of visualisation but it requires action and work to realise the desired goal.

A friend of mine had just published a book on the travel industry. She encouraged me to finish writing my book and introduced me to her publisher. I started to write the book and then thought, 'Who will read this? What makes me any kind of expert?' The self-doubt was creeping in again.

This time I took positive steps. If I couldn't rely on my own credibility, then I would rely on that of neuroscience researchers. I looked at all the techniques and actions that worked and didn't work for me and reviewed the scientific research. This opened a whole new world. I started to understand why certain things worked and others didn't, and I weaved the neuroscience through my writing. I realised that there are many myths around goal setting, and much of what I had been taught was simply ineffective. And the book was published.

I had changed. I no longer wanted roles in corporate IT. When I was unemployed, I applied for a jobs thinking 'I don't want this job'. It must have showed because I didn't get any of them. When I had the chance to take the project management role, I leapt at it; it seemed right. My confidence in what I could do burgeoned.

My approach to risk changed. Normally wary of risk, I now embraced it (with some rational analysis, of course). I got deeper into property development, and again through contacts, managed to work as a project manager on the development of an apartment building on the riverfront in Brisbane.

To assess risk and analyse obstacles, I came up with the Witch Technique: What Is The worst that Can Happen (WITwtCH). Using this, you brainstorm all the obstacles and then develop short strategies for dealing with them should they arise. Often they won't — but you will be prepared.

I now teach this in goal setting, as I later learned that focusing on the obstacles is a necessary step after a visualisation so that your subconscious is aware that there is still work to do. You see, in the visualisation, as the subconscious can't tell the difference between reality and the vividly imagined, it believes that the work is done which can reduce motivation to proceed. I told you there were a lot of myths in goal setting.

I started to see my life as value that I brought, not somebody else, like an employer, doing me a favour. I worked out what I was good at, what I wasn't, and what I liked doing (I disliked doing some things I was good at) and became comfortable with that.

I since realised that my identity, my self-concept, and self-worth were all about my job, and I thought that without the job I would have no identity. Fortunately, after many years in IT and losing some of the passion for the industry, I started looking for a side gig and got into property. Now I can say I have many professional and personal identities, such as project manager, property developer, goal achievement coach, author, mentor, teacher, spouse, parent, martial artist, network builder, grandparent, furniture restorer, student, sibling, and uncle. Yet, none of these now define me, and if I let one of them go it will not define me. Many of the most successful people I know have multiple professional identities and balance these with their personal identities.

I have learned over the years to set small goals in areas I am competent in, and then stretch them into areas outside my comfort zone. I also have a new relationship with failure.

You have heard all the metaphors about fire tempering steel, and the winds strengthening the mighty oak, struggle building character, yada-yada. But did you know that when you learn a new skill and practise it, the neural circuits in your brain are reinforced through a process called myelination? This process makes their conduction speed high and response automatic and makes the connection persistent. This process requires repetition and failure, or some working struggle, for the myelin to develop. Imagine learning to juggle — dropping those balls and continuously correcting your actions is what builds the neuronal structure for that skill. Another goal setting myth conquered.

Goal achievement is a process that involves many areas, including procrastination, deservedness, visualisation, habits and micro-habits, timeframes, loss aversion, accountability, responsibility, decision making, gratitude, celebration, failure, struggle, and obstacles, to name a few. All of these have a neuroscience basis, and neuro-tricks to take advantage of them.

Sometimes change is forced on you – change or perish. Sometimes you can decide that you simply want more, or different, and invite change. The former can be driven by fear, and the latter by desire. Fear is a great motivator, I used it all my life, but it is not the healthiest choice. You miss out on the best things from achieving like the celebration, the lovely dopamine hit your brain gets from success, the conscious acceptance of growth, and scaffolding of your confidence with each success.

Are you like I was? Is fear your constant companion? What are you afraid of? Is it failure? Let yourself have a new relationship with failure. Embrace it, it is a great teacher. It motivates activity and the desire to get it right. At Google's X laboratories where all the most audacious technology is developed (think self-driving cars), they reward their staff for making a project fail as soon as possible. From the failures they learn either how to improve, or that the project is untenable and should be cancelled. The internet is replete with stories of success after failure – just Google 'success despite failure'.

I have talked about the building of myelinated neural circuits in your brain needing failure for you to master a skill. Take throwing a ball into a bucket from 20m away, or learning a language, public speaking, driving a manual car, playing the violin, or learning to manage staff. Lots of tries, failures, corrections, and then lots of progress. Guess what happens if you stop? You fail. You don't get any better, you don't achieve. So, the trick is to keep going.

When you fail, big or small, stop and think about it. What did I do, what would be better? Should I do it more slowly? Do I need more information?

Choose a goal just outside your capabilities and target the struggle. Do, fail, rejoice, do, fail, rejoice, do, do, do, rejoice …

Failure takes many forms – sometimes skill- or knowledge-based, sometimes preparation or experience. Failure isn't an invitation to blame (oneself or others), it is an invitation to fix, to learn, and to reinforce the neural pathways.

Here are some practical steps to do that.

Journey, habits, learning

The neuroscience and empirical evidence say that one of the most effective ways to set goals is to focus on the path, the journey, looking at the process and developing habits that support the desired outcome. Also, setting learning goals is more effective than setting performance goals.

If the goal is an indicator for where you want to be, and you allow yourself to change it if needed, you can focus on the path. The path is the engine room, where the action is. It is where you will excel, make all the necessary adjustments to get to the end, where you learn, bring in supporters and mentors, have fun, focus and develop. Along the path, what do you do? You set goals. These sub-goals are the steps to the ultimate prize.

What else happens along the path? You fail, you get it wrong, you make mistakes, and you fix them. Have you failed at the goal? No, it is still intact.

Forming habits is a great way to achieve goals. Even activity towards larger goals is very effective when it can be systematised into a habit. Habits get you past fear, procrastination, laziness, and distractions. Successful people often emphasise their daily habits, and how this consistency contributed to their success.

A 2009 study funded by the US National Institutes of Health asked 1600 participants to do two extra things to lose weight – write down what they ate, and bring the diary to a weekly group meeting.

Those people doubled their weight loss compared with others. A notable participant went from being obese, a smoker and drinker, jobless, and in debt, to having a full-time job, buying a house, running marathons, and getting engaged.

When Paul O'Neill took over as CEO of Alcoa (the US' biggest aluminium company) in 1987, stock prices were down and investors were unhappy. O'Neill focused on two things – worker safety and all staff being accountable for it. Over the next 10 years Alcoa stock rose 200%.

Why? What did they have in common? They tapped into a keystone habit and were accountable to others. By concentrating on that one habit (writing, safety), they began to reprogram other habits in their lives.

Habits are trigger-action-reward loops. A trigger causes an action, which provides a reward. This works for good and bad habits. An example of a not-so-good habit may be when it's 3.00pm, you're feeling hungry and bored (trigger), so you go to the café for something sugary and a chat (action). The reward is the neurochemical hit from the sweet food (not-so-good) and the pleasure of another's company.

Bad habits can be broken by recognising the trigger and changing the action. For the above, go to the café and get an apple and have a chat. New habits can be formed by deciding on a trigger, action and reward.

Micro-habits are just the little steps. When you set a goal, break it into smaller steps, sub-goals. To get over procrastination you simply start, and then you commit to a small amount of time to the task. Same with changing habits.

A little neuro-trick to develop those habits is called an Implementation Intention (check out research by Prof Peter Gollwitzer, Professor of Psychology, NYU).

Implementation Intentions follow this form:

IF/WHEN <trigger> THEN I will <action>.

For example: WHEN <I get home from work> THEN I will <work on my project for 10 minutes>.

IF <I get offered sugary foods> THEN I will <say no and have a drink of water>.

Implementation Intentions help to disrupt cognitive states, aversive emotions, and bad behaviours that interrupt goal striving. To reiterate, habits get you past fear, procrastination, laziness, and distractions. They are, of course, more effective with a stronger commitment to the goal. Commitment is a great predictor for success and repetition is the mother of learning.

Work out the best time of day and place for you, and deliberately work on your goal every day, same time, same place. Your goal could be anything, from learning Spanish to planning a property development.

Sometimes our actions, activity or goal may be going nowhere and needs to be terminated. It is okay to change the path or the goal itself if it is not working out.

The challenge is to identify that the activity is not contributing to the goal, or that the goal is unattainable, and to disengage from it. An unattainable goal consumes resources that are better spent on achievable goals (e.g. time, money) and induces stress and frustration, and reduces motivation.

It is important to identify and eliminate unattainable goals. A balance is required so that you are not giving up too early on ultimately attainable goals. This is not failure, it is prudence.

Monitor your subconscious for the signals that things are not going as they should. You may experience negative feedback from yourself or others and notice sub-goals failing, deadlines being missed, or encounter factors you cannot control or experience significant stress. If the goal is unattainable, change it or drop it and move on.

Discovery Goals

My experience moving into property development was a Discovery Goal. I would go running and think about the goal. I had no idea how to do it or what the timeframe was but I prepared for it without knowing. I did renovations, talked to people in the industry, and researched council websites on others' developments. I invested in a property developer, did some work for them for a year for free, and then they asked me to join the project. When the opportunity arose, I was able to see it and confidently take it. I was ready.

The lesson – some goals don't, or can't, have timeframes. You can't yet see the complete path or all of the actions required to get there. Using this approach, the goals you set are preparatory goals; each step of preparation an achievement worthy of celebration. As you prepare, both the path and the goal become clearer and soon you can plan direct steps to your goal.

You may not have envisaged how to achieve the goal until the end; such is the flexibility of the Discovery Goal approach. You may try things that don't work (you fail), so you try again.

Mentor or Coach?

You will have failures; it's part of the process. You will learn from those failures, however, it's cheaper if you can also learn from others' mistakes, or another's experience. Having a mentor or coach is important for accelerating your development and ensuring that you don't have to make every mistake yourself.

'Who has mentors?' you might ask. I would say most successful people, regardless of their field of endeavour, have mentors, and many have several. Entrepreneurs like Mark Zuckerberg, Richard Branson, and Warren Buffet; presidents such as Barack Obama and George Bush (both Snr and Jnr), prime ministers such as John Howard and Paul Keating; actors like Johnny Depp and Leonardo DiCaprio; celebrity Oprah Winfrey; Nobel Prize winners from economics to physics, and some of the historical greats like Christiaan Huygens, the 17th century astronomer who mentored Gottfried Leibniz, the father of calculus, and creatives like Isaac Asimov, the science fiction writer who mentored Gene Roddenberry, the creator of *Star Trek*).

The lessons from a mentor can be categorised into characteristics (role model) or information (sage). From the role model you might take on behavioural and character traits. From the sage you gain wisdom and information and they can teach you how to do things. A good mentor can provide you with both approaches.

How do you find a mentor?

Look at people you know

- *to whom you could go to for help.*
- *through interests and courses you have been involved in.*
- *on your LinkedIn, Facebook or other social media and contact apps.*
- *who are authors of books, blogs and articles you have read.*
- *who you admire and respect.*

The worst they can say is 'no', but you will find most successful people want to give back and will give their time to someone who genuinely wants to perform.

Before approaching them

- *research them on the internet.*
- *read material they have published and watch any interviews you can find.*
- *find key points to trigger their interest when you approach them.*
- *work out what you want from them, being respectful of their time.*

If you don't get a response, keep trying. Each time you contact them, tell them what you have done for yourself, and keep abreast of their work if possible and reference it. Always be respectful.

A great way to get to meet someone is to contact them to do an interview:

- *Make a list of questions you want to ask in the interview.*

- *Approach them and ask for an interview for 30 mins, either by phone, video, or face-to-face.*

- *Provide the questions to them if they ask. They may use these to judge your knowledge, so ask good questions.*

- *Ask them if you can record the interview so that you can have it transcribed.*

- *After an interview, send some extra questions by email. This keeps the relationship developing.*

Once you complete the interviews, you can decide who you want to approach to be a mentor.

A key point – initially if they ask you to do something then do it, you are not there to second-guess them and they don't want to waste their time. They may also be testing you to see if you are serious.

Final word

My final encouragement for you is to find the joy in what you do or do what brings you joy. You know, I discovered that I learned to love things that I get better at. Joy is not a touchy-feely word here, and I am not a touchy-feely person. Use whatever word you want to convey purpose, belonging, a reason why, a love for what you do, and to do what you love. *You* define who you are, you define your identities, and they do not define you. *You* are the foundation beneath those identities, those actions, those goals, so strengthen that foundation.

About Chris

Chris Christoff is an author, mentor, goal achievement coach, property developer, IT project manager, and network builder.

Chris completed a degree in Electrical Engineering and launched a career in Information Technology, achieving General Manager and Director roles, managing large teams and building IT infrastructure in the corporate, government and university sectors.

After buying an old Queenslander house at his wife's insistence, renovating it, and finally selling for triple its purchase price, Chris developed a love of property. His projects extended from renovations to working on the construction of a riverfront apartment building in Brisbane.

On leaving a toxic employment situation, Chris did some deep life analysis and published a book, Goal Setting for People Who Can't Set Goals. The book is backed by the neuroscience of how the brain really works. Chris is now building a business centred around helping others set and reach their goals.

Chris Christoff can be contacted at

ChrisLChristoff.com

CHAPTER THREE

*Don't cling to a mistake just because you took
a long time making it.*

Nikki Ellis

Having a body transformation is by no means the most important thing in the world. Challenging, fun, intriguing, yes. But important? No.

As a personal trainer it's a privilege to work with people's bodies, but far more of a privilege to work with their personalities, philosophies, and values.

If I take a formulaic approach, my story is a simple one, and it's the version I usually tell to any new clients, should they ask why I do what I do.

Growing up, my father was an athlete, my hero. I loved being part of his exciting world where success was based on kms covered each week, and his friends were household names. In my eyes they were superstars. Even now the smell of liniment is so evocative my pulse quickens! My mother, on the other hand, was obese; she'd had two heart attacks before she was 38 and died of cancer at 51. As a child it was ingrained in my psyche that you could be either fit or fat. One choice led to a long, healthy life – and if you worked hard enough – accolades and happiness. The other (in my young eyes) led to disease and early demise. The choice was a no-brainer.

Of course, like all good stories there's more to it.

My mother was cruel and controlling. Being a minute late home from school and she would pin me to the wall, her hands around my throat, her face in mine. 'Where have you been? Who were you with? Why the hell are you late?'

My every move was watched. There were no playdates, birthday parties, or riding my bike in the street. Every day I was told I was lazy, stupid, and useless.

Her favourite game was such a hoot! She would sit making school lunches for the following day and would wait till I walked to my bedroom at the end of the hall before yelling, 'Nikki, get me the marmite!'

I'd return, deliver the marmite, walk down the hall, then ...

'Nikki, get me the butter.'

This would continue for four or five items before I'd say, 'Is there anything else you need, Mum?'

This would lead to, 'Who the hell do you think you are talking to you lazy, stupid, little bitch? Get to your room.'

I couldn't wait to grow up and I knew that the second I turned 18 I would leave, even if I had nowhere to go. It was a time of deep personal unhappiness. I was around 12 when I heard about suicide for the first time. I started to contemplate this as a very real option; I was desperate and miserable.

My very first epiphany is clear as day. I was sitting at the dining table with Mum as she hurled abuse at me. 'You are beyond useless, an untrustworthy little nothing, and bone idle – no one could be lazier.'

Suddenly a door shut in my brain, the door that allowed all these insults in. I looked at this slovenly woman and I thought about my good school results, my friends, and my own self-esteem, and I suddenly questioned why I would EVER believe a word she said. There was no truth at all to anything she uttered; she was sick. I learned to let her words slide off me.

This skill has seen me into adulthood. I'm impenetrable! I literally imagine I am a duck with waterproof feathers and anything upsetting just slides off. Try it! It works!

I also realised at this time that going to running club with my dad not only got me closer to him, but was great for my soul. Literally 'running away' felt great, and I was allowed out of the house to go on training runs. It felt like a new sort of freedom, it felt fantastic. Even today a great panacea for the soul is to get out and walk in nature, sans headphones. Get out, move, breathe the fresh air, and let your subconscious mind do its job of solving any problems.

Mum died when I was 15 and it feels sad to say that life became 1000 times happier. Dad and I struggled together with trying to cook, and in particular we struggled with the concept of healthy eating. We didn't have a clue. We were both running a lot, but even that couldn't compensate for the wild excesses we went for.

KFC, fish and chips, McDonalds – every night was a different takeaway. We also ate and drank all the things that Mum had not allowed. I happily adopted the wonderful habit of adding a dollop of cream to my coffee. Four cups a day for weeks and my lean athletic frame was changing. I can remember starting my first job; no salad sandwich for me. Every day I'd have a milkshake, a packet of crisps, and a packet of Twisties (variety!) did the trick. Then home to takeaway food! Yummy!

I didn't really notice the creep of weight gain. It was only when people would make comments like, 'Don't worry, I was the biggest I've ever been at 17, too!' that I'd wonder if they were referring to my weight; surely there was no issue! I had reverse body dysmorphia.

Despite this shocking diet I was still super active, so I made no changes. I moved to Melbourne, and into a share house with a lovely girl who gave me the rundown on things like vegetables and fruit, and I loved the stability of living with someone warm and kind, and having lots of fun. I started doing mini triathlons. I joined a gym and on my first day at my assessment I was told I was 'clinically obese'. I have no idea what I weighed because I never weighed myself, but I knew that was a horrible, unnecessary term. I came home from that assessment with my self-esteem somewhere around my socks. This incident was a massive driver for me wanting to work with clients to get fit and in great shape – but in a kind, compassionate way.

I was angry that someone like me, a normal girl, was told I was obese. Sure, I wasn't super slim, but obese? I decided I would make it my mission in life to work with people to get them strong and fit, and never ever have them walk out from seeing me, feeling terrible about themselves. Isn't it amazing how one chance meeting with a stranger can galvanise you into action? To this day I still make it my aim if I am doing a client's body composition to have them leave feeling great about themselves.

I was accepted into my dream degree (B.App.Sc – Phys Ed) at Vic Uni in Melbourne, Australia. Although they did philosophy of sport, sociology of sport, play and leisure theory, and countless other fascinating subjects, I surprisingly did not do even one hour of nutrition.

At this point I still was in a body rut. Doing mainly cardio, I wondered why my body was still not quite where I would have like it to be. Now, call me shallow, but for all the exercise I did I really wanted a particular type of physique. I'd watched *Flashdance*! I'd seen *Perfect* with Jamie Lee Curtis! Those lithe, strong dancer's bodies were my idea of perfection. How could I get that? I had a degree in physical education, and I didn't know how to change my physique. Wasn't I meant to know this?

Fast forward to 1995 where I was working as a personal trainer in a large inner-city gym. My typical exercise week looked something like this:

- *5-6 sessions on water rows (1-1.5 hours each)*
- *10 – 14 aerobics classes*
- *5 walks with clients*
- *My own weight training*

This was an exhausting amount of training. Where was my lean body?

Around this time, I was training the editor of *New Idea* and was asked to write a column and also be the model in all the pictures.

This was a huge coup for my career, and I was thrilled. About six weeks in, one of the admin staff grabbed me and handed me hundreds and hundreds of reader letters (this was before emails!) The pile was enormous!

'Fan mail!' I thought.

Letter upon letter I opened enthusiastically, and over and over I read the same sentiments:

'Dear Nikki, it's so good to see someone in a magazine NOT in great shape, so refreshing.'

'Dear Nikki. I'm a size 16, I can relate to you, my body isn't perfect either.'

'Dear Nikki. So great to see a role model with lumps and bumps in a magazine.'

Let me make something clear. I am all for different body types being represented in the media. Never at any point in my 'journey' have I been at risk of being less healthy due to my weight. My waist was smallish, and I was happy and active – all was fine!

However, I didn't WANT to be the chubby poster girl, I wanted to be inspirational! I was doing hours of exercise per week; why on earth was I not lean and defined? I didn't know what changes to make.

This was the 90s. The current dietary advice at that time was plenty of carbs, moderate protein, and low fat. Looking back, I misinterpreted these guidelines a little, I truly believed that 'unrefined' carbs were fine, as long as I ate low fat.

A typical day looked like this:

- *1 x packet of crumpets with jam only 500 + 200cal*
- *6 slices bread with jam 500 + 200cal jam*
- *Salad roll with ham 330cal*

- ***Lollies 380cal***

- ***Pasta and tomato based sauce 700cal.***

- ***Huge serve of rice pudding with generous low fat ice cream 350 + 300cal***

I was eating around 3,500 calories per day, and was well short on fibre, fruit, vegetables and healthy fats!

Basically, I was living on refined carbs. The amount of exercise I was doing meant my weight was in maintenance, but the sheer volume of food meant I was never going to have the lean body I craved.

One day I walked into an activewear shop. My work uniform screamed to the world my job – 'Personal Trainer' was embroidered on my back. The girl behind the counter smiled. 'Oh, you're a personal trainer! This is MY personal trainer.'

She handed me a postcard with a picture of a girl with the most incredible physique. A tiny waist, defined quads, cannonball shoulders. Her name was Donna Aston and she was everything I wanted to be!

'Donna gets us to have small meals frequently. I've just had a small handful of cashews!'

I frowned 'Really? Cashews are super high in fat, I never eat them!'

The conversation went on with the salesgirl telling me, to my mind, outlandish things. Higher protein, what? Protein powder? The most refined food possible? Isn't that made in a lab? Lots of veggies, surely three a day is okay? Adding healthy fats, to a meal? Ridiculous.

I left the shop unsettled. Such a radical deviation from what research was telling us made me uncomfortable. Here was a woman who looked phenomenal but ate in a completely different way to me.

I continued to go to courses and conferences where we focused on primarily low-fat eating, and I continued to miss/ignore entire chunks of education where they also talked about volume! (This is embarrassing to write because YEARS passed by before I took any action.)

Around this time 'Body for Life' became a thing. You may remember it; led by Bill Phillips, it featured hundreds of pictures of transformation contestants. In the first picture they were out of shape, glum, and pale, and in the second picture looked lean, strong, and sexy as hell. This was what I'd been looking for – I wanted to be the girl in the second picture so badly. I could taste victory.

Along with my husband I began to transform my eating, massively upping the vegetables, lowering the refined carbs, and increasing the protein. I continued with my exercise, although I was no longer teaching aerobics. My weight training and rowing became the main things I truly focussed on. The changes happened, but the fun had gone out of my eating and I felt deprived. On a 'cheat day' I'd start eating at 7.00am and not stop till 10.00pm. This was not a way to live.

My thirties revolved around pregnancy, breastfeeding, and sleepless nights. I went back to teaching resistance training at Vic Uni. I'd always loved weight training; I knew my stuff and I was strong.

After years of teaching students who loved me, there was one semester where I knew in my heart that I had lost their respect, or more likely never had it in the first place. I'd had my daughter a few months earlier but hadn't lifted for around 18 months. I was unfit, weak, and out of shape. The shift in confidence from my students was palpable, and I was horrified. Every afternoon driving home from uni I'd stop at Bakers Delight and buy a custard scroll, then miserably eat it in my car. Those 584cals per day started to add up.

Things had to change, or I needed to quit my lecturing job that I'd always loved. Limping miserably to the end of semester, I was at a crossroads. I could listen to one voice in my head that said things like, 'You are 40 now – of course you're not in great shape! Plus, you've had two kids. Sheesh! Stupid students. What would they know? Probably just a bad semester.'

The other voice said, 'You are still young, and you are done with having kids. Let's get back to training and get in great shape. Also, while we are at it, let's rework every lecture and PowerPoint so they are super up to date. It's time to get into the sort of condition the students expect and deserve. Strong and inspiring.'

So, this was where it all happened.

The years of frustration with my doughy body, despite hours of exercise. All of the letters holding me up as a role model for the less-than-slender gals. The look of 'you lost me at hello' in my students' eyes.

It was time for action.

The plan was made. My girlfriend, Sharon, would come over every day and I would train both of us. Imagine the scene at a glorified carpark with a bench, squat rack, and some free weights. It was winter; we trained in tracksuit pants, windcheaters, beanies, and gloves.

Cue Rocky soundtrack

We walked every day and lifted Monday to Friday using a split routine (a different body part every day), but most importantly we did an eating overhaul. I went cold turkey on those custard scrolls, and instead went for the actual cold turkey (see what I did there?)

A typical day looked like this:

- *oats, cottage cheese, and low fat milk and berries*
- *can of tuna and chopped tomato, spinach, and flaxseed oil*
- *chicken, veggies, and rice*
- *protein shake and berries*
- *protein and veggies*

I ate small meals frequently so I was able to get approximately 20g protein in at any meal. I used olive oil and flaxseed oil, I upped my legumes, and learned about this thing called 'moderation'. I weighed my food initially, so I didn't mistakenly have a much larger volume than I meant to (my major tendency).

Over the months my body changed and I became leaner, I felt strong in myself, and I loved being able to wear anything.

In case you are wondering how the next semester went, frankly it could be made in to a movie (I feel Demi Moore would be the perfect person to play the lead role, but I'd also be happy with Cate Blanchett) I returned to the job I love, and today have many ex-students all over the world still keeping in touch, saying I inspired them and they loved my classes. I'm so glad I didn't give up.

This is more than ten years ago now, and I've maintained this physique consistently. I don't generally weigh my foods anymore and I love my once-per-week almond croissant. I'll have takeaway food on a Saturday night, and I drink wine. My focus is on health first – veggies rule.

In terms of my job as a personal trainer, the difference has been astounding. People often come to me now because they've seen my 'transformation' pictures and want to do the same. I feel confident saying, 'I can help you' because as well as knowing how to do it (finally!), I put it into practice every day. The framework of my eating is so strong that I know exactly what and how I need to eat to feel energised and well, but also lean and defined. I'm able to live my life with no hang-ups about my body with no disordered eating, no obsession, and no guilt. It is absolutely not everyone's goal to look a certain way, and of course it is only ONE element of my being, but it's an important one as your body is what the world sees and I simply felt I could be different.

I wanted my clients to be as proud of me as the shop assistant years ago when she showed me the photo of her PT and said, 'This is my trainer'. Now, I think – just maybe – they are.

Have you yoyo dieted your way through the past few years, each time putting on a little more weight? You might be feeling frustrated, annoyed, and completely stuck. Perhaps you are beginning to truly believe the adage, 'Diets don't work'.

I hear you. I have been exactly where you are.

Let me share with you some of the things I truly wish I had known 40 years ago.

You cannot out-train a poor diet (or a diet that is well in surplus of your needs)

You need to be mind-bogglingly active, e.g. dragging a sled across the plains of Antarctica for twelve hours a day to truly be able to eat whatever you want. Be very careful not to overcompensate for any activity you do. Women in particular tend to compensate for workouts done by eating more – 'Oh, I went to the gym today so I can have that chocolate bar.' People also tend to compensate for workouts done by being less active the rest of the time – the term for this is being an 'active couch potato'.

Even when you are doing more planned activity than usual still ensure that you are staying active, do your ten thousand steps a day, and don't stay sedentary for long stretches of time.

Be careful with the volume of your foods

With the exception of leafy green vegetables, it is possible to overconsume even healthy foods. Live light. When you finish a meal look for signs that you are comfortably satiated as opposed to side-busting stuffed. Take your time, eat slowly, and be conscious of your serve sizes.

Weight train

This tip has flashing lights all over it! So many of us fall into the trap of starting excessive amounts of cardio when we want to lose weight. In short, we panic! Start lifting weights, and in particular train in a way that is progressive, keep track of what you do, and aim to lift more over time. Keep your daily steps up and do 1-2 huffy puffy higher intensity interval training sessions per week. That's it!

Eat more protein

Once you start your weight training you also need to increase your protein. As a rule of thumb, for most female lifters I would recommend 90g of protein a day as a great starting point.

Supplements, vibration plates, fat burners are not for you

Ignore all fads and seemingly quick fixes. I'm not anti-supplements, however, apart from a protein powder, when you are going on a journey of transformation get the basics right first! Don't start looking for the easy out, just be smart and get the job done. You've got this.

I am truly excited for you, because this is the very information you need to get you in great shape!

What does this mean for you? It may mean the body of your dreams. It may mean you feel strong and confident. It may mean you have more energy and get up and go, or perhaps it may mean you never have to worry about lifestyle diseases such as Type 2 diabetes or heart disease.

Importantly, it may mean freedom from the eternal loop of yoyo dieting, critical self-talk, and needless guilt. I am so hopeful for you that it means less time thinking about food and exercise, and more time to think about exciting plans, your children, and your PhD thesis! Clear boundaries allow you more freedom to create habits and lifestyle choices that lead you to being in great shape, or at the very least fitting comfortably into your clothes.

I have one last tip to share with you before I wish you well and let you get started.

Be consistent

There will be days you don't want to train, when you hop on the scales and weigh more than you wanted to. There will be many, many times you won't feel motivated. Do it anyway. Stay the path, trust the process – it works! Fat loss success is not a linear process, and there will be many blips and setbacks along the way. You have your entire life to eat and train optimally. This is the new you, and you are magnificent.

Let this be the start of your new life.

Reader Tips

- *You can most certainly be fit and fat. Our modern lifestyles make it incredibly difficult to stay super lean, and for many it isn't the most ideal or even attainable goal. For some of us it leads down the path of disordered eating and misery – the very opposite of good health. Eat healthy, nourishing foods and move that body. A lot.*

- *Be mindful of who you take advice from. Even parents can be dead wrong.*

- *Do your research. The dietary guidelines back then did place breads and pastas at the bottom of the food pyramid, but also recommended five serves of veggies and three serves of fruit. Plenty of people have got in great shape eating low fat, it doesn't mean you can eat unlimited quantities of everything else. Misinterpreting data so it reads the way you want it to can create big mistakes.*

- *If someone is where you want to be, emulating what they have done might be worth looking in to.*

- *Although at the time they might feel good, self-medicating with food or alcohol generally are not solutions to your problems.*

- *There is plenty of scientific evidence to support the link between physical strength and self-esteem, self-worth, and self-efficacy. The measurable increases in strength are brilliant for changing our bodies, but just as important – read that again – JUST as important are the changes to how we feel about ourselves and what we can achieve.*

- *Never give up, dude.*

About Nikki

Nikki Ellis is a career Personal Trainer and Transformation Coach who runs a thriving PT and Transformation studio in Melbourne, Australia.

She was a sessional academic for seventeen years in the College of Exercise and Sport Science at Victoria University where she also completed a B.APp. Sc Exercise Science. Nikki has taught and trained thousands of people over the past thirty years, written hundreds of magazine columns, and presented at conferences in Australia and internationally.

Nikki is happily married and has two generally utterly delightful teenagers.

Nikki Ellis can be contacted at

cinch.training

CHAPTER FOUR

*Getting out of your comfort zone is obligatory,
skinny dipping is optional.*

Marie Kimber

Unable to turn over in bed, gasping for breath and vomiting something that resembled the secretion from a squashed snail, the doctor said, 'Relax, you're about to be intubated.' It was music to my terrified ears.

It's 7.00am on a Wednesday in early April 2006. I've got the day off from my job as a practice manager at a General Practice in suburban Adelaide, South Australia. As I struggle to get out of bed, I soon realise that I won't have an easy day ahead of me. The ability to simply walk to the bathroom evades me, and I'm shocked to find I can only get there by holding on to the walls to stay upright.

Oh, my God! What the hell is happening? Have I had a stroke? What is wrong with me? I frantically reach for the phone to call my doctor.

At 3.00am the following morning my son carries me to the car and I'm taken to the Emergency Department. By the time a neurologist arrives six hours later, I'm incredibly anxious about my condition. Among other observations, I'm sent for an MRI scan for my brain. The neurologist then orders an MRI of my spine, before marvelling at my courage as he inserts a needle into my back. This lumbar puncture ultimately confirms my diagnosis of Guillain Barre Syndrome, and I'm admitted to the general ward.

Guillain Barre Syndrome (GBS) is a rare neurological disorder in which the body's immune system mistakenly attacks part of its peripheral nervous system. The nerves contained in the brain and spinal cord are spared, but all other nerves can be affected. People with the illness suffer to varying degrees, with a death rate of around 5%.

It is generally preceded by a viral or bacterial infection up to three weeks prior. I had a bout of mild diarrhoea 19 days ago. In a nutshell, my immune system attacked the infection, which is great, but it then got a tad confused and went on to attack the myelin sheath, the protective covering on my nerves, which is NOT great! Consequently, messages from my brain are lost in transit and not making it to the rest of my body.

Sitting on the edge of the bed, waiting for assistance to get to the toilet. The nurse assures me I'll be okay. 'I'm going to fall,' I explain huskily, my voice also losing strength. Just as I fear, I fall hard onto the floor with my first step. My young adult son looks on, deeply concerned. A shower chair is brought to carry me on to my next toilet visit. As we're nearing the cubicle, I'm horrified at the unmistakably rich scent of excrement, realising I've lost control of that, too.

A five-day course of intravenous immunoglobulin is started in the hope that the 'helpful' antibodies contained in that would overcome the 'baddies' my immune system is producing to attack my nerves. It is kind of ironic because I am a plasma donor, regularly donating at the Red Cross every month. I never expected to be on the receiving end.

Unfortunately, the baddies win out, and my condition continues to spiral downward. An ever-present, metallic taste in my mouth repulses me. My struggle to breathe scares me so much, I virtually plead to be taken to the support of a ventilator in Intensive Care.

We are told my condition will deteriorate to a certain point and will then, all going well, start to improve. The unknown factor is how long this process will take.

I'm moved from the general ward to the Intensive Care Unit on Sunday. By Monday, a tracheostomy is performed. An incision is made in my neck through which a ventilator is connected. A tube is inserted in my nose and feeds 'chocolate milk' looking liquid directly to my stomach.

For the next seven weeks, I lie paralysed, kept alive by drugs, machines, and the nasogastric tube. My elderly parents rush from country South Australia. While the 45-minute plane flight is faster than the 700km drive, they still can't get there fast enough. Dad sits at my bedside for days with his head in his hands and tears rolling down his troubled face.

Initially, I'm unconscious and oblivious to everything. However, as the weeks go on and I slowly gain more awareness, fear and horror add to my pain-filled thoughts, fuelled by medication-induced nightmares.

The nurses apply Vaseline to my eyes to stop them drying out because I can't close my eyelids. The only sense I have at my disposal is my hearing, so I strain to listen to all the sounds and voices around me to keep updated. What are they saying about me? When am I going to get better?

As Guillain Barre Syndrome doesn't affect the nerves of the brain, I am mentally sound but I can't see or communicate. It is just like being buried alive.

I endure the revolting and regular ritual of 'suction', whereby phlegm is vacuumed from my airways via a hose fed down the hole in my neck. The sound makes me cringe, but the procedure enables me to breathe more freely. I am continually either really hot or cold and I can't relay that, or any other discomfort or pleasure, to anyone.

The only sound I can make is a click of my tongue. A beautiful nurse sets up a board with letters and numbers on it as my avenue of communication. My family use this when they come to visit. They move their finger along the board, and I click my tongue when it arrives at the letter I want. They then write down each individual letter until I spell out the sentence I want to say. It is an incredibly drawn out, frustrating process, but it's my only choice.

As I had no warning of my hospitalisation, I need to give my bank account login details to my son so he can keep the wolves from the door at home. He moves his finger slowly across the top line of numbers. No click comes from me. He points to the numbers on the bottom line. Still, no click from me. He goes back over the top again and then repeats the lower numbers. I lay silent, my eyes staring blankly. The login has a zero in it, but only the numbers one through nine are on the board.

After seven weeks a tiny bit of movement returns, and I'm delighted to see my little finger move after a direct command from my brain. Awesome! I'm on my way back, I think, relieved at the glimmer of light at the end of the tunnel.

I am gradually weaned off the ventilator with increasing times of breathing on my own. My pre-illness fitness holds me in good stead, and I'm determined to blitz this stage and get talking again!

Finally, the day arrives to get off the ventilator. A doctor comes to remove the tracheostomy tube. I feel the pressure of his hands on my throat and then his words, 'There you go, it's all done.'

'Is that it?' I whisper, in a dry, raspy voice. I'm surprised the procedure is so simple.

'Yeah,' he replies, 'that's it.'

'That was quick,' I croak. 'Will I be able to sing?'

'Of course,' he says assuredly.

Then quick as a flash, I reply jokingly, 'Bonus! Because I couldn't sing before!'

I'm grateful to be able to sprinkle an ounce of light-heartedness on what has been an extremely traumatic phase.

However, I'm not out of the woods yet. I'm soon transferred to a rehabilitation facility for two more painful and frustratingly long months, weighing 9kg less than usual. After those motionless, bedridden weeks, my wasted muscles are not very receptive to the movements required of them to become mobile and functioning normally. My daily routine comprises physiotherapy, hydrotherapy, and occupational therapy, as my weak 43kg body battles hard to comply with all that is asked of it.

Most of the other patients are elderly stroke victims, so heads turn as my tiny, bikini-clad body is lowered into the hydrotherapy pool. I try hard to be indestructible during my rehab but I cry often as I gallantly try to simply stand up, let alone perform other dexterous tasks of daily living. And as for walking – who knew how difficult that could be! It takes many weeks of repetitive practice, effort, and commitment.

Once I pass the 'getting in and out of a wheelchair' test and walk a few steps aided by a walking frame, I am released from care. I shuffle back into the real world, still very much in need of further strengthening of my physical and mental state.

I am a shadow of my former self.

I was successful in my management career previously, but now I'm too timid to even answer the telephone. I gradually ease back into work but eventually resign from my position, knowing I'll be more comfortable with a simpler role.

My physical health returns quite rapidly, but mentally I am suffering. I burst into tears with even a glimpse of a hospital-based television show. Elements akin to Post Traumatic Stress Disorder linger and are soon to be in the mix with symptoms of menopause.

Noooo! That is just what I don't need! Mood changes, lack of motivation, sadness, loss of libido, self-worth, and femininity; these are not welcome additions to my already depleted confidence.

Over time my relationship starts to unravel. My partner has done nothing wrong; he is thoughtful, loving, funny, intelligent, and even helps around the house. But it is me who feels stale and needing more. I've become bored and unfulfilled. Is that his fault? I don't know. I blame myself anyway.

My two sons are married and live with their own families. Although my partner and I have made the most of this phase of life with travel and experiences, and we enjoy similar interests, something is missing.

Emotionally, I feel so empty, so sad, so worthless. Is this what post-menopause life feels like for *every* woman? One morning, as I lie hunched up on the floor, heaving loud, uncontrollable sobs of unhappiness, I wonder how much longer I can go on.

Doing my best to snap out of it, I dress and drive off, under the premise of going shopping. However, I have absolutely no idea where I'm going.

Without any conscious thought, I soon find myself turning into a beachside carpark. Again, with no predetermined notion and with tears falling, I pick up my handbag and start walking to the beach. I'm supposed to be going shopping, I'm not dressed for the beach.

'What am I doing *here*?' I question. A cool breeze sticks strands of hair to my wet, mascara-blackened face as I stride determinedly toward the water's edge. Something has led me here, some powerful force. My soul crying out, maybe?

When I arrive at the far end of the beach, I place my handbag on the sand, strip off, and walk into the calm, blue-green ocean.

Naked.

Okay, so it *is* a dedicated nudist beach, however, this behaviour is way out of character for me. But, oh ... my ... God ... it feels *absolutely* amazing. As I float on my back looking up at a cloudless, blue sky, I sense the soothing clear water wash the anguish away, and I start to gain clarity around what I need to do.

With regret and sadness, I tell my partner I am ending the relationship. I feel I will be happier on my own, instead of dealing with the perpetual guilt around being so unsatisfied when I possibly shouldn't be. He and I will remain close friends.

With the separation, I give up my security, both environmentally and financially. However, if there is one thing I learned from my illness, it is the value of life and time. It waits for no one and can be taken away from you very swiftly, regardless of your health. I consider myself lucky to have a second chance.

I now have plenty of free time for my passions of writing and photography. I had fallen in love with Italy when touring there with friends, and I now feel a huge desire to return. What better way to throw me out of my comfort zone than to book a trip on my own? I feel a pull and I need to follow it.

Stepping through the sliding doors to the airport, I am apprehensive about my first solo journey. What am I doing travelling alone to the other side of the world? Is it a whim? Is this the best thing for me now, or am I making a big mistake?

On clearing baggage screening, my instinct takes over. I need to live my life, and I need to be the writer of my own story. I'm doing this.

I spend the first day wandering the streets of Rome. I skip over cobblestones with a spring in my step and a glint in my eye. With all my senses magnified, I feel so alive. I stop off to photograph and write about the energy that surrounds me.

I sit for lunch at an outdoor table on the edge of Piazza Navona and chat with the people around me. My head is thrown back with laughter as a handsome waiter fills my glass with a crisp white wine. The aroma of pasta pescatore permeates my nostrils and makes my mouth water.

The vibe around the restaurant is lively. The classical tune of a violin and double bass wafts across the sun-soaked square, as the sounds of the casual buskers add to the clink of glasses and cutlery and joyous chatter. The memory of this uplifting day will remain with me forever. I sit writing on my iPad, dreaming that one day someone will pay me to do this.

Over the ensuing days, I discover something substantial about myself. I'm going beyond my comfort zone and thriving. Yes, I'm succeeding! Not only do I see this beautiful city through different eyes, I see myself in a new light. I rejoice in the challenge of travelling alone and making my own decisions.

Nine days in this inspiring country resets my compass and now I need to take the rudder. I dip my toes into a life that fuels my passions, and it gives me a glimmer of the competent, confident, sassy woman I'm capable of being.

It's time to create the life I want. I can now see the path to fulfilment. On returning home, I set about developing a plan to lead me there.

I start working on my mindset, because *everything* begins with our mindset. Without a doubt, it's what is going on between our ears that has the most significant bearing on how we feel. In most cases, the default setting is to 'negative'. We are traditionally geared up to think negatively more than we think positively. We can be guilty of focusing on baggage from the past and using it as the limiting beliefs that hold us back.

Yes, we need to acknowledge things that have happened to us, BUT they are in the past; they are NOT our future. We can alter only that which is ahead of us and not what is behind us. Remember, a car's windscreen is larger than the rear-view mirror.

It is time to push negative thoughts and excuses out of my mind. I continually think about what I can give, and not what I can take. What I can do, and not what I can't.

When we create a feeling of joy and gratitude, the positive vibes will overtake the negative thoughts. A healthy mindset is an incredibly powerful force. It can propel you forward while shielding you from detrimental influences.

With my decision to move on into an unencumbered way of life, I need to pack up the past. I'm ready to remove or repurpose aspects that are tethering me to a previous point in time. This includes not only physical reminders but also routines that are embedded in how I lived before.

Next, I clear out my space. Decluttering is seriously one of the most empowering things you can do. I start with my clothing and clear out everything I haven't worn for ages and anything that depicts me as a dowdy housewife.

Dowdy Housewife has left the building!

There are plenty of places where you can donate your unwanted clothing. Plus you get the benefit of 'warm and fuzzies' knowing you're helping out someone who needs your stuff more than you do.

The next phase of my transformation is what I call my 'Love Thy Self' initiative, wherein I look at my strengths and weaknesses. On a sheet of paper I draw a strengths column and a weaknesses column, adding to it as I think of items.

Strengths can be defined as the qualities we are happy and proud of. However, we can easily fall into the trap of thinking our weaknesses are our failings. By acknowledging our weaknesses, we can choose to make changes or accept them as they are.

It's now time to learn not to beat myself up over past failings. Failure is not to be feared. It is another way of learning and should, therefore, be embraced. Forgive yourself and other people. There are no winners when we hold a grudge. As they say, it's like drinking poison and hoping the other person will get sick.

How often do we take time to nurture our souls? This was the next area I focused on. Our soul is said to be our lightbulb – the essence of us that will light up a room. It is who we *really* are, not our conscience or our ego. It works in combination with our hearts and our intellect. No doubt it was what drew me to the beach that day!

We need to continually feed and nurture our soul. Only you can decide what works for you. It may include such things as connecting with nature, volunteering, meditation, exercise, long baths or reading, etc. Anything that results in a greater sense of freedom, joy, empowerment and inner peace. It helps you love yourself more, even when things aren't going to plan.

Beware the constant chatter of your ego and your fears that can hold you back from fully aligning with your soul. Because this can be seen as enjoying 'me time' it is often excluded from our list of priorities in a busy life.

By this stage, I'm on the right track to living how I want. It is now time to reward myself with a massage and beauty treatments.

During my 'Boring Housewife Days,' I'd completely lost touch with my femininity and with my sense of worth around that element. It is now time to blossom as a woman.

Being comfortable in our naked skin doesn't come naturally to most. This is often the effect of society or advertising and the resultant perception of perfection. Our body is a vehicle for our soul, so shouldn't we love and respect it? It transports our core self into all areas of our lives and into the lives of others. The confidence we gain from gratitude and self-love for our body, will radiate out to all we meet.

Even if you're worried you are too short, bow-legged, overweight, your hair is too thin, so what? Even supermodels find faults in themselves. Just remember your MINDSET!

Spending time on self-awareness and with fond memories of my unprecedented nudie swim some months prior, I begin frequenting the nudist beach. Nude swimming is exhilarating, and I find it incredibly empowering to know I don't give a shit. I don't care what I look like, I don't engage with anyone, I am there totally for my pleasure. It is time to purge my brain, switch off, and re-energise. It nurtures the hell out of my soul, let me tell you!

When taking charge of our life, it is an excellent time to look at the personalities around us. Are we mixing with positive people who are supportive of us? Or are we surrounded by the negative naysayers who want to inflict their toxic views on us? These people are all over social media, so be mindful of what you're consuming.

I now have the mindset to challenge myself and go out of my comfort zone. Wanting to do something significant in this my 60th year, I competed in a short-course triathlon after just eight weeks of swim, cycle, and run training. I was the oldest woman in the field and felt prouder of my training discipline and commitment than actually finishing the race. The value was in the journey, not the destination.

Since my illness, I've developed a massive respect for life. From the moment I was diagnosed with Guillain Barre Syndrome, I was grateful. Grateful that I had something I could recover from, not an illness that would beat me. I was one of the lucky ones who went to the lowest point while grasping onto a return ticket. I was fortunate to have a wake-up call with time to make amends. I wear the permanent scar of my tracheostomy and am reminded of my fortune every time I look in the mirror.

Don't waste your time being tied to your devices. Get out and enrich your own life instead of getting caught up in the lives of others. My dear dad, who has since passed away, never lacked appreciation of the earth's beauty. I'm proud to say he instilled those values in me.

Have the courage to live a life true to yourself, not the life others expect of you; I certainly have! Now at age 60, I vigorously pursue my passions of travel, writing, photography, and helping others live their best life. From sitting in Rome with a dream, to now where someone does actually pay me to write!

Through the avenues of public speaking, mentorships, and hosting small ladies-only group tours, I can help make it happen for others, too.

I live my best life, have more passion and connection in intimacy, and am free from issues that were tethering me to my past. I'm proud of my unique self, I exude confidence, I've attracted the right people in my life, and I have a clearer vision about my future.

Change does not have to be made in leaps and bounds. Stringing together baby steps can start the momentum. Stay focused on the life you want, keep building toward it and don't be afraid to seek help to get there.

Your life is a journey, and if you fall in love with the journey, you'll be in love forever.

About Marie

Marie Kimber is a travel writer, inspirational speaker, mentor, and hosts small group international travel tours.

In 2006, fit and vibrant 46-year old Marie woke one morning to find she couldn't walk.

She was diagnosed with Guillain Barre Syndrome, a highly debilitating illness, and spent seven weeks totally paralysed in Intensive Care, kept alive by drugs and machines. After a further two months in rehabilitation, Marie wheeled her wheelchair out of hospital, to contend with life a shadow of her former self.

Aching with unhappiness, she realised she had to make a change. Marie used her illness as a blessing and a wake-up call, closing the door to death and opening the door to life. She transformed from dull and disinterested to vibrant and sassy.

Now at 60 years young, Marie lives her best life and shares her journey of discovery with others. She hosts small group, ladies-only tours overseas, using her life experience to lead other women to confidence and curiosity.

A grandmother to five, Marie lives on the beach south of Adelaide, adjacent to the wine region of McLaren Vale.

Marie Kimber can be contacted at

mariekimber.com

CHAPTER FIVE

In order to become who we're meant to be, sometimes we have to let go of who we wanted to be.

Naomi Holland

When standing on the cliff edge of our dreams, contemplating whether to jump or not, we're told to trust that we will grow our wings and fly.

But have we ever stopped to consider if flying is the only way?

With the explosion of the motivational movement, we've created a mentality that we can be anything, do anything, achieve or obtain anything we want. Provided we set our mind to it, provided we set out a carefully curated plan and we hold a vision of what we want, it will eventuate, as if it's written in our future.

That when we jump, we know we're going to fly.

We're often made to believe if we don't achieve or obtain what we want, then we're not trying hard enough, that we don't want it enough. Making us believe we're doing something wrong, often leaving us feeling as if we are somehow flawed.

But rarely do we ever stop and consider that maybe we're not the problem; maybe the goal is. That maybe the way we're trying to achieve it isn't right for us. That maybe there's a way more perfectly suited to you than you could have ever imagined. If only you'd let go of trying to control how it turns out and allowed life to show you the way.

If only we'd stop believing the illusion that flying was the only way.

When I was 17, in my final year of high school, I came face to face with the reality of letting go of everything I had ever dreamed of, not knowing that this would allow life to deliver me more than I ever wanted.

Growing up in a small country town in Australia, my earliest memories of the city were looking up at the tall buildings towering above. We would drive into the city and I would stare out the windows, in awe of the buildings flicking by. I knew then that that's what I was going to do with my life. I was going to design them. Not just an architect creating the vision, but the one responsible for taking that vision and making it stand up.

At the age of 13, I was determined with everything I had to make that dream a reality. I was jumping. I was determined to fly. And I knew exactly how it was going to happen.

I had it all planned out. I was moving to the city. I knew which university, which campus, and I was going to design those buildings. Any doubt that rose was squashed before I allowed myself to believe it, pushing it into the abyss, refusing to let it derail my plan.

But life had a different path for me.

One night, in the middle of my final year of school, I was sitting at the kitchen bench, trying for the millionth time to write a personal story about my life for English class but the words refused to come. For some reason every time I attempted to write I just felt empty. My stomach would knot. A lump would form in my throat. My shoulders would tense, my chest would become heavy, and my mind went blank. I couldn't put words to what was happening. And I guess I didn't want to.

This night I was on the verge of tears, without knowing why. Struggling to write, I looked at the TV. A reality show was on. One of the female contestants was talking to her close friend, discussing their return to 'normal' life. As I watched it, this woman who seemed to have it all together was standing there in tears, declaring that she didn't want to return to her normal life because she didn't like it.

My stomach dropped. Tears welled in my eyes. Picking up my pen and paper as quietly as I could, hoping I could hold it together long enough to retreat without my family noticing, I walked straight to my room and shut the door.

I slumped, defeated, onto the floor. She had said the words I just couldn't, that I didn't want to voice. *I didn't like my life.* The words reverberated through me. And I cried that night for the first time that I could remember.

Tears streamed down my face. I felt numb, empty, desolate, void of any motivation or inspiration. I felt like an emotionless shell of a person. I didn't like anything about my life, yet there was nothing inherently wrong with my life.

I grew up in a typical country town with 10,000 people, not the smallest but not the biggest either. I was raised by two parents who were doing the best they could, working hard at whatever job they had – because that was how their families raised them. Completing high school wasn't seen as a necessity and university wasn't something anyone within my extended family had ever managed to attempt, let alone complete.

Career and life advice consisted of: find a respectable working-class job (typically an apprenticeship or a job in the community), work hard, save money, buy a house and raise a family. It was how most people I knew were raised.

My family wasn't the most financially successful, with Dad spending a big portion of my childhood out of work and Mum not having much of a choice other than to become a pastry cook and support the family. Financial and professional success seemed to elude my family at every turn.

Yet here I was, with an incredible intellect and academic ability; dreaming of the day I would rise beyond their story; get into university and smash through the glass ceiling, every member of my family seemed unable to break. And I was choosing the male-dominated engineering field and I wasn't going to settle for mediocre-sized projects either. But here I was, on the verge of an emotional breakdown.

Sitting on the floor that night crying my eyes out, I felt the weight of it all. The pressure I placed on myself to succeed. The unspoken expectation of my family to do something great with my life. To go beyond the working-class struggle that was so entrenched within the family.

The weight was just too much to carry. I didn't have anything left to fight anymore. But more than that, I didn't have the energy to keep suppressing the real reason I was fighting so hard for that life.

I started crying that night and I didn't stop for a week. I was so broken, yet I couldn't verbalise what was wrong other than saying 'I'm not okay and I don't know why.' I spent the week staring out the window because looking at the TV pushed me over the edge. After a second week of not being able to mentally and physically function, and a diagnosis of post-viral depression, I started to let go of the idea of university and of engineering. I physically couldn't make it to school, let alone finish Year 12 with the results needed for engineering.

So I chose to let go of the only thing I had ever wanted; the dream of making those big buildings stand up.

I let go of the idea that I would ever grow wings and fly.

The days I couldn't make it to school because showering, eating, and dressing were physically and mentally too difficult, I sat on the veranda, looking at the trees and listening to the birds. When I wasn't crying, I wrote. I didn't want to talk to a professional therapist, nor confide in anyone. So I talked to myself. I wrote my heart out, exploring what was really going on underneath it all, why letting go of this was so hard, and why getting that life in that way was so important. Through writing, I uncovered why I was so broken and why I needed it so much.

Whilst my life didn't seem bad, underneath it was a story of endless hardship. My early childhood years weren't easy. My parents were 28 and 32 with two kids under 4, trying to navigate marriage, raise children, rescue a failing business and avoid bankruptcy, whilst trying to live out their partying youth. My teenage years didn't get much better, either.

I was obese for the majority of my childhood; not just the chubbiest in the class, but one of the biggest in the school. The onslaught of teasing was horrible. I didn't have many friends and the ones I had seemed transient. My little sister was gorgeous and most people in high school knew me as her sister. My family, struggling with their own issues, seemed to constantly remind me of my flaws; stubborn, selfish, opinionated and self-centred, but reminded me at least I was smart.

It was also the small-mindedness of the town. No one really left town when they finished high school. They left temporarily, only to return later in life, coupled up with someone from childhood, and had children. No one ever really escaped the image and identity that was formed throughout their school years because they continued to be surrounded by their childhood. It seemed like a cycle many repeated and were unable to escape.

Whilst it was by no means a life or future to be ashamed of, it wasn't for me. It would have destroyed me staying there, surrounded by the same people who did nothing but judge and label me throughout my childhood. It would have sucked the life out of me. I wanted to escape the cycle, escape my story, escape the identity that I seemed to be drowning in and the future I didn't want.

The only thing I had going for me in life was my academic ability. It was my ticket out of there. However that seemed to be slipping from beneath me.

Again, through writing I uncovered the reason I so desperately wanted that career and attend that university. It meant receiving external validation that I was intelligent. It was the prestige of rising above my family history and cycle of financial and professional hardship. It was outdoing everyone who put me down, in various ways, throughout life. That by achieving my goal I would show them that what they said about me wasn't true and that I was someone. I wanted an abundant life and believed professional success was the only way to achieve it.

I also believed it would re-write who I was; that I could elevate myself beyond the stories of my childhood and my upbringing. That it would provide me with status and this status would prove my worth as a person.

What it really was, was me trying to prove to myself that I wasn't the person that I believed people thought I was. I felt deeply unworthy of an incredible life. Other than my academic ability, I had nothing to offer the world, and without it I would be nothing. I believed I would be fated to live the same life as everyone around me. A fate I was trying desperately to escape. A life filled with labels, judgement, and struggle.

As the shame of who I believed I was and the fear of a future I didn't want bubbled to the surface, I let it break me. Instead of suppressing those thoughts and feelings, or trying anxiously to fix them, like I had done so often, I began to embrace those broken parts of me; the sad little girl who felt she was worthless.

I didn't judge myself for what surfaced, or how I viewed those around me. I just witnessed the thoughts, the feelings, and the emotions, and I held as much compassion for myself as I could. I was a depressed 17-year old holding space for the sad little girl inside of me who was watching her dream life slip away. There wasn't much I could do other than watch her let it go and help her find peace.

I wanted to escape my story – my life, my identity, the person I believed I was – so badly that I was clinging to an ideal future because I tied my worth as a person to it. I needed that future to happen because I believed it would prove all the labels and stories wrong. I was trying to control the outcome because I didn't believe I could be happy any other way.

I was clinging to my plan, terrified it wouldn't eventuate. Afraid I would be resigned to the person I believed I was – worthless, unattractive, an incompetent failure, unable to amount to anything in life.

Instead of fighting harder for my goal, I allowed myself to feel the suppressed emotions. To find peace with any future that may unfold and what I feared most; to find gratitude for what I had, and embraced who I truly was – not the labels or stories I carried.

Through self-reflection I've learnt we often dismiss the undesirable beliefs of ourselves. We banish them within our minds and bodies, generally the same place we hold the desire for our dreams, only underneath them.

We look outside of ourselves at ways in which we can cover over the hurt, proving the undesirable views we hold of ourselves, untrue. As if by obtaining what we desire most, it will magically dissolve the unpleasantness underneath.

But it is this suppressing and band-aiding over that causes us to fight and battle against life, against ourselves. Trying to obtain dreams and goals through clinging and grasping only seems to perpetuate struggle; locking us into believing there is only one way to achieve our goals, creating tunnel vision in the process. It prevents the perfect path from unfolding because it's covered in fear; fear of failure, of unworthiness, of inadequacy.

To truly release the fear and open ourselves to receive what is meant for us in the way it is meant to arrive, we must open the area which not only contains the dream and the desire, but contains the fear and the unworthiness, as well.

So I sat and I opened to the fear.

I allowed the unworthiness, the inadequacy, the 'not enough' to be felt.

I grieved the future I wanted.

I felt the disappointment of not accomplishing what I believed I could; what everyone around me believed I could.

I felt the sadness and anger that surfaced as my pride shattered.

I allowed myself to hear all the name calling I screamed at myself.

I erased the image of how I believed my life would look.

I shed the identity of who I believed I would become.

I let go of the idea that I'd fly in the way I wanted to.

And I made room for the person that I was; motivated, determined, kind and caring.

I found compassion for the little girl who felt deeply unloved, ostracised, worthless, and not enough.

I found gratitude for what I had around me. A loving family who only wanted me to have the best opportunities and succeed in ways they wished they could have.

I found appreciation for the close friends who had always been there, the beautiful friendships I had dismissed because I was so determined to escape every other part of my life.

And I started paving a new path; a path that wasn't an old escape plan or a ploy to gain validation and worth, dressed in different clothes.

And my physical and mental health started to improve.

Each day got a little easier. Each day I found a little more gratitude for all I had and all I was. I was no longer solely focused on engineering as the answer to all my problems, but had opened to a new way of living. I started living life in gratitude. Finding joy in what I already had. Living with an expanded outlook and belief in endless potential. Saying yes to opportunities I would have otherwise dismissed because it wasn't in accordance with my 'perfect' plan.

As I returned to school, it was no longer about aiming for high grades, but just passing and to consider other career options.

Apparently my dream was not a lost cause, as there were alternative pathways into engineering I hadn't needed to consider before.

And that's when I found the course that was more perfect than I could have ever imagined. The course was entirely to do with structures, minus all the subjects I was not looking forward to; no damn engineering, no transport, no roads, and no civil. And it was at a university with a government initiative to encourage students who weren't the most academic to enter engineering. Maybe I wasn't going to fall off that cliff after all.

I chose not to get my hopes up or cling to the idea as a lifeline. I was still at peace with just allowing myself to focus on my mental health and enjoy life as it was, regardless of what my future might look like.

Fast forward through ten years of the most unorthodox career path into structural engineering, where I was standing on a city footpath. Looking up at a building towering over me, designed by me.

I stood in awe, in front of me a $600 million project, with three 30-storey buildings towering above. I had never been prouder of what I'd accomplished, or more appreciative of every challenge that helped create the woman I had become.

Having been unable to sleep the night before I saw the completed project, I was a nervous mix of emotions. Excited beyond words, and in disbelief that it actually happened, I remembered the little girl who stared out the car window mesmerised, inspired, and motivated to go after her dream. I also remembered the teenage girl sitting on the veranda staring at the trees; exhausted, defeated, broken, believing she would never amount to anything. And I cried for both of them, just as any proud parent would. I cried with happiness for that little girl accomplishing her dream and I cried with admiration for that teenager for not allowing life to defeat her. They finally got the very thing they'd spent most of their life wanting and working for, yet repeatedly letting go of.

We'd done it. Despite feeling like life was punishing me, life had my back, and it worked out better than I could have ever planned.

Prior to depression I had been terribly afraid I was only as good as the judgements, the teasing and the worthlessness my environment seemed to reinforce. I believed engineering, in a very specific way, was the only way to prove all of it untrue. But that plan was created from brokenness, from unworthiness, from inadequacy, and it almost killed me.

I was chasing a dream with a pathway that wasn't meant for me. My relationships were superficial and I was running on empty, because my identity and my worth as a person was completely dependent on this dream transpiring.

I was giving ~~150%~~ 100% of the time to one area of my life, believing everything else would magically change, that who I was would magically change once I succeeded.

Over the years, even as I was succeeding in my career, some days it felt like those towers were never going to happen. Whenever I felt like I was failing, like I was losing control of the outcome, I'd come back to the process of letting go.

And you can, too.

I invite you to think of something you are anxiously anticipating; desperate to accomplish.

Visualise your dream. What does it look like, what does it feel like? The euphoria, the accolade, the sense of accomplishment.

Now breathe in, and breathe out.

Feel how much you want this; the desire, the determination, the need.

Breathe in, and breathe out.

Notice your feelings; anticipation, nervousness, anxiety, fear.

Notice any sensations; gripping, grasping, clenching.

Now breathe in, and breathe out.

Allow your emotions to surface; anger, sadness, grief.

Feel them. Notice them. They're just emotions. They won't hurt you. You will come out the other side.

And breathe.

Relax your shoulders, expand your chest, untie your stomach.

Breathe.

Loosen your grip, unclench your jaw, relax your hips.

Breathe in, and breathe out.

Now let your dream fade, dissolve in front of you.

Breathe in, and breathe out.

Find calmness in your body; allow the stillness to remain, make peace with the loss.

Feel appreciation for what you have, feel gratitude for all that is present, feel pride for everything you have already accomplished.

And breathe.

This will allow you to move forward, open to all possibilities, yet unattached to a particular outcome.

Moving forward without a perfect plan or an intended outcome can be an overwhelming experience. It requires trust and faith. Yet the more at peace you can be with a feared outcome, the easier it will be to seamlessly move forward with a willingness to embrace any potential opportunity. You'll be less likely to act out of desperation, fear or unworthiness. You'll be able to move forward full of inspiration, belief in yourself, and pride for who you are whilst choosing opportunities more appropriate for you.

The depression allowed me to peel back all the identities and the images I was trying to live up to. It peeled them back so I could discover who I was without the status, without the label of success. It gave me an opportunity to come back to the incredible person I was and build my career and my future on that foundation of personal admiration and recognition that any success, regardless of size or prestige, would be enough; that that was a milestone in and of itself.

Wayne Dwyer, the internationally renowned self-development author and speaker once said, 'When you are unattached to nothing, you are open to everything.' This has never been more fitting, not just for my career, but for my life.

When you let go of controlling an outcome, you open yourself up to the future that is truly yours, that was meant for you in every way, that cannot escape you.

You enable subtle clues that life presents you to be seen. Like little crumbs showing you the pathway to your future, you have an opportunity to move forward in the way that is perfectly imperfect for you.

So rest in the knowing that when you jump, regardless of whether you grow your wings and fly, you will never fall more than you need to because life will be there to catch you, placing you in the water, enabling the realisation that you can swim to sink in.

How else are you ever going to find your treasure at the bottom of the ocean?

About Naomi

Naomi Holland is a structural engineer at a leading engineering firm, a keen photographer, speaker, and a transformation and self-mastery blogger.

Using her logical and analytical thinking, she takes all modes of healing from mainstream motivation techniques to transformative energy work, as well as philosophical ideas, breaking them down into poetic, instructional steps anyone can apply to their life.

Using various self-exploration exercises and healing techniques, through her blog Naomi can help you uncover the source of your unhappiness, make peace with your past, and embrace all that you have to offer the world.

Through the process of self-awareness and self-mastery as a pathway to personal transformation she will help you become the person you are destined to be; whole, complete, fulfilled, in love with life and who you are, irrespective of your external environment.

Naomi is deeply passionate about teaching people how to uncover who they truly are, embrace all that life has to offer and obtain fulfilment in their own unique way. You can start your transformation today by heading over to her website.

Naomi Holland can be contacted at

naomigraceholland.com

CHAPTER SIX

What if you could honour your truth without people implying you are 'faking' your pain, when you are actually 'faking' that you are okay?

Carmen Taylor

This has been the basic mantra behind me choosing intentional living and conscious experiences rather than bottling and hiding my pain and emotions. 'Faking it until I make it' never worked for me. I choose to live an authentic life by not masking my chronic illness.

I am so incredibly passionate to share this message, especially with all those living in pain who are silenced by the stigma that you need to fake being okay to get by. What if you could stay true to yourself and get by in life by actually enjoying it? By really appreciating all the parts of who you are, the parts you may perceive as good and the bad?

I spread belief that it is possible to live such an amazing life, even if your body has been handed what can appear as an awful card. I purposely write the word 'appear' because over the whole 31 years I have lived with this, my perspective has drastically changed.

I grew up having no idea how to handle my body, believing that I had been dealt the worst card that life could hand. I had no gratitude or any positive perspective of my life. I lived each day with chronic pain from a condition called Ehlers Danlos Syndrome, and because this genetic condition I was born with is so unknown and heavily under-researched, there was nowhere to go for help.

Ehlers Danlos Syndrome is a connective tissue disorder that affects the whole body either directly or indirectly through the supporting parts of the body. This includes the skin, muscles, ligaments, joints, bones, blood vessels, organs, tissues … practically everything.

Oh, how I wish I knew someone like me when I was young, or that the internet and social media was available so that my mum could reach out to someone for help. There was only one person who I genetically inherited this from, and he would not be someone I could trust or rely on for any form of help or support.

I became a mother on December 28th 2016 to the most beautiful girl. Gabriella coming into my life hit me with a huge realisation that if I didn't master my life living with chronic illness, how could I help her if she inherited it?

Becoming a mother is the best thing that ever happened to me, and Gabriella is my inspiration for taking control of my life and my disorder. My story of change is about a collection of moments before motherhood where I collected tools and then developed many game plans to live my best life possible.

I was never one who really wanted to die; each time I 'tried' I knew deep down it was never because I actually wanted to leave this earth. I didn't want to impose that kind of pain on my loved ones. I never had much self-worth, but I knew that I always had my mum in my life who loved me so much. I could never put her through that, despite her always being first witness to the painful life I was living.

I was just in so much pain. Every ... single ... moment ... of my day. I needed to escape, and reflecting back with the knowledge I have now, I was craving attention. I was so lost and needed attention and guidance. I needed someone in my life who knew what I was going through and could reach their hand to me when I was in my darkest moments.

When I was a child my mum searched for answers. We saw doctors and I was given many diagnoses. The one that we settled with was, *'It's just growing pains'*. Yet as I grew older these *growing pains* never disappeared. My mum had no idea what was happening to me. When I was younger, I wasn't able to articulate where the pain was originating from in my body; it was too intense, and I wasn't yet skilled at assessing my body (a skill I have become so good at as an adult). I wasn't lucky enough to find a helpful doctor who was able to explore this unknown disorder until I was in my late twenties. I had to however do my own research. Growing up, I was unfortunately misdiagnosed so many times. One doctor sent me home saying I had sprained my knee; it turned out I had broken the top of my tibia, ruptured ligaments in the knee, and torn the cartilage, too. I'm not one to judge a particular doctor – all I know is the lack of awareness of Ehlers Danlos Syndrome in the medical world has unfortunately been to my detriment. I have luckily come across some amazing doctors and professionals who have helped me as an adult, or been eager to learn more about myself and EDS.

I used to believe I was handed the worst card, but if you ask me now I will say with absolute belief and conviction that I have been blessed with the life I have been given. Over a collection of many moments in my life, I changed my perspective.

In the past I associated EDS with unbearable pain and depression. Being wheelchair-bound, on crutches, in slings, I would watch the world go by. At school I would be off to the sidelines while I watched everyone else playing and having fun. There's a quote that says something like, 'Depression arises from feeling that the present moment can't get any better, and anxiety arises from the fear that our future is worse than our past.' I feel like this summarised my childhood and teen years.

I hated myself ... true hate. From the moment I was born all I knew was the constant pain from my body. So many hospital trips, heart troubles, dislocated hips when very young, broken bones, sprains, torn ligaments, broken ribs, severe gastrointestinal situations where I have been hospitalised for days, where once there was mention of a stoma bag! Lots of nose bleeds, and wounds struggling to heal, as well as slowly going deaf due to several perforated ear drums, daily dislocated jaw, fingers, knuckles, shoulders, knees ... the list literally goes on and on. If you can think of a bodily function, it's most likely that having a collagen deficiency will have some impact.

I have strange distorted memories, and blacked out moments in time that I still cannot recall. Then there are the clearest of memories, the ones imprinted in my brain.

I grew up resenting everyone. When I was 15 I remember seeing a girl in my class fall. She had dislocated her knee and the pain was so much that she passed out. Then when the ambulance arrived she was given laughing gas. I watched her with jealous eyes. That had been me many times on the ground with a dislocated knee, broken leg, or sprained or broken ankle, and because I had somewhat built up a resilience, my brain never gave me a reprieve.

I never passed out. I never cried or yelled. In fact, I would go so deathly silent and cover my face with both my arms like a shield. Then whenever I could muster up the strength I would say, 'I've dislocated my knee' or, 'I've broken my foot'. And because I was somewhat calm, there was never an urgency. My mum would be called, I would wait in sick bay for what always felt like forever. The whole time knowing that she believed me and was rushing to get to me as fast as possible.

She would help me hobble over to the car and open the back door as I always sat in the back with my leg propped up across the backseat. Then there'd be a discussion – we knew the drill: did we go to the hospital, GP, surgeon, or just go home and try to relocate or fix the joint ourselves? Each time was somewhat different.

I had a pain filter over my mind and it consumed my every waking thought. They say that it takes hitting rock bottom to truly find yourself. I feel like I hit rock bottom several times and then got stuck under a rock.

There was however, this one significant day that I remember so clearly. Maybe this is where my story of change starts? As I said it's a collection of moments, but if I were to pinpoint it, then this would be it.

I drove out of the Knox Private Hospital car park, skidding my tyres on what was then a gravel surface. I was alone in my mum's burgundy 1996 BMW blasting the song from the film *Honey – I Believe* by Yolanda Adams. I had tears in my eyes, stabbing in my stomach, my heart was racing, and I was raging mad! I had just left my surgeon's consultant room with more terrible news: I had been told to give up my martial arts, karate and boxing at the time.

This broke my heart! I wasn't sure of much in my life, but I was sure I couldn't survive without martial arts as an outlet. It is the only thing that takes my mind off the constant daily pain. I screamed so loud in my car and hit the steering wheel so many times. I WAS SO OVER THIS! I was raging mad at my life. I hated myself so much, and despised my failing body.

I literally had two paths right here.

The dark path was easier, it was familiar, and it was comfortable. I was used to self-hate, and it was incomprehensible to imagine a life where I didn't hate myself. To be free of this broken body was a day I had always dreamt of, and I was hit like a ton of bricks with the realisation I would be living with this for the rest of my life. There was a moment I contemplated driving into a tree – I just could not see myself ever living a pain-free life.

I parked the car and slapped my face several times. I took a deep breath and decided I could no longer live like this. I wasn't done yet. And I settled with the belief that there had to be a reason I was given this challenging life. This is the significant moment where I decided to live my life with intention, and I set out on a quest to ensure I learned to love my life.

It was here that I decided I was going to keep training. I was empowered, and I passionately chose to take a path of intentional living, instead of the dark path I had too frequently travelled in the past.

I took control of my life right there; I decided I would determine what my body could and couldn't do. I turned from rage to passion in the space of half an hour and was screaming the song lyrics, 'I BELIEVE I CAN!' Onlookers stared with confusion and concern.

I did all the rehabilitation exercises that my physiotherapist gave me, then went back to training. I was beating all odds! I had EDS-related speed humps, but those didn't stop me. In the past my martial arts training was scattered, and although I always returned to it, it was always by recommended guidelines that were essentially limitations. This was the first time I tuned into my body and started listening to what was right for me. I felt so empowered! Months went by, then I dislocated my knee again.

'No, no, no, no, NO!' I repeated over and over again. I didn't care about the pain! This was my new knee! I had an organ donor graft in here, I saw it as my bionic knee! This was supposed to work! HOOOOOWWWWWW?! Gosh, I felt like a failure. I felt so much anger towards my body. 'Who am I to take control of my life? My body controls me.' And just like that, I was in a dark mindset again. And it shocked me how I was so easily thrown there.

I saw my surgeon and ended up having scans and another operation. It turns out that my body rejected the organ donor graft. They removed the remnants of the new ligament, as well as the screw in my tibia. It turns out that the pain I had in that spot was because there was not enough tension from the new ligament in there to keep it firm in place, so it essentially became loose and wobbly.

This was the time where I heard the words, *'You may never walk properly again, and may quite possibly end up in a wheelchair very young.'* I was devastated, but I didn't stay devastated for very long.

Each time I was in a 'flare up', bedridden, or in hospital I searched so hard. I read so many books, blogs, and articles about how to deal with living with chronic illness; each time adding little bits that resonated with me to my toolbox. I would learn more about myself, build resilience, and realised I needed to look towards feelings of self-love and respect.

The reality is that my body is seemingly getting worse each day as I get older, so if I kept with my self-hatred pattern, I just wouldn't be around much longer. I realised that reclaiming power and control over my life, through inflicting pain on myself, just wasn't the right way. Treating my body with love and respect gives me the mental strength to handle all the pain I experience daily.

I came to an underlying belief over time where I realised that no matter what was happening in my body, I could still love it and myself. I don't know when that belief entered my subconscious thoughts; all I know is that I realised that to control my body it was imperative to master my mind first. Once my mind was strong and I saw things with gratitude and self-love, I started to gain clarity on everything that then must happen. Each time I hit a low, the darkness wasn't as dark anymore, and I stayed there for less time each time.

Confucius said, 'He who says he can and he who says he can't are both usually right.' I love to relate this quote to my body, and the belief of mind over matter.

I was that self-pitying person for years, that one you see at a family gathering and avoid. I used every chance possible to victimise my body. I wanted people to feel sorry for me, as I believed that would heal me some way, or make my life easier to live with. When I spoke about my fragile body people didn't know how to respond. I made them feel uncomfortable, and although I was speaking my truth, it just puts people off, or they would feel so sorry for me, I would bring them down to my energetic level. It was too much for them to comprehend when I would explain how I really was.

When I became aware of this, I went the complete opposite way; I didn't talk about my body and no matter what I always smiled and said that I was great! I began to 'fake it'. But this sucked, too. The voice in my head was still so loud! I was so convinced that I was living the worst absolute hell of pain and that no one else could know. I had learned to exercise to punish my body ... I felt genuine joy the more bruises I saw from training. Bruises and being sore from training made me feel so free! I was choosing what kind of pain I felt. It was liberating, but it wasn't healthy.

I went from a place of hate and disgust for myself to bottling up all my truth and pain. Neither treated my body with love and respect. Neither honoured my truth, because the truth is I have EDS and I shouldn't be ashamed.

What truly worked for me was choosing to see it as a blessing, to connect with my body and all the weird and wonderful things it can do. Choosing a life of gratitude and truth over hate and anger. I like to think that I have somewhat found a balance. Writing out game plans has worked wonders for me throughout my life.

I can genuinely now say that I treat my body from a place of love, gratitude and respect. Oh yes, the pain is still there. But my mindset is so strong and my game plan is flawless for me. I've had a lot of practice to master it and I feel unbreakable. I can truly say I haven't been broken mentally by having EDS for quite a while now.

It took time to develop my self-care and self-love mindset. And I have learnt that there is no final destination to reach. I will and always will be learning more about myself. I find it so exciting to know that I am yet to learn new tools to add to my game plan. We never stop learning, and to think we have reached our final destination in attaining knowledge is truly sad.

My game plan isn't about getting rid of pain or numbing myself from all the negative emotions that we human beings are gifted with; without the negative how would we even comprehend the positive? I do not use terminology such as negative or positive when talking about emotions, normally – I used them here to convey the message, as I struggle to convey it any other way. Emotions just *are*; I believe that if we honour and respect all of them, then we can find our truth. If we choose to deny certain emotions we are denying certain parts of ourselves and aren't living an authentic life.

Here's how you can write out your game plan. It's simply a mind map with multiple bubbles floating.

- *Get a blank piece of paper and write your name in the middle. Then write out all the things you perceive to disrupt your flow in life.*

- *Around each of these subheadings write down all the feelings that this situation would bring up. Dive deep into this and allow yourself to remember every single detail; nothing is too small or too big.*

- *Then write down a game plan for each. You can number it, or use dot points, or even write them out as little bubbles coming of each 'disruption'. The game plan has to be catered for you; for example, if you know meditation doesn't work for you then don't put it in. This doesn't mean meditation will never work for you – continue to discover and develop new tools to add to your game plan, just don't put it in until you are comfortable using it when you are in a state of distress or feeling overwhelmed.*

- *Share your game plan with loved ones for the times your mind is too consumed, and try your hardest to make it a non-negotiable task in your life when you are needing it the most.*

Here is a very brief write up of one of the pathways for me within my game plan.

Always write your name in there and claim ownership of it. This is so important because you can trust yourself. When you are overwhelmed you will know that when you are in your normal state, the one person that you should be able to trust is yourself. Even if you do doubt this, you will have the memory of being in a loving mindset when you wrote it. And hopefully that can drive you towards following the game plan.

Carmen – Game plan for whole body flare up and inflammation

a. Ask my loved ones to take over running EFMA, my business.
b. Ask loved ones to help with Gabriella.
c. Sleep or rest in bed for 1-2 days. I allow myself to take this time, and feel all the feels. Although I come from a place of love for my body, I can predict (as I've been in this state thousands of times in my life) that I will have a whole array of different emotions flare up.
d. When I'm able to, I do some self-love meditations, and EFT tapping (Emotional Freedom Technique tapping).

e. Sometimes when I'm at this stage I'll do a post on social media to inspire others through my experience. Not always, as it would then flood the majority of my posts.
f. When able I do mobility work, flowing movements, and yoga sequences that feel good for my body. At this point I can usually return to my life the day after.

Please always remember that it is your RIGHT to live an amazing, authentic life. No person or situation can take this right away from you. People who have what may appear to be the bleakest of situations may live happier lives than those who have everything in the world you could have. I personally know people who have bodies without chronic pain, illness, or injury who live a less active, less grateful, or happy life. Yes, of course this is my own perception looking in, but I hope you read this example for what its intention is: to highlight that you will always have a choice.

YES, shit happens that will throw you down. You are human and are allowed to crumble, but it is a choice whether you pick yourself up or not. It has been so freeing to acknowledge this! I really thought I had no choice in how my life played out and that to be truly happy I would need to escape the darkest emotions and be pain-free. This is so far from the truth, and the sooner you realise this, the closer you are to living an amazing life!

The game plan changed my life! And I hope it can change even just one person's life because that would make all that I have been through so worthwhile.

Much gratitude and love to all those who have read this book! We are a collection of amazing people with unique inspiration.

About Carmen

Carmen Taylor was blessed with a chronic disease called Ehlers Danlos Syndrome from a very young age, and has lived a life in and out of hospitals, doctors' clinics, and specialist centres.

From her darkest moments of living with chronic pain. Later in life, Carmen made the decision to change her outlook on life. She now spreads awareness not only about the life she lives, but also her beliefs and values around living an amazing life despite what might appear as limitations. Her strongest belief about herself is that she's here to inspire people to find their authentic self, and live their most amazing life possible.

Carmen Taylor is the owner of Exclusive Fitness and Martial Arts, more commonly known as EFMA. She is also the founder of Carmens Blog EFMA and Worldly Women in Martial Arts. Training with some of the best martial arts coaches in the world.

From being told that she wouldn't be able to walk again, she is now a world champion martial artist! Once told she was just a young and naive girl and that she would get nowhere in a male dominated industry, she now owns her own business!

Carmen Taylor can be contacted at

efma.net.au

CHAPTER SEVEN

Self-care is not selfish ... it is essential.

Jo McKenzie

The definition of self-care is the practice of taking action to preserve or improve one's own health, wellbeing, and happiness. Any decision we make to do something deliberately to take care of our mental, emotional, and physical health reduces anxiety, decreases stress levels, and helps to improve our moods. When we take care of ourselves and our cup is full, we are better equipped to be more loving and patient in our relationships, more resourceful and productive in our careers, and have a positive effect on those around us, as well.

There are many times in our lives when we find ourselves at a crossroad. Sometimes these are major crossroads and we do not know which path to take. Do we move forward in a completely different direction? Do we stay where we are in our comfortable place even though we do not feel happy or fulfilled? Do we take baby steps forward and keep our safety net in place, or do we take a giant leap of faith into the unknown with the belief that there has to be better out there? The hardest thing about these crossroads is that the decisions we make and the paths we choose usually affect others, as well.

Such a crossroad occurred for me at 34. I felt depleted, trapped, and unhappy. I knew the time had come to decide to either stay in my marriage or venture down an unknown path and create a life for myself and my children. I knew the path I was choosing was not only going to shape and change the course of my life, but also that of my children. To stay in my current situation meant financial security would continue, but at the cost of an extremely stressful and emotional home environment.

I decided to leave my marriage and commit to creating a peaceful, happy, and stable home environment for my children and me. I knew I would never have that if I chose to stay. I chose the unknown path which held the promise of a brighter future over the one I felt I was guaranteed if I stayed.

My decision was not made lightly, and it challenged my own family values having grown up in a small country town with parents who had been married since they met in their teens. Leaving a marriage, especially when children are involved, is one of the hardest things anyone will ever have to go through. There is so much uncertainty and so many questions without answers; questions about finances, shared arrangements, special occasions and holidays, schooling, etc., which can all feel very overwhelming.

However, staying in a relationship that is not good for you can lead to anxiety, depression, and illness. I was feeling a constant state of anxiety and stress in my relationship, and I strongly believe that if I had stayed I would have eventually gotten sick. Leaving a relationship that is not healthy or good for you takes courage and strength and shows that you value yourself and your boundaries.

My decision meant I was faced with a new dilemma. I was now a single mum with two small children aged 2 and 4. I had no job. I had given up my career to support my husband's business and raise our children. I had no family nearby, my closest girlfriend lived interstate and my confidence and self-esteem was extremely low. Life seemed overwhelming and scary when I looked too far ahead but I knew in my heart I had made the right decision.

At the same time, I felt strangely free – free to create a new picture where I was doing the choosing and making the decisions about what I wanted to do and how I wanted my life to be. I now had a clean slate to move forward and find myself again without feeling wrong, or selfish for wanting what made me happy. I felt like I was making the shift from being a passenger to being in the driver's seat, taking control of steering my life and where I wanted it to go.

My goal became to create a peaceful, safe, caring, and loving home environment for my children and me. I couldn't change the fact that they would not experience the idealistic traditional family of both parents in the household, but I could make a commitment to make sure their experience at home with me was as stable and encouraging as I could possibly achieve. To take care of them properly, I had to make sure I was looking after myself.

I practiced taking time for me again; simple things I could manage while manoeuvring life and two small children around to preschool, swimming lessons, appointments, play dates, etc. Life was busy, however I wanted to make sure things continued along as normal as possible for them. I learnt that I had to prioritise the things that really mattered and let the other things go and not beat myself up. Spending quality time with them and taking some time for myself was more important than stressing over how perfectly clean or organised the house was. I did not realise at the time but taking those small positive steps for me ended up playing a huge part in the direction my life took.

As I was very conscious of the fact my children needed me, and that they deserved a healthy and happy mum, I put my focus on developing a positive mindset. I have always loved reading, but instead of spending time reading novels or watching TV, I spent my time studying personal development and motivational books and materials. I practiced being grateful and enjoying and appreciating the 'moments'.

I exercised whenever and however I could fit in around the children. I ran around the backyard, I went to the park nearby and did exercise while the children played. I purchased some home yoga and fitness classes and I kept as active as I possibly could.

I learnt about low-carb eating and I introduced more lean meats, fruit, and vegetables, and tried to limit the amount of processed carbs such as rice, cereals, breads, and pasta. I dropped the extra kilos I had gained during pregnancy. I was looking and feeling healthier and slimmer, and that was helping to build my confidence.

I was using good quality skincare products and created a regular routine. I tried to apply at least a little makeup on my skin every day. I felt that taking that 2-3 minutes at the start of the day made a substantial difference to my confidence and how I felt during the day.

The combination of everything I had been doing started to take effect and I now looked and felt much healthier. I felt a lot calmer and less anxious and my confidence was slowly building. I started seeing glimpses of my old self again; the light-hearted, fun, and playful side of my personality. I was feeling much more in control.

Taking those small steps of self-care enabled my confidence to grow enough to feel ready to put myself out there and apply for work. I applied for a part-time job as a beauty therapist at a nearby salon. I felt extremely nervous at the interview and my nerves increased even more so once I accepted the job. I had lost a lot of confidence being out of the working environment for a few years and I worried if I could do this. I felt like an imposter playing a part who would be found out. I had to practice some positive self-talk and push the negative thoughts out of my head when they would appear and replace them with ones such as, *'Of course you've got this, you'll be fine'*.

It was challenging at the time, however I had no idea how those steps would end up playing a huge part in my future. That job restored my confidence and reinforced that beauty therapy was my passion. It was also the catalyst for making the decision to open my own business from home which would enable me to do what I love, earn an income, and provide the flexibility I needed to work around my children.

I had talked about wanting to work in my own beauty business for a long time. It had always been my dream; I felt in a way it was now or never as I could no longer blame anyone else for not living life the way I wanted. The only thing stopping me was my own fear of failure. I had to keep telling myself, *'You can do this'* or, *'Find a way or make one, because failure's not an option'*. I am quite a proud person, and I did not see myself – nor did I want anyone else – to see me as a victim. It was important to me that I could take care of myself and my children.

I started my business from home and was determined to make it work. Over time my business gathered momentum, and I found myself fortunate to have a steady and consistent client base. I was grateful that people were coming to me, however I was so focused on making the business work that I lost sight of taking care of myself. I was not prioritising my health and wellbeing, which eventually took its toll. I ended up with chronic back and shoulder problems which was making it increasingly difficult to do my work, and was the sign I needed to make some changes.

I was referred to a sports massage therapist. When I turned up, I was surprised to find a man in his seventies. Asking about my work and lifestyle, he gave me a warning: 'You are going to burn out if you continue what you are doing, and you will not be able to continue working in your business. I give you about 12 months at this rate unless you make some changes'. I was all ears. This man was twice my age and had been running a busy clinic for many years and was still very hands on massaging clients, which is extremely physical work.

He said that unless I prioritised looking after myself, I would not be able to help anyone else. We came up with some strategies to make changes, and I never looked back. I am extremely grateful this man crossed my path; it was the wakeup call I needed to rethink, make changes, and prioritise myself once again.

I think I was destined to be a beauty therapist from a young age; my mum caught me staring intently at the lady next door's face. She had very lined skin and, much to my mum's horror, I came right out and asked, 'How come you have so many wrinkles?' My fascination with faces has continued, and I have made a career out of helping people correct and improve their skin concerns. I certainly hope my approach is a lot more tactful and subtle these days!

Many years ago I worked as a volunteer at the Look Good Feel Better workshops, a free community program dedicated to teaching cancer patients how to manage the appearance-related side-effects caused by cancer treatment. The theory behind these successful workshops is as the name suggests; when we 'Look Good', we 'Feel Better'; taking the time on your appearance can make a substantial difference to your state of mind and the way people react towards you. Illness can change your looks, and it can be distressing for you and family members to see you looking different or sick.

As a cosmetic tattooist and skin specialist, I have had the privilege of helping other women build their confidence through change and transformation on the outside, and witnessed firsthand the difference it can make to how someone feels on the inside. The way we look does affect the way we feel about ourselves, and when we know we look our best, we have more confidence. I have worked with many clients who have lost their eyebrows due to Alopecia, illness, or medication. I have cried with them when they see themselves with eyebrows again for the first time in years and thanked me for making them look 'normal' again. I have watched the transformation of young acne clients from hiding under a hoodie or avoiding eye contact to blossoming into the wonderful, confident young person they are meant to be. Increased confidence can help us to make changes in our life, and take chances and risks we would not have otherwise considered.

If something is holding you back or affecting your confidence, do some research to see what your options are to fix or improve it. The answer may be a lot simpler than you think and the benefits to your confidence over time may far outweigh what the solution requires.

Self-care takes many forms, and it is all about doing whatever it is that makes a difference to you. It could be prioritising time to exercise, reading, having a regular massage, or having a laugh with a friend. The point is that you recognise that you are worthy of time for you, and that you do not come at the end of the line after everyone else's needs. You will become depleted and resentful which eventually leads to illness. Self-care is important to our self-esteem. When we take time for ourselves, we are investing in ourselves and saying, 'I am worth it'.

All those years ago when I made the decision that I matter, and took back control of my life and the direction I wanted it to go, those small things I started to do for myself were building my confidence and self-esteem. I reduced my stress and anxiety levels, which had a positive effect for my children, as well; they benefited from a happier, calmer, and more patient version of their mum.

The small steps I made for myself gave me the confidence to get back to do what I love, which led to making my dream of owning my own beauty business a reality. I had no idea that when I made the decision to prioritise and take care of myself that I would have the privilege to make such a difference to the way other women look and feel about themselves. Through looking after myself initially I ended up being in the position to make a lasting and positive impact on others.

I hope my story of personal transformation from single mum with two small children, no job, and no family support close by, to owning and running a successful skin and beauty clinic for the past 20 years encourages you to prioritise yourself.

My tips for building confidence

- *Be kind to yourself, make time for yourself, value yourself, and others will value you, too.*

- *Start by doing what it takes to build your confidence – small acts of self-care.*

- *Taking time to nurture yourself helps you relax, unwind, and reduce stress. Not taking time for yourself leaves you feeling tired, depleted, burnt out, and irritable. It may affect your sleep and lead to illness which has a negative impact on your work and personal life.*

- *When you know you put your best face forward you feel more confident. This improves your state of mind and allows you to create positive change, to take a chance, and step out of your comfort zone.*

- *As we gain confidence, we are more likely to take risks, explore new ideas, new relationships, friendships, new job and career opportunities, new interests, and hobbies.*

- *Feeling good about yourself from the inside out radiates outwards in your posture, body language and gestures. Nothing is more beautiful than someone who knows they look their best and exudes confidence, vitality, and warmth.*

- *If something about your appearance bothers you, find out what you can do about it. Getting a professional opinion can save time and money by getting the right advice and solution upfront.*

- *Skin is something we can transform and change. It is possible to turn back the clock and erase your skin's past, giving a more youthful, healthier look. Look your best at any age.*

- *Grooming is important. People react differently to you when you are well-groomed and take pride in yourself and your appearance. It says to the world, 'I value myself because I matter'. It could be applying a little makeup, styling your hair, or for men, shaving. Just a few minutes a day well spent on you can make the difference.*

- *Real beauty comes from within. It is about feeling your best, not about pleasing someone else or trying to fit someone else's version of you; the youngest, freshest, most radiant and confident version of you. Positive self-views = self-esteem, and believing you have worth.*

- *When we feel negative, we do not believe we 'deserve' or are worthy of great things. When you believe in yourself and invest in yourself and radiate confidence, others believe in you, too.*

- *Do not compare yourself or how you look to anyone else. You are unique, you are one of a kind.*

My tips for change

- *Make a positive choice to make the best of your situation, even if things have not worked out the way you hoped. Setbacks and challenges happen to everyone, and some things we simply do not deserve. Accepting a situation for what it is and making the most of it is within our control. You must try to make a conscious choice to move forward, not be too hard on yourself, and turn life's' challenges into opportunities to learn and grow.*

- *Do not beat yourself up about the way things have worked out.*

- *Our experiences teach us compassion and empathy for others. We cannot relate to other people's pain unless we have encountered similar experiences and situations. The challenges and low times in our life teach us to be appreciative and grateful for the good times.*

- *Think about what makes you happy. Spend as much time as you can doing the things that make you feel good. This is not selfish. You cannot give from an empty cup – you must fill your cup first, and allow it to overflow to the people most important to you (i.e. your kids, family, friends, etc.). We are like bank accounts – you cannot keep making withdrawals without making deposits.*

- *Look after your health. Eat well, make time for exercise, limit alcohol intake.*

- *Take one step at a time. Be kind to yourself, ask for help, and try to surround yourself with people who support you and are good for you to be around.*

- *Remember that sometimes you just need to take some time out and enjoy fun times with family and friends, and forget about everything that is going on. It will all get sorted out in time, but you will not get these precious moments again, so give yourself permission to put your troubles away and just enjoy what is in front of you!*

- *Expect that at times life may feel like a roller coaster of emotions and experiences, but keep reminding yourself you are moving forward and that with each step you are moving closer to creating the life you deserve.*

About Jo

Jo McKenzie is an Advanced Skin and Beauty specialist and business owner who has operated her clinic, Envisage Beauty in Melbourne, Australia, for the past 20 years. Jo is also the author of Envisage Your Beauty Business – the Ultimate Guide for Setting Up and Running a Successful Salon From Home.

Jo brings almost three decades of experience and knowledge, and is passionate about helping women look and feel their best. Jo specialises in creating change and transformation through corrective treatments and products.

Jo is known for her caring nature and positivity amongst clients and friends, and in business for being motivated, professional, and driven.

Jo created her business from home initially to allow her the flexibility to work around her family when her marriage ended and she found herself a single mum with two small children to raise, no job, and no family support close by.

Jo lives with her son, James, who graduated from university and works in the finance industry, and daughter, Alana, who has followed in her mum's footsteps opening her own beauty business.

Jo is in a healthy and loving relationship after meeting her partner in 2016 and enjoys personal development, keeping fit, good food and wine, travel, and fun times with family and friends.

Jo McKenzie can be contacted at

envisagebeauty.com.au

CHAPTER EIGHT

The Universe whispered, "I had to make you uncomfortable, otherwise you never would have moved."

Paula Johnson

I've learnt to find change exciting, not something to be feared or resisted. Through choice or circumstance, I've reinvented myself so many times, I've become comfortable with change. It's something I welcome - keeping life interesting and keeping me growing. But it wasn't always this way…

Being diagnosed post-menopausal at the much too early age of 29 was a major catalyst. The *change of life* coming way too early and changing everything started a chain reaction of decisions and events that have led me to where I am at this moment in time.

Of my many stories, the one I'm sharing with you comes later in my life. It's my journey of how I have become a female digital nomad in my mid-fifties, moving from place to place with my laptop, having no fixed income or home to call my own.

Our upbringing has a massive part to play in how we live as adults. It is our deeply ingrained beliefs that shape how we operate in the world. These beliefs are downloaded into our subconscious (our auto-responding part of the brain) during our first formative seven years from birth. There's nothing we can do about it, it's automatic, and it's the same for everyone.

My beliefs were shaped from my stable family background. I only ever knew one family home (my parents lived there until they died in old age) and I continued the tradition of always having my own roof over my head at all times and never leaving a job until I had another to go to; it was something that was instilled in us by our parents from a very young age.

My basic foundations were strong – I knew where I belonged, where my safe home was, and that I would grow up to spend my days earning a reliable living ... *there was comfort in my security.*

As an adult my circumstances allowed me to travel, which in turn completely opened my eyes and my heart to the plight of others less fortunate. After a particularly life-changing trip in 2010, travelling seven weeks through Vietnam, Cambodia and Bali, my inner compass did a complete 360 degree turn that suddenly had me questioning my *Groundhog Day* existence. I now felt caged by my privileged first world circumstances ... *but there was still comfort in my security.*

Coming back from that trip had me examining everything. Surely there was more to life than this? I became disenchanted with my superficial-feeling life in New Zealand. My heart was calling me to do more. To be more.

When your heart is calling, it's for a reason. That reason may not be absolutely known to you right now, but by you taking the courageous step to follow the call of your heart, no matter how ridiculous it may seem, you will grow and evolve and learn what that reason is.

That trip was the catalyst for an inner transformation that absolutely and completely changed my entire life.

I never had any previous desire to go Southeast Asia. I was in a new relationship and my partner invited me to go with him. I said yes.

My deep desire to explore something completely new, was much greater than the fear I was feeling. *There was comfort in the security of me being with him.*

Tip: Become a YES person and watch your world open.

My next life-changing step was the following year in 2011. I resigned from my reliable finance job, said goodbye to my bodywork clients, my car, my river-side cottage I adored, left my belongings in storage, and went to live in Bali for five months with my partner, volunteer teaching underprivileged kids in a poor fishing village.

Was it easy? Hell no! I was way out of my comfort zone, every single day. I had no teaching experience and there were countless times I wanted to come home, the discomfort was so great. But I stayed for the children. I stayed for a cause bigger than myself. And by staying for them I stayed for me. I learnt how to keep going, through the fear, anxiety, and the intense feelings of worthlessness, of not knowing what the hell I was doing and feeling like I was letting everyone down.

Tip: You build strength and courage being of service to others.

That was my training ground for how I live my life now. Am I fearless? No. I've just learnt to keep moving through the fear until I get to the other side, because the deep inner knowing that if I don't, I'll stay stuck, is just not an option. *There is security in following my heart.*

Bali was now my second home and its pull on my heart was strong. In 2013 I went back for an initial three-month period, the first month with a friend as we planned to get stuck into our writing projects. Ha-ha, yeah right. We did everything but write! We ate delicious food, we explored on bicycles, we had healing sessions and massages. We had an amazing time. Then it was back to do some more volunteer teaching for a few weeks, spending time with my sponsor children and their family. I never did get fully comfortable with the teaching, but I did it. The desire to make a difference to these children, to give them knowledge that may help them have a better future, was the motivation that kept me going.

In order to stay in Bali as long as I could, while stretching my limited budget, I regularly checked the Ubud social media group for accommodation alternatives. It was here that the synchronicities of the Universe came together to help me. Responding to a post in the group, I spent my last six weeks helping a charismatic French writer. She put a roof over my head free of charge, in lieu of me helping her create a website and organising her computer files. This sowed the seed of how I wanted to live my life ... being a digital nomad, living wherever I desired and working independent of location. My initial three months in Bali now turned into five ... *there was comfort in my freedom.*

I was greatly influenced by the lifestyle a much younger friend and her husband were living. They were travelling the world teaching online courses, blogging, writing, coaching, and filming mini documentaries to raise awareness of poverty and environmental issues. They were my idols and I dreamed of living a similar life one day.

When I got back to New Zealand, I secured a long-term house sit and endeavoured to start a Virtual Assistant business with the intention that once I had regular clients I could work from anywhere. But while my head thought it was a great idea, my heart wasn't fully in it. After a few months struggling along, I decided I needed to get a job.

Tip: If your heart isn't in it enough to face all the challenges thrown at you, it won't work.

So, I succumbed to my comfort zone of an office job once more and landed a role at a large corporate company. Now I had a regular paycheque it also meant I could afford to rent a place on my own – yay! *There was once again comfort in my security.*

The next two years my heart and soul would call me home to Bali. Whenever I stepped off the plane back in New Zealand after each trip, I would steel myself for the long 10-month work slog to be able to go again. I hated it. Here I was back in the box.

Tip: Sometimes we need to take a step back in order to take two steps forward.

I would dread Monday mornings. My heart heavy as I got out of bed to go to a workplace where I was dictated any small freedoms in my day. There was no flexibility. When I requested a shorter lunch break so I could leave earlier in the winter months I was told, 'Not possible. You are on the new contract which is 8.00am-5.00pm with one hour for lunch. If we change it for you, we have to change it for others.'

In March 2016, I requested to use three weeks of my annual leave and take one week leave without pay for a month-long trip to my beloved Bali. I waited three weeks for a decision.

I was told the news on Friday as I left work for the week that my leave was declined. The reason given, *'If we do this for one person, we have to do it for everyone.'* My similar leave for the previous two years had been granted without issue. I was gutted and I was angry. As I drove home, I realised I couldn't carry on. I was done with all the rules and regulations, feeling like I was being treated as a number on the payroll instead of a valued employee and individual. They really had no idea who I was as a person and what was important to me. This was the final nail in the coffin I needed to make a change.

That weekend I went through every conceivable option, riding the fear and emotion behind each of them. *'If I don't have a job, I'll have to move out of my house, then where will I go?'* That was my biggest fear. My home. My nest. It was such an important part of my security. Remember, I had been brought up in the same family home since birth. Having that stability was an integral part of my psyche.

But I knew deep in my heart what my decision had to be. My health depended on it. I had developed acute physical issues that weren't going away, and I knew it was work related. I just needed to find the courage to follow it through.

My contract called for four weeks written notice, so I followed their rules for the last time. I had planned to go to Bali in August, so I waited four long months until July to hand in my resignation. I told no one my plan. Giving notice in July gave me one more month and then I would be gone.

The day I walked out of that corporate job, head held high, was a major turning point. This time I felt it deep in my heart, and while

I didn't have a definite plan, I knew I had absolutely made the right decision.

As I pulled into my driveway and turned off the ignition, a volcano of emotion suddenly erupted out of me. I started laughing, and then I started sobbing. I felt like a crazy woman as it all flooded out – the relief, the absolute soul-full relief in knowing I'd escaped – with my life. That may sound melodramatic, but within days of leaving, the health issues I was experiencing disappeared. That environment had sucked the life force out of me.

Tip: Don't underestimate how much stress affects your health!

I flew to my beloved Bali. In between nourishing food and swims in the cool pool water, I slowly came back to myself, deciding to row my own boat from now on. I remembered back to when I had been helping my French friend, how much I enjoyed the ability to be in another location while also contributing my skills to someone who needed them. How could I make that happen again? Although this time I would need to earn an income, as I still had to live in the real world.

I listed all my skills, from more than 30 years in administration and finance roles, plus my business from previous years as a holistic bodyworker, where I had created advertising material, newsletters and my blogging website. I knew I could go back to my bodywork practice but that was more suited to staying in one place. It needed to be something I could start straight away, that I could do from anywhere, and help clients worldwide.

I did a daily dip into the Ubud social media group, and it was here that the synchronicity of the Universe aligned once more. I responded to a woman who needed help with her website and as I jumped on the back of the Ojek's motorbike (motorbike taxi) to meet her the next day, I felt a rush of excitement. My dream was coming true.

I arrived back in New Zealand, with my first paid project in progress from that Bali meeting. I advertised my services through social media and community noticeboards and also called the local thermal spa to see if they needed any massage therapists. I met the owner the following day and had my first massage client booked there for later that afternoon – the flow was starting.

Tip: This is manifestation in practice. Have the clear intention in your heart of your dream. Start taking the action towards that intention. The inspiration and people to help make it happen will come.

And there began my foray into self-employment once more. From people responding to my advertising and word of mouth referrals, I started building up my clientele, both bodywork and online.

But it wasn't easy. At first I felt the stirrings of freedom but then all sorts of emotional detritus started surfacing. The lifetime habit of working regimented office hours, to now not having to wake to the alarm clock. Being able to go to the beach with a takeaway coffee in the middle of the day if I wanted had me feeling uncomfortable. It was like the old comfy shoes didn't fit anymore. I had to learn to break in new shoes and start having gratitude for being able to create my day how I wanted. Because now I could.

Financially I was also taking a hit, my income greatly reduced and expenses high, as I was still renting. As a woman in her early fifties who was comfortable on her own, the thought of having flatmates in my small house wasn't an option I wanted to look at, so any shortfall in living expenses was taken from my dwindling savings and using my credit card. Many would say that was unwise, but for me my freedom of choice to work the hours I wanted, doing work I loved and being of service to clients directly was the only way I could now feel any sense of fulfilment. And I still had my bigger dream to reach – to be able to travel and take my work with me. I had to keep going. I had to make it work.

With my irregular cash flow my home was now a stress, feeling like a heavy ball and chain. And emotionally it was hard. When I doubted myself, there was no one there at home to give me a hug and tell me, *'You're doing great', 'Keep going', 'You can do this, I've got your back.'* Even though I had wonderfully supportive friends and family, at home there was just me. I was it. Having all the decisions, responsibilities, fears and sleepless nights full of angst. At the end of the day, the burden was totally mine. I swam alone in this chapter of my life.

But it was also my choice. I had the choice to give it all away and go back to a job at any time. But my deep heartfelt dream kept me going. I started my online work so I could be location independent, working from anywhere while travelling. I couldn't see that dream die.

In my heart I knew something had to change, but I had so much fear around it. I put myself through hell over the decision to give up my home. Every time I thought about giving it up, I would feel the panic in my stomach. My home was my nest. It was safe. It was mine. For two years I agonised over my decision. There was comfort in the security of my home.

In the end I had to be stern with myself. 'Paula, you're stuck and you're in fear, that's the only thing holding you back. If you don't make a change, things are going to just stay the same.'

I remembered one of the quotes I love from Anais Nin – 'And the day came when the risk to remain tight in a bud was more painful than the risk it took to blossom.' It was now time to start blossoming.

With my heart leading the way like it was charging into battle, pulling my logical reptilian brain kicking and screaming along with it, I made the decision. I was going to give up my home, sell and give away belongings, put the rest in storage and house sit indefinitely. This meant completely letting go of all attachment, surrendering to complete uncertainty – a single 55-year old woman with no secure home and no secure income, essentially living the lifestyle of a much younger and carefree person.

Decluttering was so liberating. I eliminated so much stuff I had been carting around for decades. I didn't need the hindering energy of those things anymore – after all, I'd well and truly moved on. With my remaining worldly possessions neatly stacked inside a 3mx2m container, I finally felt light and free, all fear was gone. *There was comfort in my downsizing.*

Tip: When decluttering, a really great process for chunking down what can be an overwhelming job is to get rid of things daily.

For example, on the first of the month you get rid of one thing. On the 2nd of the month you get rid of two things. On the 20th of the month you get rid of 20 things, etc. It gets harder as the month progresses, but you learn to get really ruthless. Start in one room and work on from there.

For nine months I was enjoying my new nomadic lifestyle, when out of the blue, Covid-19 struck our shores and we had to go into lockdown. My house sits (and lifestyle) stopped immediately.

I had learnt over those nine months to trust and be in flow. I was never in panic over where I was going to stay, something would always appear just at the perfect time. So, when lockdown arrived, I trusted I would be looked after. And I was. A friend's small flat had become vacant, and even though I was paying rent again, I knew it wouldn't be forever.

Tip: Trusting instead of panicking had allowed the solution to surface.

When most people had to stop work, many even losing their jobs, my online work didn't diminish. In fact I got busier, with more referrals coming through. I realised the blessing of having different streams of income ... *there was comfort in my success.*

I am so grateful I kept going in the times I felt like giving up. It's damn hard work being self-employed, it's not the rose-tinted glasses dream you imagine. Yes, you have certain flexibilities that you don't get with many jobs, but you never rest from it. Your business is always in your mind in some form or another and some days it's just plain exhausting. But you get to row your own boat, in your own way, and there's huge fulfilment in that alone.

Tip: Building strength and courage to move through change is just like building a muscle in the body. It takes practise, lots and lots of practise. The fear will never go away, you just learn to live through it to the other side until the next fear arises, and then you do it all again.

If you are experiencing dread at going to work on a Monday morning, have an idea for a business you'd love to get off the ground, or are just super passionate about something you'd love to share with the world, then you owe it to yourself to make the change. The world needs your passion!

Hey, it's not going to happen overnight – my digital nomad journey has taken seven years. It's a baby step process that you must choose every day – *'Do I go backwards to my familiar comfort zone or do I continue forward to growth and expansion?'* The only way forward to growth is by pushing through your fears, again and again. Change-fear-growth, it's a cycle.

Tip: It's your journey, no one else's. Don't compare yourself to how fast someone else achieved their goal. One thing I've learnt is you're not ready until you're ready. It will happen when it's right for you. But if you don't take that first step, and then the next, it's never going to happen – is it?

Navigating change is an inside job. You're trying to shift habitual ways of being. Habitual ways you've made yourself be, in order to be accepted. But you're the captain of your own destiny and no one is coming to rescue you to do it for you (sigh).

The only boundaries are those we put upon ourselves – how low is your glass ceiling? Are you ready to break through it?

My number one tip for you when facing your fear of change, is to listen to your heart.

If it excites you and lights you up, it's right. It only comes down to one thing in the end: *How much do you really want it?*

Have I got it all figured out? No. Am I fearless? Definitely not. But I know when I'm stuck and I move through it quicker. I now embrace change – it makes life challenging and interesting.

Change is a constant in life. We all go through it, sometimes by our own making and sometimes it's completely out of our control. Resistance is futile. If we can learn to make friends with change, the easier things will flow and evolve. Because that's what change brings – evolution. The people you'll meet, the experiences you'll have, the new things you'll learn, the internal shifts that you go through … that's the journey, that's the gift. Please don't say no to the gift.

About Paula

Paula Johnson is a Champion of Change. From a very young age she was always seeking, exploring, learning, and growing. She has reinvented herself so many times, change is now exciting to her, not something to be feared or resisted.

When diagnosed as post-menopausal at the young age of 29, the change of life coming way too early and changing everything, she began a journey deep into the mental, emotional, physical and spiritual. Finding meaning became her mission. Why had this happened? Why was she here?

A seeker, a wanderluster and a creative, her practical skills have seen her work in a variety of jobs and self-employment – from office work to preserving wedding bouquets; holistic bodywork to website design. She has organised and hosted women's retreats in New Zealand and writing retreats in Bali. She is currently a middle-aged digital nomad, creating websites while travelling and house sitting.

From blogging to writing a memoir, and now invited to be an Influencer of Change, Paula is here to share her experiences and help others move from fearing change to embracing it.

Paula Johnson can be contacted at

paulajohnsonnz.com

CHAPTER NINE

What if you are living an unconscious life?

Sean Nicholas O'Leary

I was unconscious. From the age of 12 until I had turned 42, I was living an unconscious life. In my head I thought I was doing well. I thought I was being the best I could be. I thought I had strong values. I thought I was successful. And in many ways and in many moments, I was. But for the majority of my life, I was living unconsciously.

How did I come to know of my unconscious life? At 42, the freight train of reality hit me and I was forced to wake up. It then backed up and hit me again, and to make sure I was truly awake, it backed up and hit me yet again. The reality I had unconsciously created was not a good one. I was not the best I could be. I was not living through strong values. I was not truly successful. It was all just a façade, an illusion, a brave and happy face to show the world.

Inside me was turmoil, stress, anxiety and ill-health. My failed marriage, my exit from a business that wasn't working, my large amount of debt, my 135kg obese body, and my very long list of health issues (which included constant headaches, migraines, back pain, and IBS), proved that my reality was not what I had imagined it should be. At this pivotal moment in life, I had to make a choice: to give up or go on. I had been shocked out of my unconsciousness by seeing that my reality was the furthest thing from success it could be.

I was on the edge of hopelessness, trying to look for a reason to go on. I couldn't see a way forward. For months it was just a matter of surviving. It was only the vision of my three children's future that encouraged me to go on. As I imagined what the impact on their life would be if I gave up, I knew there was no other choice than to somehow go on.

But how could I go on? I felt like everything I had done in my 42 years had compounded into a tragic crisis. Everything was shattered. Even though I had big successes in work and family life, such as being a consistent high performing business development manager, leading multi-million dollar projects and helping raise three wonderful children, I had also, through many unconscious choices, had massive failures and those failures had compounded into a cavernous collapse. I was broke, broken and alone.

I was feeling lost. I was feeling overwhelmed, not having an idea of what to do next. In this darkness looking for an ember of hope, I decided that all I could do was to set an intention of just being better: a little bit better every day. To focus my attention on what I needed to let go from my life, so I had space to become a little bit better. This letting go was like cleaning out my metaphoric shit bucket and not allowing it to keep filling up. Letting go of thoughts, feelings and behaviours that didn't help me.

The ember of hope that I clung onto was that I had a choice to think, act and behave differently. That I had a choice to be and do better. I was realising that the only person that could really help me shift toward being better, was me. I was the common thread in all my successes and all my failures. The one relationship that I had to wake up to, understand and be clear with, was the relationship with myself. It was this relationship that had caused me to live unconsciously for so long.

In this realisation it was up to me to shift, to move beyond my current experience. I decided to let go of all my previous thinking. I realised I didn't have the answers. I didn't even have the right questions. I had nothing. I had to start all over again. I had to give up any thinking that I could work this all out by myself.

I made a big shift to put my faith in humanity. Faith that somewhere amongst the seven billion or so humans that inhabit this planet, someone somewhere would be able to help me.

I was still full of shame and embarrassment to share my tragedy with too many people, so I searched for the wisdom I needed in the great vault of knowledge called the library. I started slowly and diligently going through the sections where I believed wisdom would show up. I trawled the library shelves that held all the books on Philosophy, Religion, Spirituality, Psychology, and General Information. Book by book, I read the title and blurb, hoping that the wisdom I needed would appear. If something sparked some knowing I would sit there in the library and read the book in more detail.

Over several days, I travelled to all the nearby libraries and sparks of wisdom started to appear in those vaults of knowledge. I gained some profound insights and understanding about my thinking patterns, my personality structure, and my emotional energy. Enough understanding to realise that both my success and my failures were all my doing. That it was my heightened conscious behaviours that lead to my successes and my detached unconscious behaviours that lead to my failures. I was living on a scale of conscious to unconscious behaviours. Operating either from a heightened sense of awareness, or amidst a frenzy of unconscious compulsion and coping. This new understanding opened new hope for me.

For the first time, I felt hopeful that I could influence my change. That I could work at being better, at being more aware, more conscious, making better decisions. That I could raise the scale of consciousness to think, act, and be better. And so my journey shifted into one of intentional transformation. I started absorbing more wisdom to understand and develop my personality structure, thinking patterns and emotional energies. I shifted into making small but compounding changes that built on each other to deliver better behaviour. I focused on raising my self-awareness and catching the times I slipped back to my previous unconscious actions, so that I could quickly adjust my behaviours and actions. It sounds simple, but 42 years of unconscious living makes it hard to get back to living consciously.

For the next 12 months my focus was developing my psychological, emotional, and spiritual consciousness. I wanted to become more aware and active in responding to life, rather than being bound by compulsive coping strategies like eating and watching TV. Even though I wasn't following any particular health and fitness plan, by focusing on living more consciously and cutting out crap food and stress, I began to have more energy. 12 months into my transformation I was still obese. The long list of health issues I was suffering started to scare me. I was still at risk of my health deteriorating into high risk health issues, such as diabetes and a fatty liver.

One night, as I stood in front of the mirror, the impact of my unconscious life hit me again. I experienced overwhelming sadness and remorse for what I had become. It was the first time that my obesity was so obvious. Even though I had lost a few kilos, down from my largest 135kgs, it was the obese mass of a body in the mirror that I could finally see. I was the *elephant in the room*. I was huge, obese, and in poor health. For so many years I didn't see it, and surprisingly no one in my life had made me aware of how obese I was. It could have been that they tried, and due to my lack of consciousness I didn't acknowledge it. Either way, the reality was I was fat and sick.

I worried that I was on a slippery path into deteriorating health, that I'd be in and out of the hospital, pumped up with medication to treat all my chronic symptoms. And that it wouldn't be long before I was spending my days in a dialysis chair coping with the inevitable consequences brought on by diabetes. It was here in this gloomy and depressing view of my future that I knew I had to make another conscious shift.

I set my intention to make a shift back to good health, I raised my conscious awareness to observe people who were living a healthy life. In my close business network, there were a few people practicing health and fitness at an elite level. When I observed them and listened in to their conversations about food, nutrition, and fitness it was like I was listening to a foreign language. How they were so passionate and explicit with their discussion around meal plans, macros, and muscle building simply boggled my mind. For some time, I was transfixed on watching, observing, and listening, hoping to get some gems of wisdom that would help me, but it was all foreign to me. I had started on my first diet when I was 15 and continued on and off diets over the years. Here I was, after dieting for 27 years, obese, and here were my colleagues, Wes and Luke, living at an elite level of health and fitness.

One day I met with Wes and the conversation came around to my intention to shift toward a healthier lifestyle. This was just the invitation he needed to open a discussion on the virtues of nutrition. I was like a rabbit in the spotlight; I sat there stunned by his passion for the way he nourished his body. I heard sounds coming from him and saw his hands and arms moving as it seemed like he was encouraging me to join the cult of elite meal preppers.

Wes reached into the small bar fridge behind his desk and produced a small sealed food container with one of his passionately prepared meals. As he brought it to the desk, he exclaimed how much I was going to love it and that it was the secret to shifting into an elite level of health. As I wondered what this superfood concoction would be, he opened the lid of the container to reveal his treasure.

Lack of understanding about nutrition showed prominently on my face and must have screamed unconsciousness to Wes. He still reminds me of my reaction to this day. I was looking at him as though he was an alien who had just landed with some science fiction snake oil that he was promising would solve all my diet and nutrition issues. This snake oil was smaller than my two hands and consisted of a less than palm-sized portion of a pale white meat-like substance and a handful of bright green organic plant material. As I tried to digest visually and cognitively what was presented to me, Wes energetically pronounced the virtues of a pint-sized meal of steamed chicken and broccoli.

I felt like I was in a dream. Never before had I seen such a small, unappetising meal be so passionately described as the secret to all my food and nutrition issues. It was more than foreign, it was alien. It was obvious to me I had to shift into a whole new world if I were to have any hope of regaining my health.

As I left Wes that day, my consciousness had shifted a little bit more. I became more focused on making changes to my nutrition. I then reached out to Luke, who had been running a fitness and nutrition program for elite athletes. I asked him if what he did for the elite athletes would help me. His casual reply that 'it wouldn't hurt' was a surprise, for I was wanting, out of desperation, a more certain answer that this was finally the one diet plan that would work. But him saying he would be there to answer any questions along the way convinced me to give it a go. This time I was going to try with a more alert and aware consciousness.

For the 12-week timeframe of the program I set a powerful intention to follow the plan in every detail. I focused my attention on just reducing my waist size, which was where most of my body fat resided. I set up my environment to create and maintain momentum. I created a space in my shack for the fitness session, downloaded an app on my phone to guide me, cleaned out all the crap food, restocked the fridge and pantry with only those foods in the plan, and set aside time in my schedule to do the fitness and mindset activities.

After a few weeks of reading through the plan and setting up my environment, I was ready to start. On 25 October 2013, with a new level of consciousness, a powerful intention and a focused attention, I started the toughest but most rewarding part of my transformation. Following the advice Luke had given me, I focused on just one week at a time. As the week progressed, I planned for the next week ahead. The plan seemed simple, but it wasn't easy. I found it tougher than anything I had ever done before. Mostly because I was battling against 42 years of unconscious conditioning. My biology had been wired over time to think and act in certain ways. Every day was a battle against this unconscious conditioning, like eating to reduce the feeling of anxiety, taking the convenient fast food option, or putting off exercise until I felt I had the energy to do it. Every day was just a string of conscious micro choices: little wins over the patterns and beliefs that had led me to obesity.

The struggle started in the first week. The plan was to exercise 20 minutes a day, three days of the week for the first few weeks. I was so out of shape that 20 minutes of high intensity interval training seemed like torture. I didn't have the belief that I could do it. My enthusiasm and mental motivation to make this happen was suddenly decreasing when I was faced with having to do the actual work. To get over this, I had to consciously return to my intention before I could find a way to start. I assessed my options, and realised that I had to make some micro steps to get started.

I found the simplest fitness routine on the app I was using: a beginner level routine that ran for just 13 minutes. When I saw the 13 minutes, I felt a tiny sense of belief in myself that I could do this. Thirteen minutes seemed like a reasonable effort; it was more than 10 minutes, but a bit less than a strenuous 15 minutes. So, with my tiny sense of belief that this was achievable, I chose to commence with my 13-minute fitness plan. I did find a way to extend it to 20 minutes by adding a three-minute warm up and a four-minute cool down. I know I was cheating the program, but this micro step was the only way I was going to create momentum.

It was all about the momentum. Even with the intention to follow the plan in every detail, I had realised that I was in a big battle. I was so out of shape mentally, emotionally, and physically that some mornings I would spend 20 minutes playing mind games to get out of bed before I did my 13 minutes-and-a-bit fitness routine. It was inevitable that I gave into the cravings and rationalised my choice for cheating the plan. But, I consciously decided that if I slipped, I would use the next morning to hit the reset button and start again. I used the daily reset button to revitalise my focus to do better each day. I started, restarted, and started again and again.

The weeks passed and I followed the program with a focused, but not perfect, attention. I thought it would get easier, but the program increased with intensity and it felt like each week I was back to square one. It was the mindful practice part of the plan that made the difference; the practice of focusing my attention on just this day, sometimes just this hour, to do what I needed to keep the momentum going. When I slipped or stalled I focused on doing whatever I could to keep progressing.

Millimetre by millimetre, I watched my waist size reduce. It was like a time lapse video of a balloon deflating. The micro changes were slowly happening to help me overcome the results of my unconscious life, piecing together a profound transformation.

As the momentum of these compounding shifts increased, I was starting to realise what was possible. I was starting to go beyond my previous experience and transform into a new life.

Four weeks into the 12-week program my health had started improving and I had amazingly reached my goal of reducing my waist size down to under 100cm. At this point my mind was completely blown. I wasn't totally transformed, but I was shocked at how quickly the results had started to show. I was just focusing my attention on what I needed to do and sticking to my intention of following this plan through to the end. I had transcended what I had thought was possible. I was shifting into a new way of being.

I shared my enthusiasm during a check-in with Luke. I was so excited I had surpassed my goal, but I was also confused on what I had to do to keep going, because I still had eight weeks of the program to get through. Luke simply advised me to set a new goal. I had shifted to a new peak and as he explained, I now had a view to the peaks ahead. I had to hit the reset button again, return to my intention, focus my attention on continuing with the plan, and keep the momentum going.

With this simple but sage advice I started again. The result over the next eight weeks wasn't as rapid as the first four weeks but I lost another 10cm off my waist. All my high risk health issues had dissipated away and my energy levels were at a lifetime high. I was fitter and stronger than I had ever been in my life, even stronger than I was as a teenager and young adult. I had dropped five clothing sizes. I had truly transformed. I had become a new man. At the time of writing this, I am older but still living a fit and healthy life, continuing to expand my consciousness to do and be better every day.

What I learned from my profound transformation is that I did not know what was possible until I shifted beyond my current reality. More importantly, I couldn't grow and transform until I woke up to my conscious reality. My encouragement to you, is to firstly, wake up to what your reality is. Open your eyes and raise your awareness to what is. What is your current reality? Do you need to acknowledge the elephant in the room?

As you move forward in this more conscious and awakened mode, remember that your most important relationship is with yourself. Transformation is possible because it's personal. So, explore and become more aware of your thoughts, feelings and behaviours. Get to understand why you do what you do. Understand your personality structure and get to the core motivators of your bad and good behaviours.

Once you understand why you operate the way you do, you will be able to shift into a new direction. When you're ready to shift, you need to set a clear and powerful intention that will guide you like a beacon. An intention that will energise your efforts and keep you heading in the right direction, amongst all the distractions, diversions and temptations that threaten to derail your progress.

To shift into progress, you'll need to focus your attention on what you need to do, how you need to be, and where to spend your energy. This includes minimising or eliminating distractions and allocating space and time for you to focus on what you need to do: raising your consciousness so that you can take action.

Finally, you need to create and maintain momentum. Momentum is the force that will shift you from where you are to where you want to be. Momentum is taking the next step: taking consistent action, no matter how small, toward your clear and powerful intention. If you're having trouble creating momentum, take a smaller step, then add onto that one small step with consistent compounding action.

Now is the time for you to wake up and shift into a more conscious life, a transformed life, a life of good psychological, spiritual and emotional energy. Now is the time to acknowledge the elephant in the room and intentionally shift its direction onto a new path. As you wake up, set your intention to be and do a bit better each and every day. Focus your attention on one thing that can guide you to a more conscious life. Create and maintain momentum through resources, tools and wisdom that will make it easier for you to shift toward your goals and aspirations.

If I can do it, so can you.

About Sean

Sean Nicholas O'Leary is a growth and transformation expert.

Combining his career in business growth and development with his personal transformation experience, Sean has now created a coaching business where he uses a suite of transformation tools and techniques, helping people grow and transform from where they are to where they want to be.

Through Sean's personal transformation journey, it is now his mission to help people create their own success, without stress. Sean is passionate about helping people tap into the energy that can help them transform their life and business.

To many, Sean is simply known as The Transformed Man. He hosts a podcast by the same name, featuring expert advice, insightful interviews, and inspirational stories.

Sean Nicholas O'Leary can be contacted at

seannicholas.com

CHAPTER TEN

*Walking confidently with your imperfections
makes you stronger and empowered.*

Donna Campisi

Most of my life growing up, I just wanted to fit in. I enjoy uniqueness in a creative sense, but I wanted less attention, and for nobody to look at me. I didn't want to stand out or look different from anyone else or walk differently from any other person. *I just wanted to be normal and walk, just like everyone else.*

I dreamt of having a body that didn't have any differences, complications and imperfections. I didn't want anyone to take a second stare at me when they saw me limp towards them. When I felt their stare, my right hand would instantly sneak up with my elbow bending in a stiff motion. My wrist curled even more, almost like a nervous reaction from the physical spasticity and self-conscious mind reaction I felt from those awkward stares. *I just wanted to be seen as walking normally.*

I wanted my arm and hand to hang normally from my shoulder, like everyone else. Swinging in motion with a perfect walk, like any another normal person. I wanted simply, to fit in.

I worked hard every day to hide my hand from the spasticity that developed from my stroke, I would hold it down and cover it with my *good* hand. But really, who was I trying to fool?

At the age of seven when I had my stroke, it was very serious. I was placed in intensive care, doctors not knowing at first what was wrong with me. They called me 'The Mystery Girl.' Eventually, after many tests including a lumber puncture, my diagnosis was found; I had meningitis, staphylococcal septicaemia, splenomegaly, endocarditis, osteomyelitis, aphasia (loss of speech), and a right hemiparesis from a haemorrhage on the left side of my brain. I was left unable to walk and use my right hand. Then at fourteen, I found myself in another critical condition, diagnosed with Type 1 diabetes.

I have been through long and difficult rehabilitation to get back on my feet and get as much use from my right arm and hand as possible. Luckily, I wasn't in the wheelchair for years; I learnt how to walk with physiotherapy most days for approximately a year until I was confident without hanging on to a hand, walking stick, or wall.

I am grateful to be standing, walking, talking and being alive. But whether my effort of trying to hide my hand and walking with my head down to see where and how my right foot would land on the ground when I walked, was from my awkward teenage years or my ailment (perhaps it was both) my constant awareness was always there. The awkward feeling of being careful not to fall, or break another limb, sprain or twist an ankle, bruise or scratch a knee, and fracture my arm or wrist ... multiple times, was always apparent to me.

Many times, I'd fall with laughter, shaking my head, and get straight back up, but other times I'd land with tears, always a concern to those around me. *I just wanted to walk like normal people do.*

I even recall my older brother going to grab my hand when we were crossing a busy road once ... I was in my thirties! This memory makes me chuckle, but also makes me grateful for my brother's care and shows the concern of those around me.

I am lucky to have that care and love from my family, but I also felt like the odd one, *'the sick child'*, the hassle in my family. Feeling watched over, like waiting for the next trip, fall or seizure.

From a child and into my thirties, I would feel a sense of embarrassment. I was different, and I had a silent fear of my ticking time bomb going off, never knowing when or where I would have a seizure ... and keeping this a secret as much as I could. My family and doctors were aware of it, of course. I consumed tablets every day, but it was never a conversation I would openly discuss.

It was not until I reached my twenties that they put a name to the sharp painful beating sensation I would feel all the way up the right side of my body which would stop me in my tracks. It was epilepsy. I did not want *another* diagnosis on my list, for people to be concerned about, making me even more *different*. But I was immensely pleased with eventually getting the dose right from my neurologist. I finally became seizure-free at 30, but there was still that silent feeling of wanting to be normal.

My physical life changing condition has left me with a slight weakness on the right side of my body. I wear a leg brace on my right leg and a 2cm heel lift on my right shoe, and an insulin pump for the diabetes.

With all the devices and medication to make my life better, for a long time I secretly still had that thought in my mind of *'Why is that person looking at me? They must be looking at my limp. Yes, they're looking at my weird hand, too.'*

I know this sounds strange, especially to people who know me well, as I've always shown determination and strength, wanting to strive and do better, appearing reasonably confident. *But still I secretly just wanted to be normal and walk, just like everyone else.*

All my life I thought I was clumsy, always tripping, falling over any little bit of nothing. It was ending up as a joke between friends and myself: *'There goes Donna, on another trip.'* I would fall hard; these were painful trips that I just learned to get used to. I wasn't told until I was in my twenties that I had 'foot drop,' from the effects of my stroke, even though when I left hospital I was given a caliper to wear on my right leg which attached to my shoe. This was removed by my physiotherapist when I was still a child. The feeling was that there was no need for it anymore. I was super pleased about that, as *I just wanted to walk as normal as everyone around me.*

So the announcement to wear a modern version of a caliper, called an AFO (ankle foot-orthosis), in my twenties left me with mixed feelings. An AFO is a brace placed inside my right shoe that goes all the way up the calf or shin (depending on the design), and straps around the leg just under my knee. It is intended to help raise my toes when walking and place my leg into a more *normal* position. To help me walk with less effort or accidents, adding to that a 2cm heel lift was attached to all my right shoes. This was another flashlight to the world that I wasn't *normal* like everyone else. But I learnt to live with it as another attachment to what felt like the 'Bionic Woman,' but I knew this was to improve my walking. *As I just wanted to be normal and walk, just like everyone else.*

I am super grateful and proud of my determination to be in the physical state that I am currently at. Many times, I have said *'there is always room for improvement'*, so using these aids and attachments meant they would help my aim to improve.

You could say my determination of wanting to be *normal* was a huge focus for me to strive and achieve what I have achieved so far, in life.

Admittedly, I would always be surprised in my early years when people would keep saying, *'You should write a book, Donna!'* This became a frequent statement. I realised my story gave people hope; they would be amazed and share their stories with me of knowing someone, or a friend of a friend who would be inspired by knowing my story and what I had achieved.

I thought I lived a fairly *normal* life in the way of my daily living, my upbringing, and my job, etc. I didn't look at myself as being super inspiring, as this is what I knew as my *norm*, in my life. But I could see people's faces light up when I would chat to them and share my story, or when they asked about my limp or wonky hand. This is where I found I could make a difference, perhaps, or maybe I could help change someone's life for the better.

So, in my thirties I decided to steer my own ship with a new career path. I studied and trained to become a qualified trainer and speaker. While studying, I made it my purpose to inspire people by telling my story.

Even though I appeared confident in my everyday world, I was still nervous about people looking at me; looking at how I walked, looking at my stiff awkward hand, wrist, and arm – more so when I felt people stare, especially those who I didn't know. So how on earth was I going to get up and be a confident speaker in front of so many eyes staring at me?

I knew I had to change; change my outlook, change my self-doubt, change my mindset, and change the way I thought people were looking at me strangely. Change to inspire others, instead of hiding or joking about my 'faults.'

I asked this question to a speaker I knew: *'How am I going to get up and be a confident speaker in front of many stares, when I am concerned about my hand?'* I revealed my message to him of how I wanted to inspire many people by telling my story, but also wondering how was I going to do this while battling to hold my awkward claw from my nervous spasticity of my right arm and hand.

At that moment he took my wonky hand and held it between both of his warm hands, looked me in the eye, and said *'Donna, just love it.'*

Love it? Love what?!

'Love your hand. Give it love. Show it love. Don't hide it. Treat it with love.'

I want to be able to tell you right now, with a rejoicing orchestra playing in the background, that *instantly Donna sailed off into the sunset after she heard those magnificent words, 'Love thy hand' and was healed and lived happily ever after as a perfect professional speaker.*

But I walked away that day with those words in my head, kind of confused to be honest. It's just a stiff wonky hand! How am I supposed to love it? What is this guy talking about?!

I limped in my way, covering and holding my nervous awkward hand, even making lame jokes about it as I got up on stage to tell my story. I thought it was easier to do that instead of facing the truth of my own insecurities.

Still, for many years after I was advised to wear the AFO, I would wear jeans and long pants to hide my obvious strangeness. I would even cover it with long boots in the winter if I wore a skirt, and worked out in the gym with long tracksuit pants, even on ridiculously hot days, never daring to wear shorts or leggings that would reveal my abnormality, trying so hard to be *normal*.

When I was 40, my partner at the time and I would go for long walks together regularly. One particularly hot day he encouraged me to wear ¾ length cargo pants on our walk while wearing my brace instead of long, hot tracksuit pants. This was a huge deal for me; I always covered my AFO, and never showed it off. So, he talked me into it that day, I felt like it was a huge moment for me, to face the world and show my strange leg brace in public. Clinging onto his hand as we went on our walk, as if I was about to face a stoning, only to find out the world didn't give a damn.

The moment I faced that fear, I realised the change was being made to my outlook on myself, and my image. Change was made toward my awkward feeling when initially meeting strangers, always thinking to myself that I had to prove I was *normal*. Looking back this seems rather lame to the *normal* person

My confidence grew internally by accepting who I was and being grateful for how far I had come, and openly talking more about my story without feeling like it was embarrassing and not important to share.

Overall, my life has been great. I have a supportive family, good friends, better health, and a great appreciation for my life, and those around me. I have no problems making friends, talking, and laughing with people, even strangers on the street.

Helping others is a huge part of my life. I enjoy working as a professional speaker, an author, podcast host, adventurer, goal setter, and supporting people in mental health and disabilities, along with training and coaching people. I would definitely say I love my life!

It is over forty years since having my stroke. I am a woman, able to speak, I am out of the wheelchair, and out of that insecure and embarrassed mindset.

I have worked on my self-development, including my mind and body, and moved passed the awkward feeling of thinking *I needed to be normal and walk, just like everyone else.* I realised later, I learned to love my hand. I stopped hiding it and used it more and treated it as *my normal*. I actually speak with it more on stage now, as any Italian speaker would.

I even created a challenge at age 42 to learn to run again. I tried one day on my own, a little fearful of doing a *'Donna trip'*. I faced the fear and gave it a go, and I managed to run 30 wobbly steps. Yes, I counted the steps!

Excited to reach 30 steps, I sought help with a coach to see if he thought it was possible for me to run a 4km distance, not really knowing how far that was at the time. I knew it was a big challenge, but it turned into a huge challenge when my coach suggested I run a marathon. After much thought I agreed to do it, with the initial purpose of wanting to share this challenge as a fundraiser for a cause that was close to my heart, supporting the hospital that saved my life more than once. But I also wanted to use this opportunity to encourage people to follow their dreams, face their fears, and take action on what it was in their life that they wanted to change or achieve.

I trained hard and faced hurdles along the way. I even created a campaign based around the charity, and inspiration I was passing on to a following that grew through the media, social media, and speaking events.

For eleven months I trained for my marathon challenge, which meant I needed to create change in my life and take action both mentally and physically.

Some days were hard, some fun. Some days brought a huge smile on my face for even the smallest accomplishments I gained, or the bigger achievements would make me jump with excitement. Some days I had doubts in my mind, *'Can I actually do this?'* Some days were difficult to control my blood glucose levels. Some days were spent with an ice pack. Some days made me chuckle, others left me in pain, bloody and bruised. I had trips and falls (even with my AFO), and there was lots of sweat, tears, frustration, and admittedly many calls or SMS messages to my coach.

I also changed my habits, my time, my training, and food. Making many changes to what was not my everyday norm.

Why I share this marathon story is that all the time while doing this, having people watch me daily through social media, I was showing the world my AFO and wonky hand and wobbly run with a smile.

I'm grateful for the encouragement I received from many people, it's a lesson of surrounding yourself with people who cheer you on and help you get to your goal, the change you want to make in your life today. I completed the marathon, raising over $36K while inspiring many people. My goal achieved through change.

I finally truly embraced my not-so-perfect body. I'm okay with sharing my story with whoever will listen – I even wrote a book about it – and I'm still sharing it now, here. The book cover even has a photo of me wearing my AFO in full view!

I write this smiling at how far I have come through changing my focus. As this is my *normal*, and if it inspires others or encourages people to take action or simply be grateful, I am happy with walking confidently with my imperfections.

This is about making a choice with change in your life and realising the opportunities, benefits, and progress you'll gain such as confidence, better self-esteem, success, happiness, financial freedom, more family time, time with your partner, a body transformation, new career, turning a negative change into a positive, less stress, growing your network with positive people, giving yourself a boost, going on that holiday, and more, by simply making a choice to *change*.

I came to the realisation that we cannot control the way people behave around us. They may stare, laugh, mock, doubt us, or make us feel insecure, etc. We can only control our behaviour, our thoughts, our feelings and actions.

So, I decided to walk with my head held high, show my leg brace to the world, face the fear, not allow my worries of *'What will they think?'* and *'What will they say?'* overwhelm me.

I have grown to realise that by being me, talking openly, smiling about it, speaking confidently and not hiding my imperfections is empowering. I gained confidence by showing up.

The question I ask others and myself now is, 'What is *normal*, anyway?' You are unique and don't need to be like everyone else. That, to me, is more interesting and empowering.

Are you hiding and holding yourself back because you are scared of change? Or maybe you think you need to be perfect? I had someone mention to me recently how she was fearful of speaking in front of crowds as she was comparing herself to other professional speakers around her. You don't need to be perfect!

Then there's others who I've seen who think they cannot launch a new idea, project, or business because their website isn't perfect, or they don't have one yet, or they think they need a business card.

Then there are physical changes of wanting to get fit, active, diet, or lose weight – *'Oh, now isn't the right time as my birthday is coming up, or Christmas, Easter, a bar mitzvah, or it's too cold, too hot, or too ... anything!'*

I've learnt through my imperfections. We just need to show up and take action, even if it starts with small baby steps. The time, place, or situation will never be perfect. It disheartens me to see people let time or opportunities pass them by as they wait to be perfect, or for that perfect time. You may have missed that opportunity; go now and create it, and make it happen.

This is how I look at most things now, and I encourage you to, also.

When you think about change what comes up for you?

To encourage you to take that step, make that change that you've always wanted. Or perhaps ideas have come to you through reading this inspiring book.

Here are my most essential tips I want to give you to help you embrace change. Be honest with yourself when addressing these points:

- *Are you waiting for that 'perfect time'? My advice is to stop hanging onto perfection. There is no perfect person, place or time.*

- *Focus on what you can do, rather than what you think you can't do. This will give you a head start. What do you have already that will help you move forward?*

- *Ask yourself 'How can I?' rather than 'Can I? You will find a way. You'll be creative enough to think of other possibilities or solutions.*

- *Openly share the change you want in your life. You may even get help, feedback, or encouragement that will help you create the change you need or want. Surround yourself with positive people.*

- *Will your change help others? Will it help you financially to give you more time with your loved ones? Will it create ease in your life, less stress, and grow and help others? Helping others may give you more incentive to change.*

- *Are you too busy focusing on your faults? Have you noticed that when you focus on the negative, it tends to hang around? Stop it!*

- *Embrace change. So many positives can come from change. Sometimes we're forced to change, from circumstances out of our control. How do you deal with that? Do you sit and complain forever? Or do you find a way to steer your own ship and move in a positive direction.*

The change you want to create is maybe something you think is scary. I encourage you to get out of your way! Walk confidently with your imperfections, it will make you stronger to make that change.

Change is not a scary word.

About Donna

Donna Campisi is a passionate woman, inspiring people around the world to turn their dreams into reality by hosting a podcast called Ready! Set! Goal! *She is a Keynote Speaker, Author, Coach, Mentor and Adventurer.*

Donna inspired many people with her stroke to marathon challenge; from only being able to run 30 tentative steps in 2012 (after a childhood stroke and diabetes) to completing her marathon goal in 2013, while encouraging many along the way that there's no such thing as can't ...

Donna coaches people to achieve their goals and step outside their comfort zone by organising awesome adventure activities, encouraging people to face their fears in a fun and inclusive environment.

She is the author of Turn Dreams into Reality, Inspiration Bible, *and* The Unlikely Marathoner– *proving there really is no such thing as can't ...*

Her background includes business development, and mental health and disability support. Donna is qualified in Coaching, NLP Practitioner, and Training and Presenting.

Donna's recent project is where she brought 10 inspiring Change Influencers together who have made positive change in their life, mentoring them to share their stories and insights in their compelling chapter. This book is about inspiring readers to embrace and make that change. Donna is very proud to bring this project to life: CHANGE is not a Scary Word – 10 Influencers Leading the Way.

Donna Campisi can be contacted at

donnacampisi.com

Afterword

After reading this book, you may now be pondering, 'When is a good time for me to make the change I've always wanted?

A good place and time to start is exactly where you are right now! Life is too short. Some of our authors and people who have contributed to helping put this book together have experienced life lost or near-death situations, on a personal level and while writing this book. We encourage you to act now.

This book you're reading is an example of me creating the opportunity and making it happen, now. It may have even been considered a not-so-perfect time to create this book for some. But I have seen greatness come from this book – I have seen the authors grow in the writing process, collaborating with co-authors they are honoured to surround themselves with and learn from, and most importantly, inspiring you and many people by sharing their story in this book. It is gold to me, and a privilege to watch the growth, enthusiasm, excitement, pride, and the CHANGE. I wish that for you also, for you to grow and make that change that you want in your life.

Let's be honest, some change decisions are not easy! It's not all sunshine and rainbows. As you read through these chapters you would have seen that every author faced doubts, barriers, struggles, fears, or doubters along their journey of change. Many times when we, the authors of this book, gathered in our Zoom calls to meet (as we are from different cities), the repeated comment I would hear was how they loved meeting together, being among positive, like-minded people who would lift each other up.

This I definitely agree with, and have always encouraged people when mentoring, writing, keynotes, or speaking on my podcast the importance of surrounding yourself with positive people.

This is the beginning of you creating your opportunity to make a life you've always wanted, rather than waiting for that opportunity that you may have missed or it may never come by your way.

Where do I start? Where do I find these positive like-minded people? you may ask.

I encourage you to re-read the bios of these amazing authors at the end of their chapters to see who you connect with. Feel free to check out their website and reach out to them. There may be one or more who could help you make that first step in creating change in your life, and living a full life you love, with purpose.

Love and gratitude,

Donna Campisi

Acknowledgements

Producing this book has been a *game changer* project for me. Admittedly, I hadn't created a book of this kind before. It started out as an idea in my mind, and here I am six months later with the completed book. I am super proud of this book.

This book would not have come together without the awesome team at Busybird Publishing. Thank you Blaise van Hecke and Kev Howlett for your ongoing support, humour, and guidance when needed.

Thank you Jessica Waters and Laura McCluskey, our awesome editors. Editing a book with ten authors has its challenges, and they handled this with patience, eagerness, and a smile.

Thank you to the amazing authors of this book, who were willing to come on this ride with me and share their story, insights and tips to the world.

I'm especially proud of the authors for their efforts in following my sometimes overly-enthusiastic and crazy lead! It can be hard to keep up with for some people, but they did it with enthusiasm to join as one, even through some tough and challenging times. We got through it! So, a BIG thank you to Nikki, Chris, Paula, Sean, Carmen, Naomi, Marie, Jo, and Malka. I am truly grateful for the enthusiasm and courage to share your stories. Some stories are revealed for the very first time to the world in this amazing book. Thank you for being raw, honest, and vulnerable, with the knowledge that you'd be helping others with your story. I am truly grateful.

We'd like to acknowledge the influencers in our lives, there are many:

The negative people or situations we experienced to push us even further. The bad health, career, mindset, and the stares. The anger that others brought to us, the pain, the hopelessness, the disease, the elephant in the room, the guilt, the friendships lost, the voices in our head that challenged us or doubted us, at times.

The positive role models we follow and have learned from, the people who led us to where we are now, the books we've read, the education we've gained, the cheer squad we've created, our deeply supportive and loving friends and family, and the positive connections made from writing this book. Both positive and negative, this is what has shaped us and lead us to step up and face change for the better. Thank you!

Donna

www.ingramcontent.com/pod-product-compliance
Lightning Source LLC
Chambersburg PA
CBHW070107120526
44588CB00032B/1373